FIGURE STUDY
MADE EASY

ADITYA CHARI

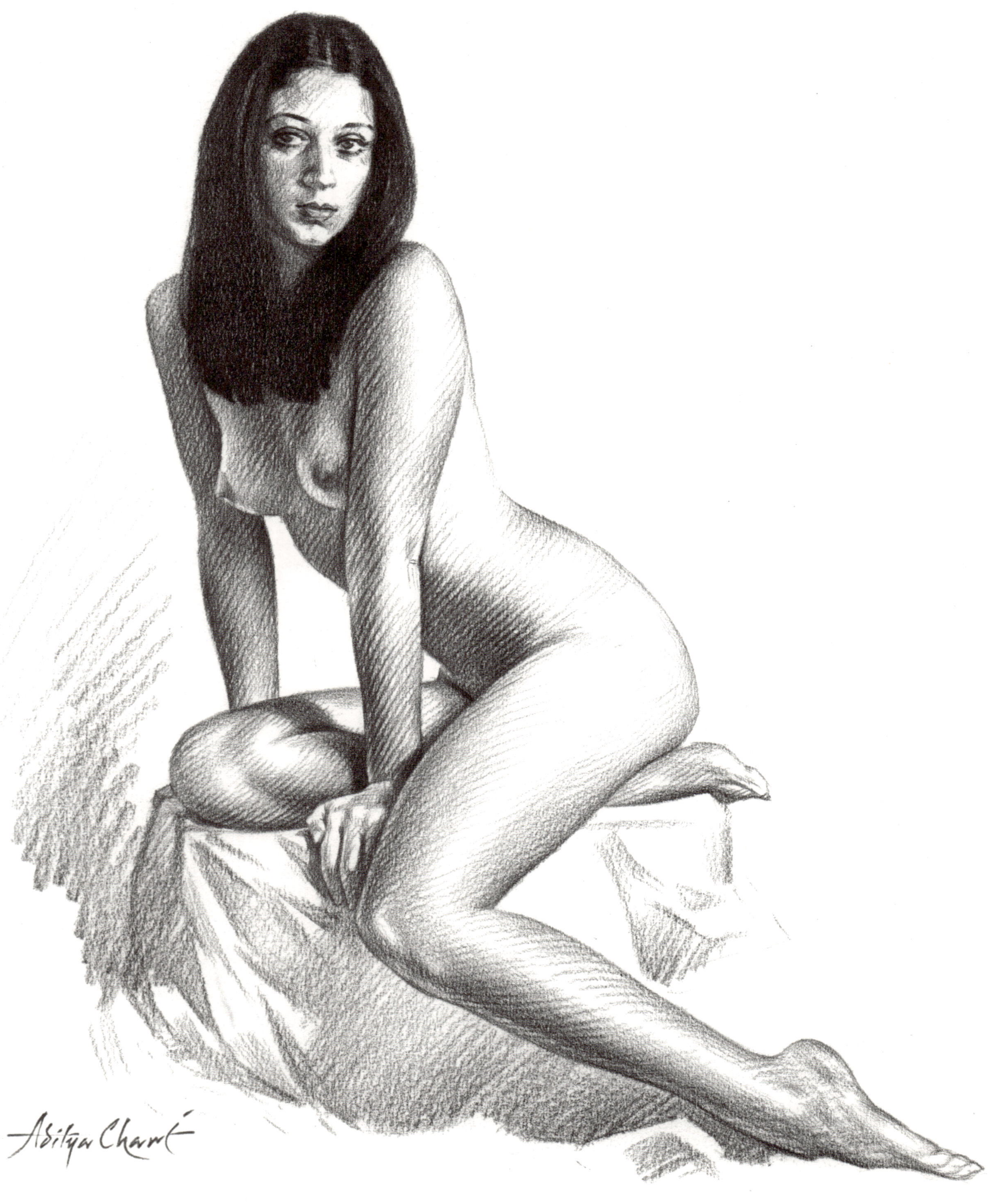

GRACE™ PRAKASHAN, Arts De Trio, 183, J.S.S. Road, Girgaum, Opp. Gaiwadi, Mumbai-400 004, INDIA.

Published by: Vikram P. Ubale
For **GRACE PRAKASHAN,**
Arts De Trio, 183, J.S.S. Road,
Girgaum, Opp. Gaiwadi,
Mumbai-400 004, INDIA.

e-mail: artbooks@graceartbooks.com
Visit us at: www.graceartbooks.com

Scanning & digital Imaging at:
Wayout Visual Communications
e-mail: bommy@vsnl.net

Printed at:
Superlekha
9, Tantia-Jogani Ind. Estate,
J.B. Boricha Marg, Mumbai-400 011.

Figure Study Made Easy
by **Aditya N. Chari**

ISBN 81-900890-9-9

1st edition Jan 2005

Rs. 300/-

RAVI PARANJPE
Painter - Illustrator
Shivaji Nagar, Pune

The rare ability to draw a good figure is perhaps the most coveted thing every true art student aspires to possess. But the road that leads to the fulfillment of this aspiration is not an easy one. It is full of pits & falls. On this road frustrations are galore and difficulties unending, provided one is able to 'see clearly.' This 'clear seeing' involves a number of problems concerning proportions, planes' structure, volume construction, knowledge of anatomy, gesture, foreshortening, drapery, rhythm, and the craft of drawing.

Learning to draw well is learning to meet these problems squarely and with confidence. Learning to draw well is also learning to put 'clear seeing' to its logical end with emotional precision. It is this meaning of the word 'Drawing' that the gifted artist Aditya Chari reveals in his book 'FIGURE STUDY MADE EASY'

Aditya Chari's approach to 'Drawing' reaffirms Michelangelo's statement that 'Drawing is Design'. And, it is this design aspect that gets percolated in the mind of any one who studies this book with discerning interest. Every single page of this book is well designed, and
What's more, it also underlines an extremely methodical approach to 'Drawing.'

A special word of appreciation is for Aditya Chari's innovative rendering techniques, that make FIGURE DRAWING such a scintillating visual experience.

I hope 'FIGURE STUDY MADE EASY' by Aditya Chari will tremendously benefit discerning Art students, professionals, beginners and hobby artists who want to reach out to the roots of the great human faculty called Drawing.

Ravi Paranjape

John Fernandes
Artist
Mumbai-400092

This book will guide both students and teachers, in drawing the human figures. The book is rightly aimed at working & developing the drawing skills. The text is short and to the point.

JOHN FERNANDES

John Fernandes

DEDICATED TO

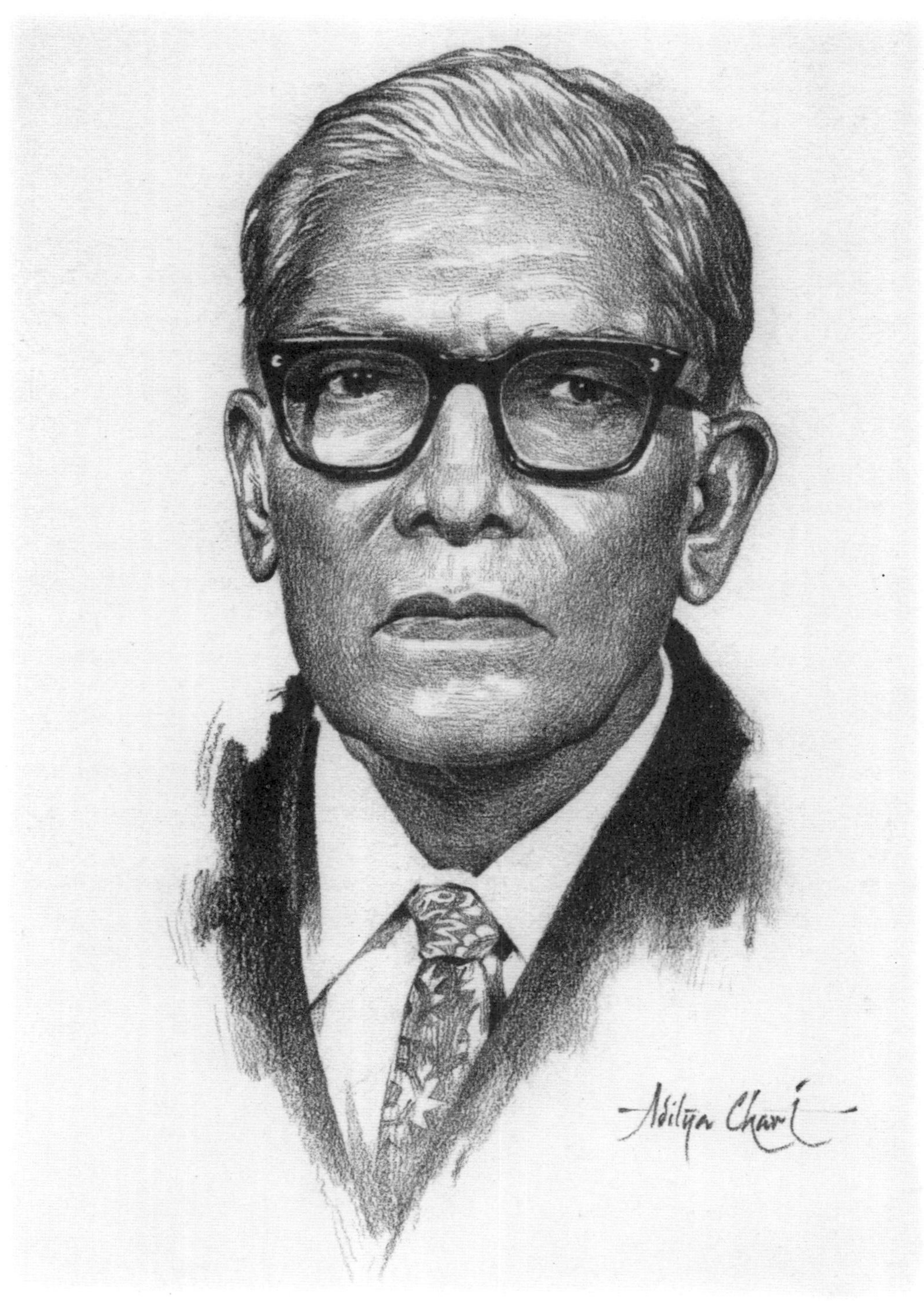

Late Mr. John V. Ubale

FOREWORD

In the year 1947, India became independent and during the years 1948 and 1950, I was very fortunate to be appointed as the first Librarian of Sir Jamsetjee Jejeebhoy School of Art, Mumbai. During this period I was in very close touch with the students, particularly of the Drawing and Painting Department; many of whom like V.S.Gaitonde, Mohan Samant, S.H.Raza, B.Prabha, B.Vitthal, Prof. Baburao Sadwelkar, Gade, Tyeb Mehta, Akber Padamasi, Prabhakar Barve, to mention a few who became internationally known in course of time, were all ardent readers of Art Books from the School of Art Library and were also keen sketch book users.

The number of good books for study of human figures are comparatively very few. This book, " Figure Study made Easy", by Aditya Chari which is a sequel to his earlier successful book "Portrait Techniques made Easy", is equal in all respects to any foreign publication. This book will not only help in study of human figure but will also acquaint you with animation drawing.

I suggest in future Aditya Chari should also bring out separate books on subjects like Animation, Computer Graphic, Cartooning, Birds and Animal studies and Fashion drawing.

Mr.Vikram Ubale of Grace Prakashan, has done great service to the field of art education by bringing out these outstanding publications. Aditya Chari and Vikram Ubale both deserve high encomiums.

At the end I would like to quote here the last words of Michaelangelo Buonarroti which he uttered at the age of 89, they are "I have hardly learnt the ABC of Art, I have not yet started my real work".

Prof. Vishwas Narhari Yande
G.D.Art (Drg. Ptg.)
Former Head of the Drawing & Painting Department
Sir J.J.School of Arts,
Mumbai-400 001.
Jan 2005

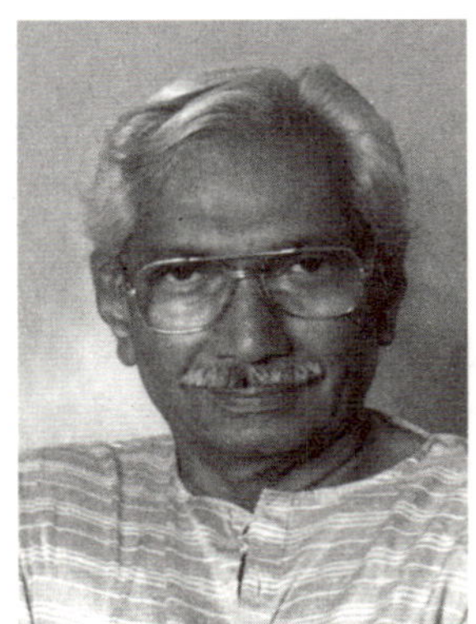

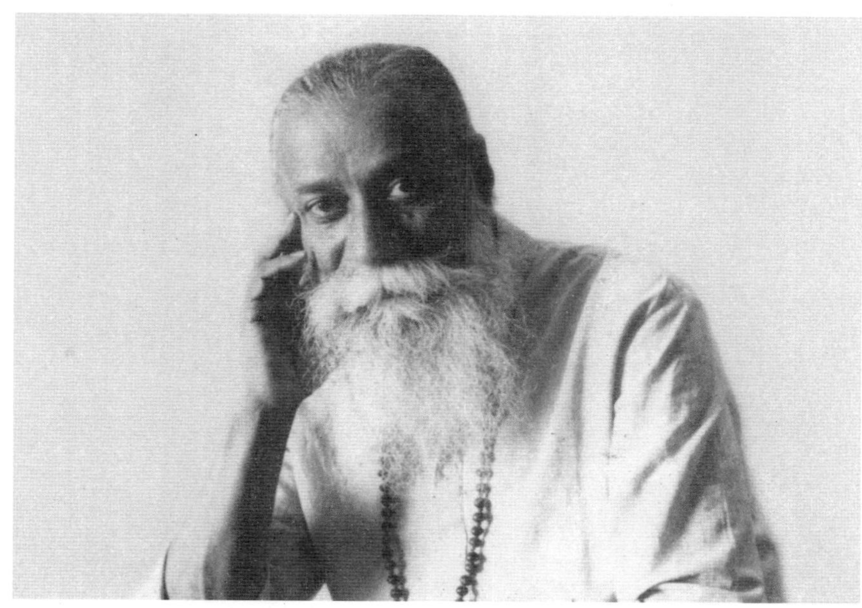

In fond memory and blessings of my grandfather
Chitrakar Kalamaharshi
Late **Dr. S. M. Pandit**
G.D.Art (Mumbai) F.R.S.A. (London)

PREFACE

The Study of Human Figure has fascinated me from the past few years. A study of various Art Masterpieces made me aware that since ages great masters had devoted their substantial time and talent portraying the human form.

This book is a result of my search for useful information that helped me solve actual problems faced during practice sessions. I was very fortunate to have excellent guidance in figure drawing from my grandfather, the Late KalaMaharshi Shri S. M. Pandit and my father Shri Nagraj Chari. They taught me to observe and express human form, as ideal teachers and keen critics. Criticism is a must for improving one's work. Guidance and advice by such 'Masters' is always cherished for a life time.

An Artist has to study proportions, modeling, balance and various movements of human forms. These observations can be studied from living models all around you, at places like bus-stops, railway stations or among one's family members & friends, etc.

I started my serious study of anatomy by keenly observing the work of my grandfather. I was also inspired by the monumental figures of Italian Renaissance artist Michelangelo Buonarroti. Besides, I always kept by my side the book 'Anatomy and Drawing', by Victor Perard, which helped me learn various facets of the human body.

The human figure is a three dimensional structure of solid blocks having weight and to draw it convincingly you must learn how to create an illusion of solid form on a two dimensional sheet of paper.
An understanding of human anatomy is a must. You will soon discover that what you see and draw depends on your keen observation. Once you understand the structure of bones and muscles, you can never forget them. This process will then spontaneously reflect in your work. Once you have mastered the basic forms, you should attempt to move subtle and creative interpretations of human figure. Regular practice will result in this confidence.

The topics in this book are arranged conveniently in step by step sequential chapters, which will show you how to capture the spirit and evolution of the figure. This will streamline your thoughts and result in capturing the essence of the figure in the shortest time. The approach of this book is based on the teachings of the great masters of this subject which resulted in figure drawings of unforgettable strength and beauty.
Remember the key to successful drawing of the human figure is to practise one concept at a time.

This book explains all the necessary guidelines towards the proper study of the human figure. Whether you want to learn figure drawing as a hobby or make a career out of it, the simple instructions in this book will help you in achieving that goal.

I would also like to thank Mr. Vikram Ubale of Grace Prakashan for giving me a second opportunity to express my skill and knowledge, which I always wanted to share with all friends and art lovers who are interested in figure drawing.

Aditya Chari

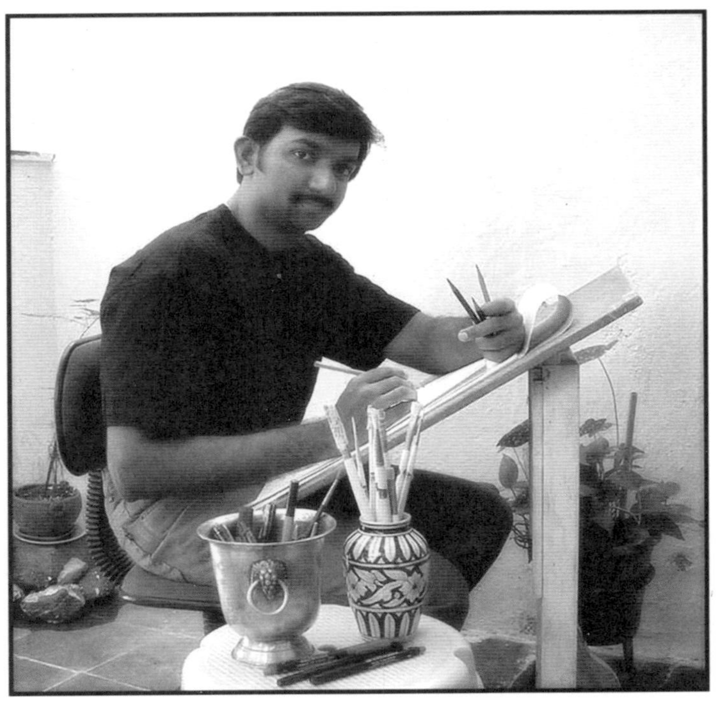

Aditya N. Chari
(B.F.A. from Sir J. J. Institute of Applied Arts in 2000)

Date of Birth: 6th Sept. 1976

Personal Projects
Author cum Illustrator of Book called 'PORTRAIT TECHNIQUES MADE EASY'
(Published in 2001)

Drew sketches for a Film called 'YUGPURUSH' and provided works for Television also.
Portrait demonstrations given in an exhibition of 'Karnataka Chitrakala Parishad', in Karnataka.

One man show exhibition held in Vashi, New Bombay, in March 1993
of 60 Portrait Sketches of Famous Personalities.

Portrait Sketches done around 700 till now, including many celebrities and politicians, and many of them are sold in abroad.

WORK EXPERIENCE
Worked for many leading companies of India like the Reliance Infocomm Ltd.,
Futurethought Production Pvt. Ltd. (Animation studio),
Clubgreetinga India Pvt. Ltd. (Electronic Greeting Site),
holding various designations as a Visualiser, Graphic Designer, Senior Animation,
Senior Layout cum Background Artist, etc.
Also woked as a freelancer for the leading organization of India like MTV Asia,
Lowe India (Lintas), Ambience D'Arcy India, Gey Worldwide, Leo Burnett etc.

GROUP SHOWS:
Participated in Group Shows of 'BOMBAY ART SOCIETY,' 'ART SOCIETY OF INDIA',
'CHATAK SHOW', etc.

EMAIL ID: adityachari11@yahoo.com

CONTENTS

GESTURE DRAWINGS

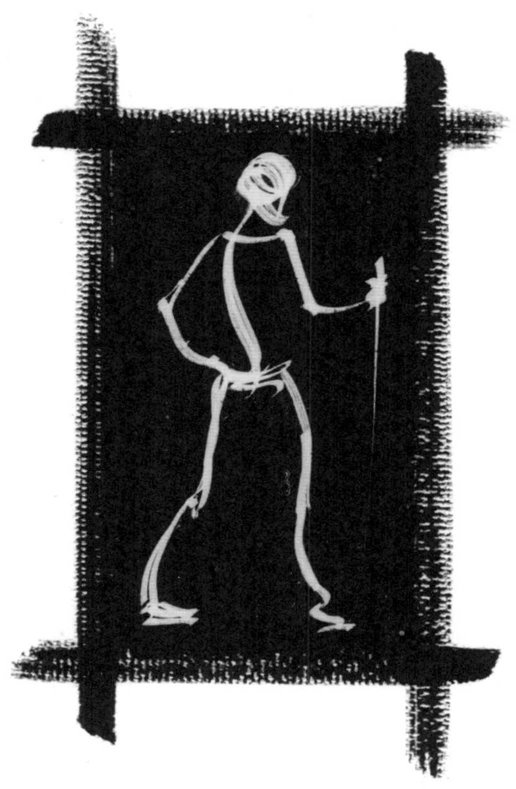

Gesture drawing means drawing very quickly capturing the essence of the form. Speed drawing is the first step in drawing. Once you begin and adhere to the quick drawing approach, the proportions you draw will be accurate and the drawing will have life, spirit and fluidity. The best way to start sketching is in a loose gestured style.

Gesture drawing demands your full involvement, which will result in better understanding giving strength to your work, and increases your understanding of various forms. Don't think about what the form is, like a face or a leaf - just draw the outline/contour. Once you finish with that, you can draw the inside contours and details, for example, the features on the face, or veins on a leaf. Do not use an eraser for this exercise!

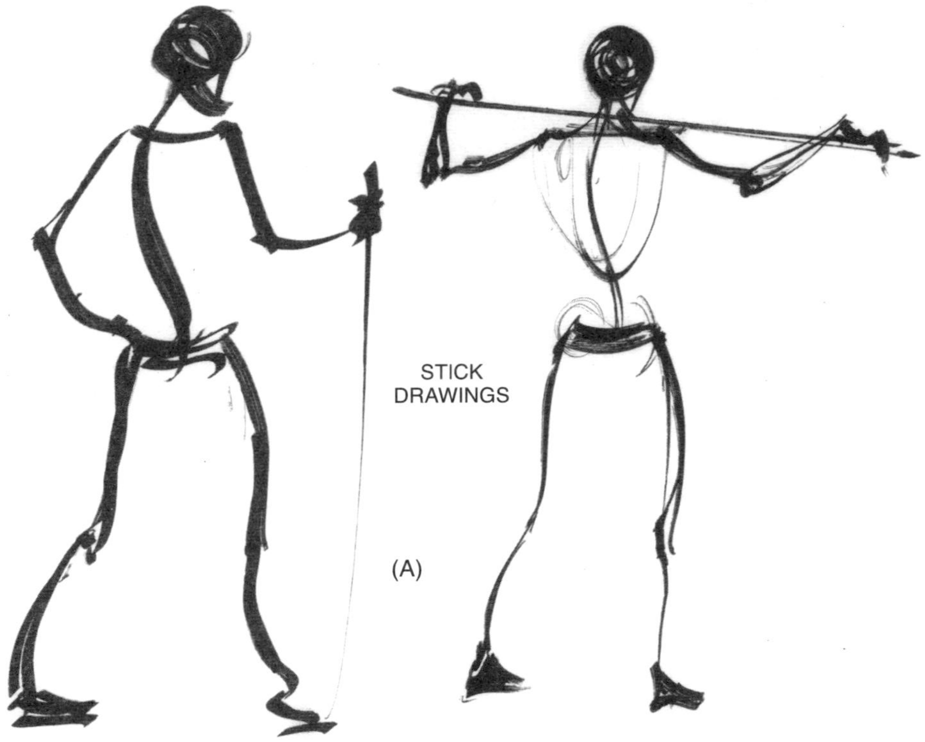

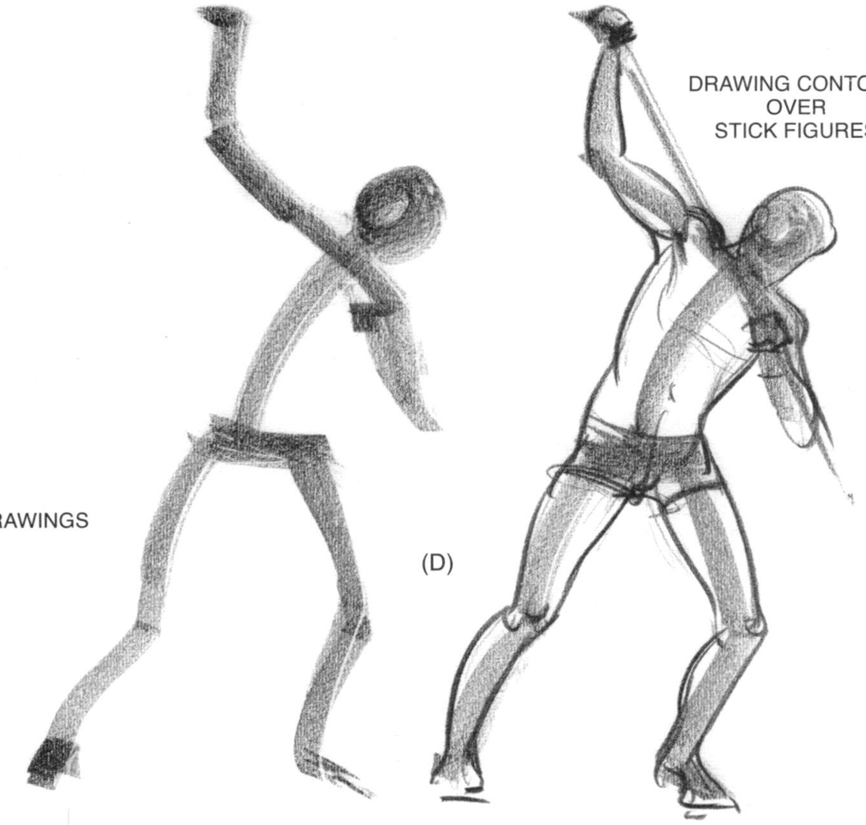

STICK DRAWINGS

(A)

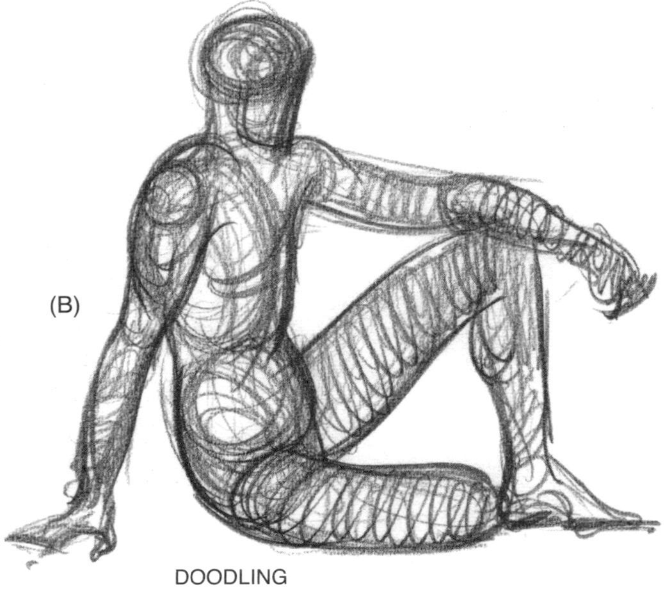

(B)

DOODLING

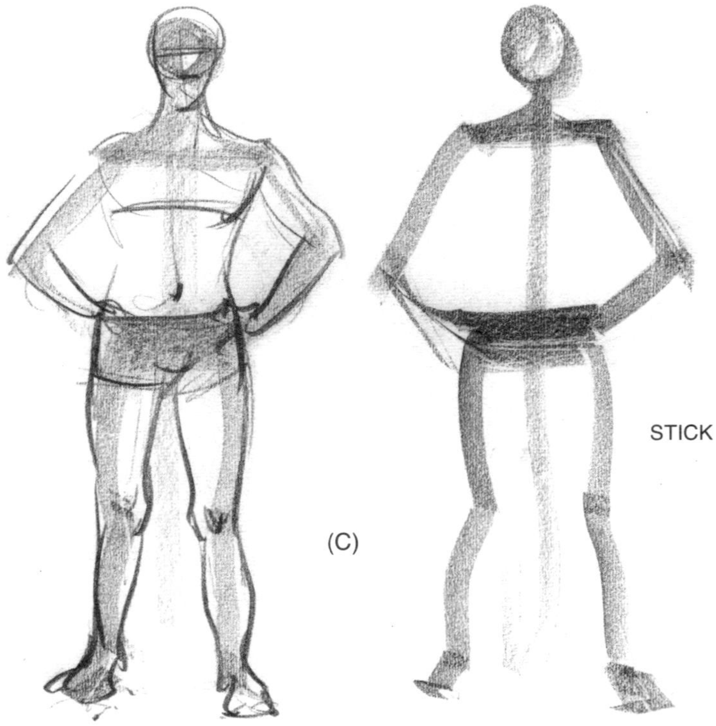

DRAWING CONTOUR OVER STICK FIGURES

(C)

STICK DRAWINGS

(D)

You should take no more than 30 seconds when you attempt Gesture Drawing. The urgency created by swiftness adds energy to your drawing. Unimportant details are kept to the bare minimum. Observe in detail, the main axis of the body, right from the top of the head to the tip of the spine. With a single stroke, try to show the flow of the spine. Always pause to observe and study a pose. Try to find what makes each pose exciting and different in its own right. When you are ready to begin drawing, try the speed drawing method, and on completion, compare your drawing with the actual model. Ask yourself whether or not your drawing has captured the spirit and fluidity of the pose in front of you. What you are looking to create here is a direct and simple drawing. The purpose behind minimizing drawing time is to maximize the concentration for a short period to obtain a given objective. For you it is an exercise to enable you to draw a figure in its most simple and immediate form. You will be surprised at how powerful these quick sketches can be. The economy of lines suggests a remarkable force and the superficial traits of the model give way to a far more expressive statement of weight, movement and mood.

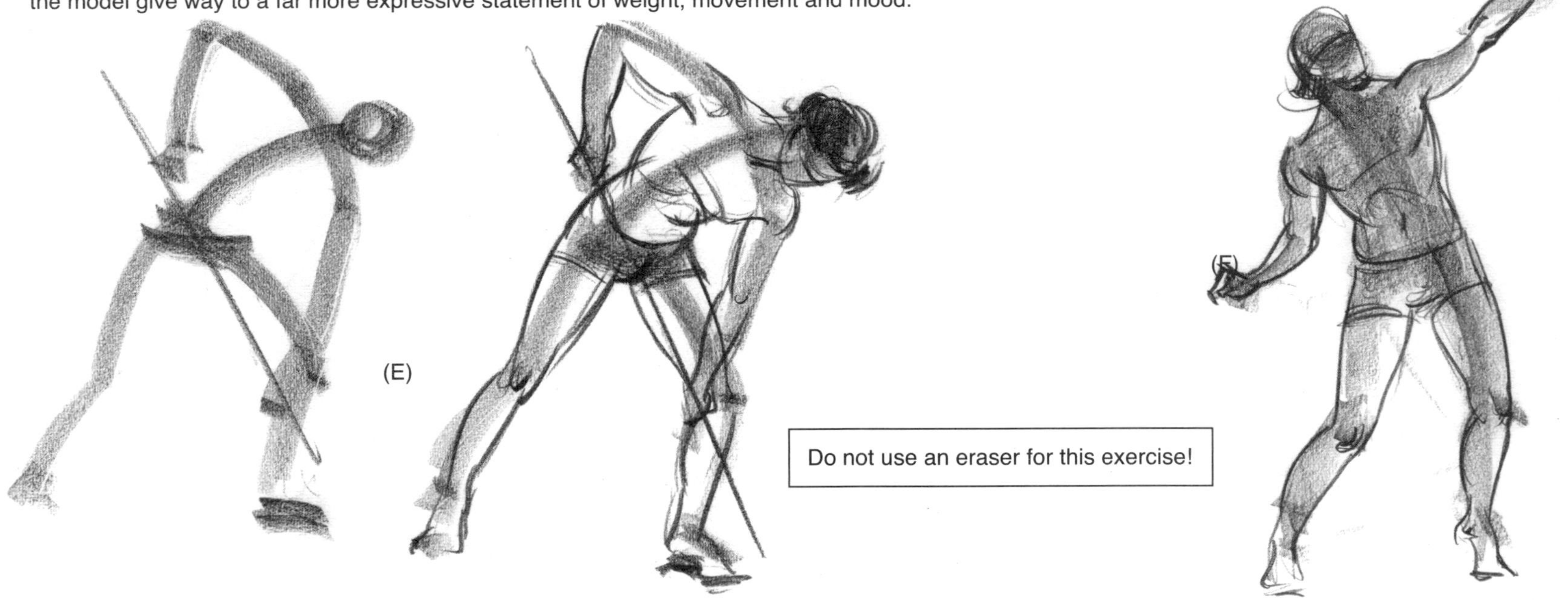

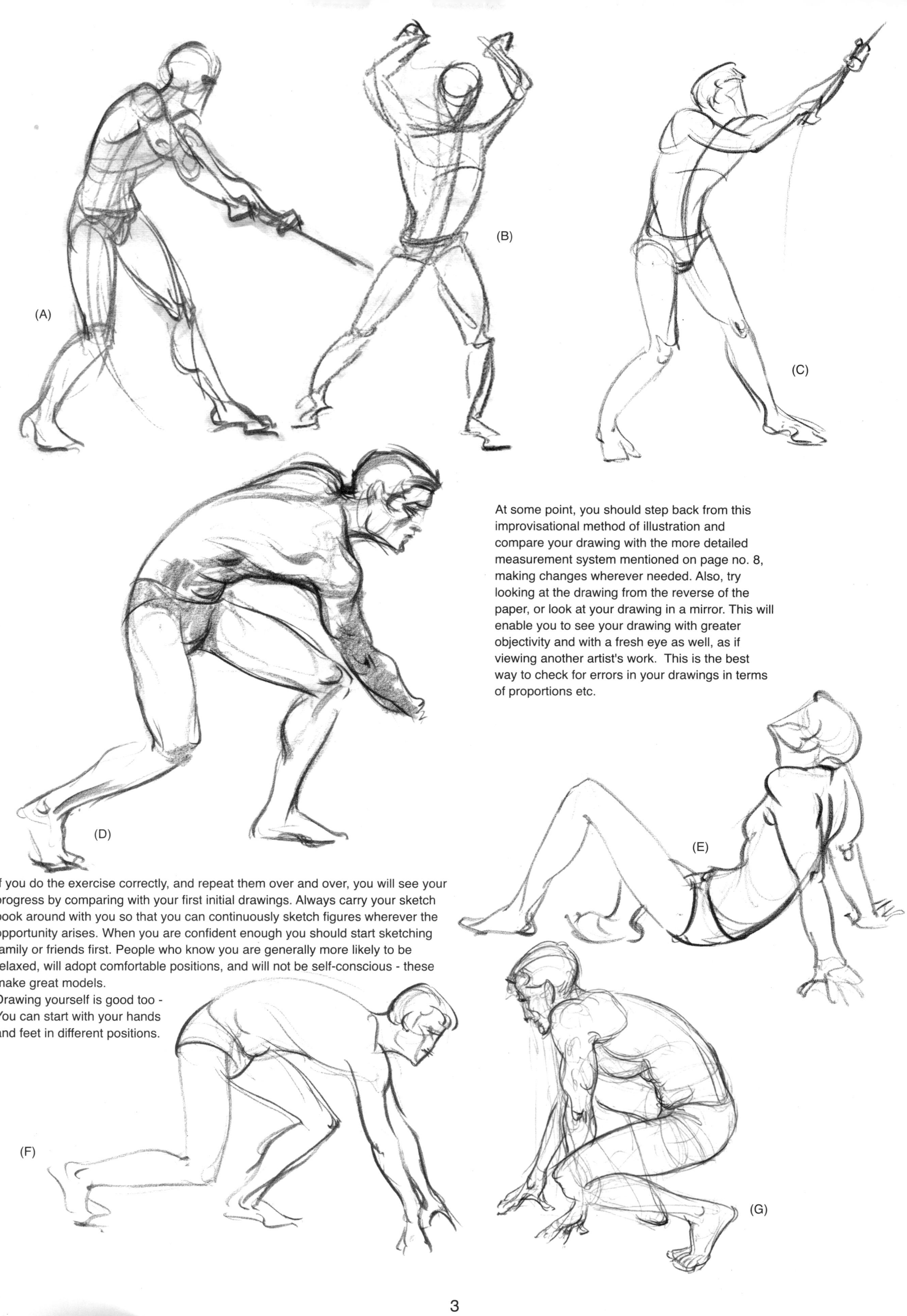

At some point, you should step back from this improvisational method of illustration and compare your drawing with the more detailed measurement system mentioned on page no. 8, making changes wherever needed. Also, try looking at the drawing from the reverse of the paper, or look at your drawing in a mirror. This will enable you to see your drawing with greater objectivity and with a fresh eye as well, as if viewing another artist's work. This is the best way to check for errors in your drawings in terms of proportions etc.

If you do the exercise correctly, and repeat them over and over, you will see your progress by comparing with your first initial drawings. Always carry your sketch book around with you so that you can continuously sketch figures wherever the opportunity arises. When you are confident enough you should start sketching family or friends first. People who know you are generally more likely to be relaxed, will adopt comfortable positions, and will not be self-conscious - these make great models.

Drawing yourself is good too - You can start with your hands and feet in different positions.

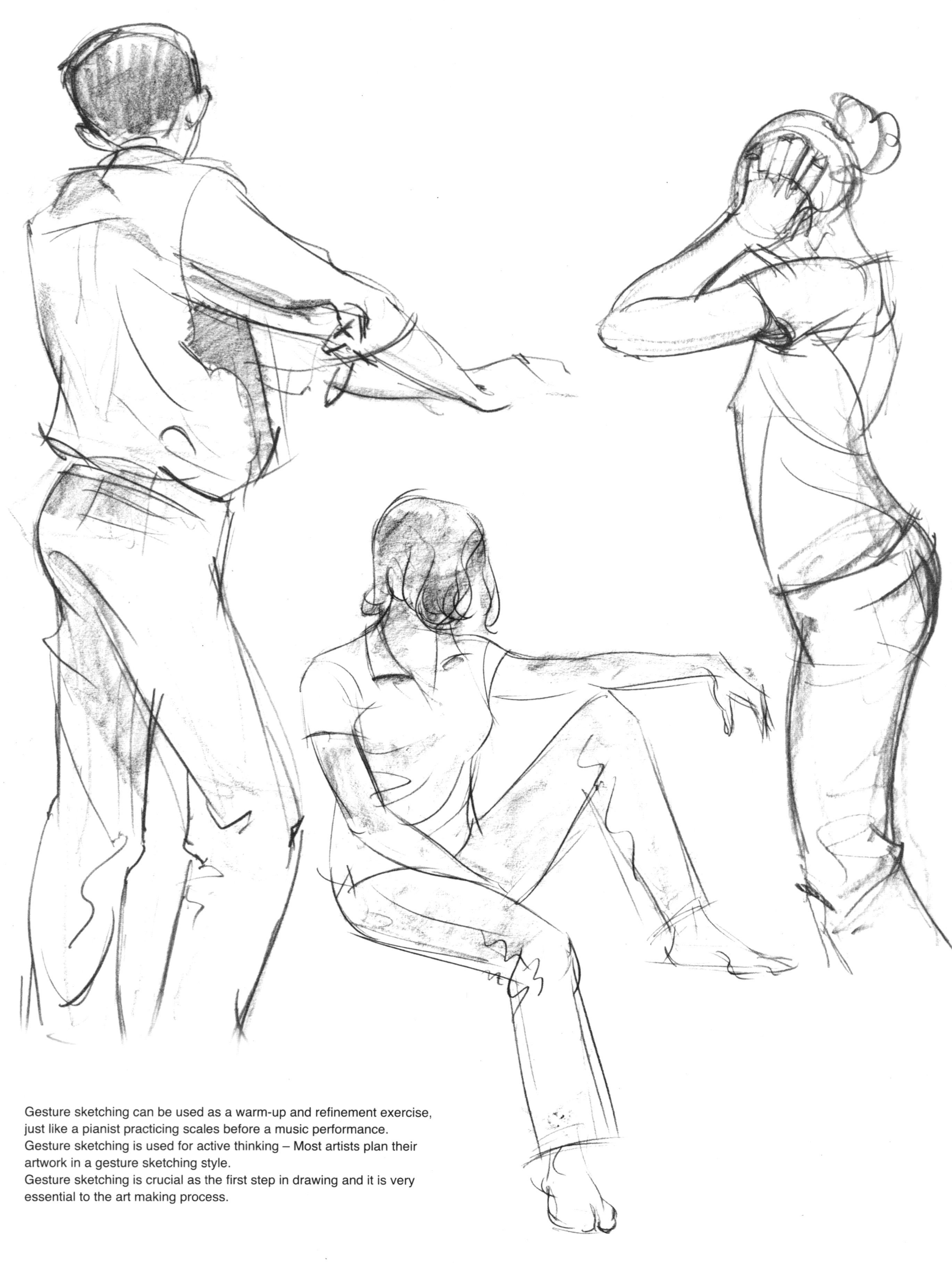

Gesture sketching can be used as a warm-up and refinement exercise, just like a pianist practicing scales before a music performance.
Gesture sketching is used for active thinking – Most artists plan their artwork in a gesture sketching style.
Gesture sketching is crucial as the first step in drawing and it is very essential to the art making process.

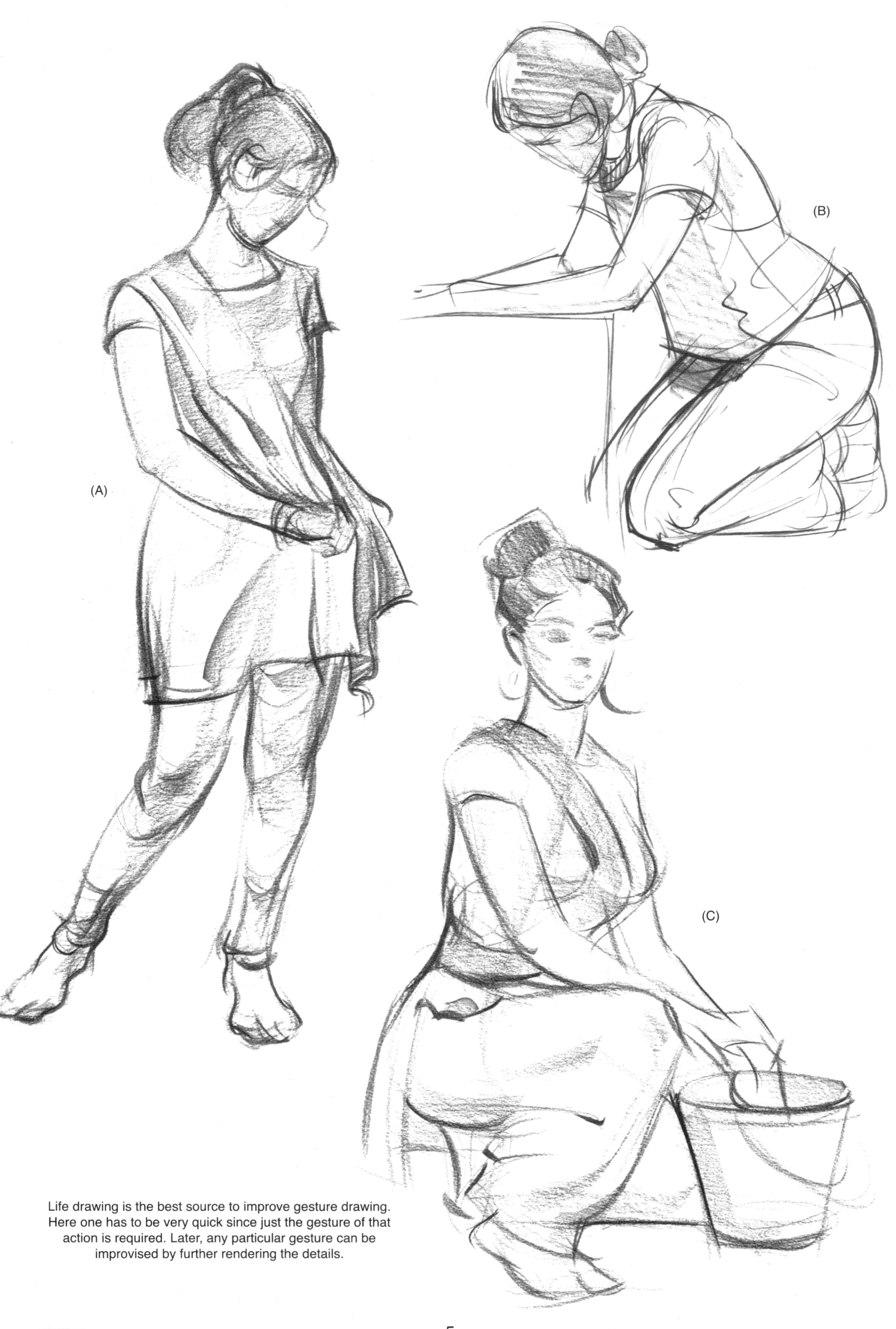

Life drawing is the best source to improve gesture drawing. Here one has to be very quick since just the gesture of that action is required. Later, any particular gesture can be improvised by further rendering the details.

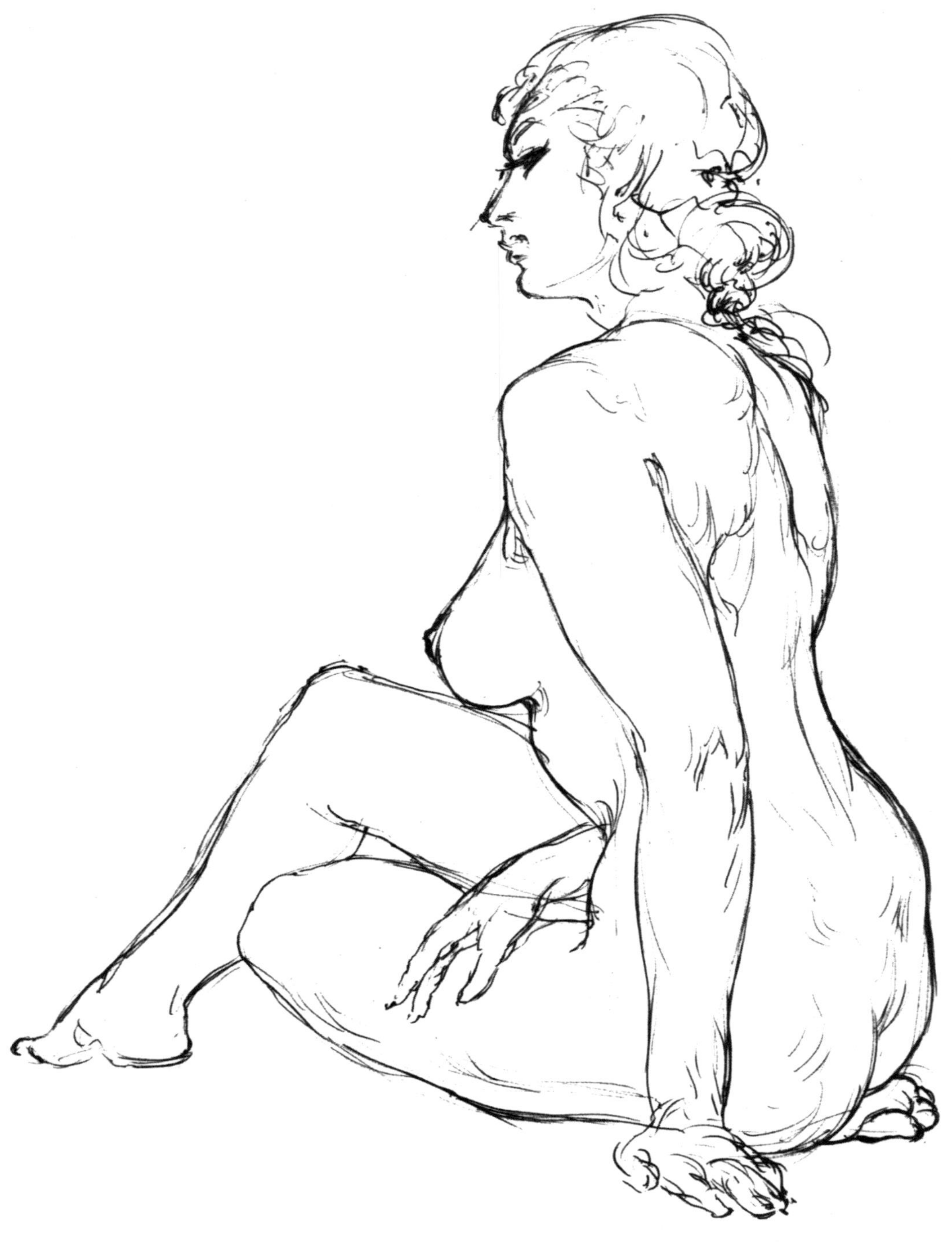

BASIC PROPORTIONS

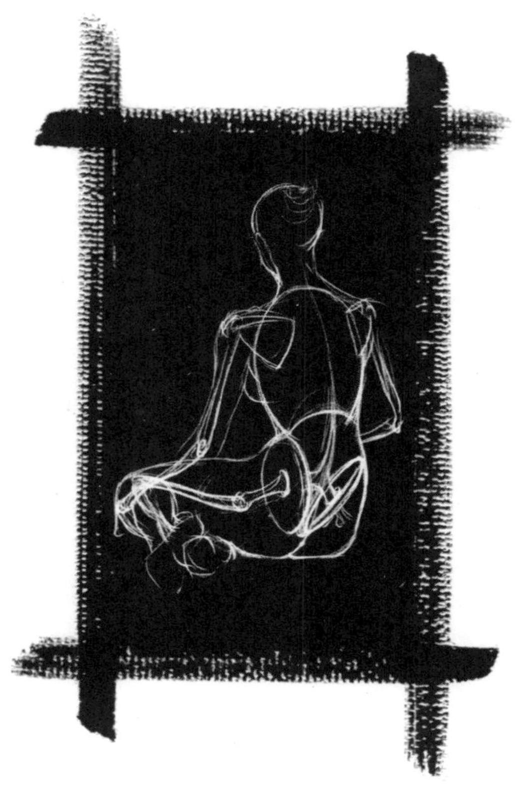

Proportions change according to the age. An adult's total height is around seven and half heads compared, to a baby's figure, which is only about four times the height of its head. Taking the approximate proportions of an adult, draw a figure in three different positions – namely: front, side, and back. Pay keen attention to the measurements of the shoulders, hips and calves. Some other interesting points you will notice are: there is only one head unit of spacing between nipples; the waist is slightly broader than one head unit, the wrist descends just below the crotch, the elbows are just above the line of navel, the knees are fractionally above the lower quarter of the figure.

The proportion of a child's body changes according to the age. An infant has a large head with a long torso, while the arms and legs are very short. As the child grows, these proportions change. If you observe the chart you will notice how the limbs - legs and the arms, get longer as the child grows older. The head grows very slowly. An older child will have the proportions closer to those of an adult.

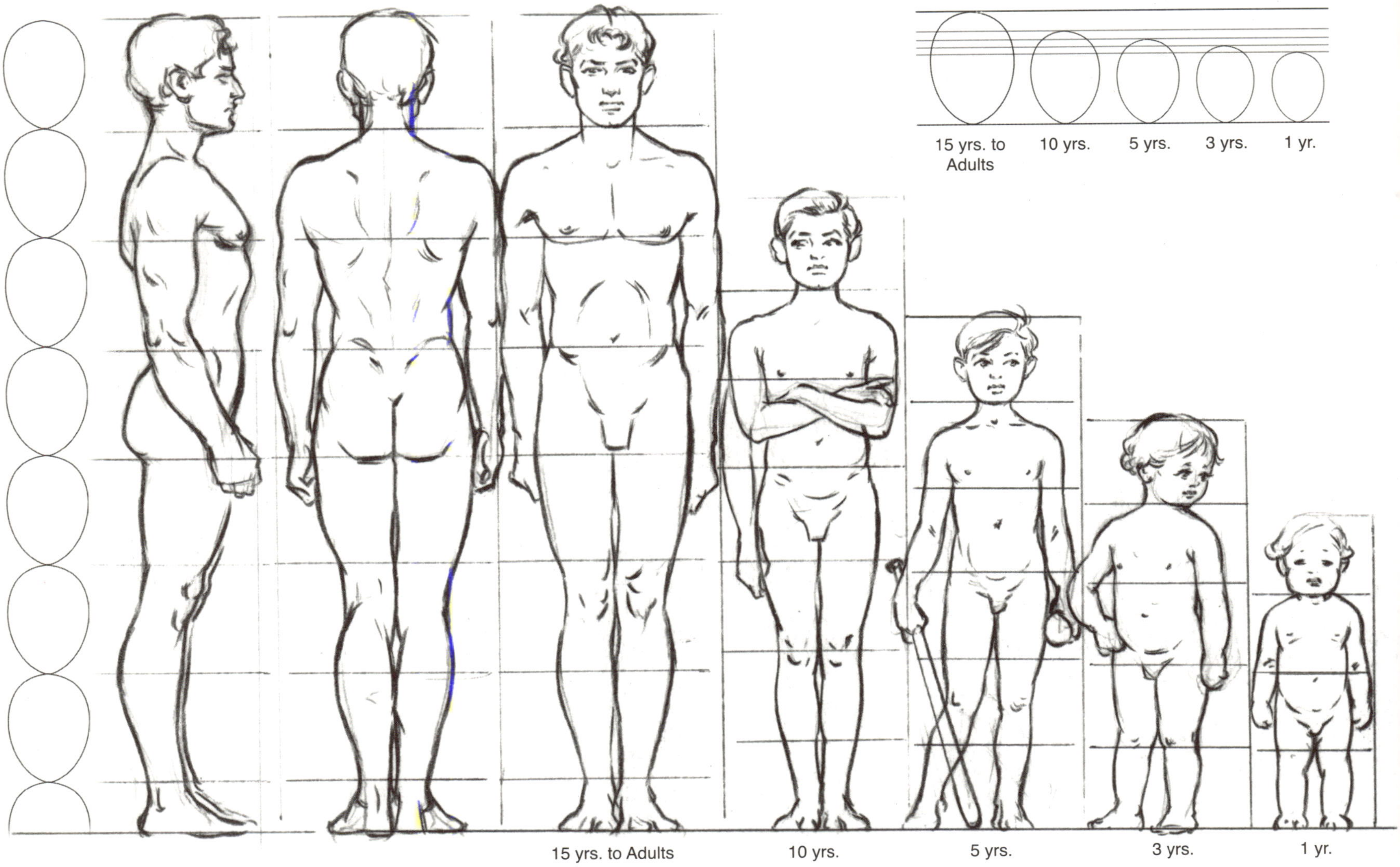

15 yrs. to Adults
10 yrs.
5 yrs.
3 yrs.
1 yr.

15 yrs. to Adults
10 yrs.
5 yrs.
3 yrs.
1 yr.

PROPORTION CHANGES AT VARIOUS STAGES

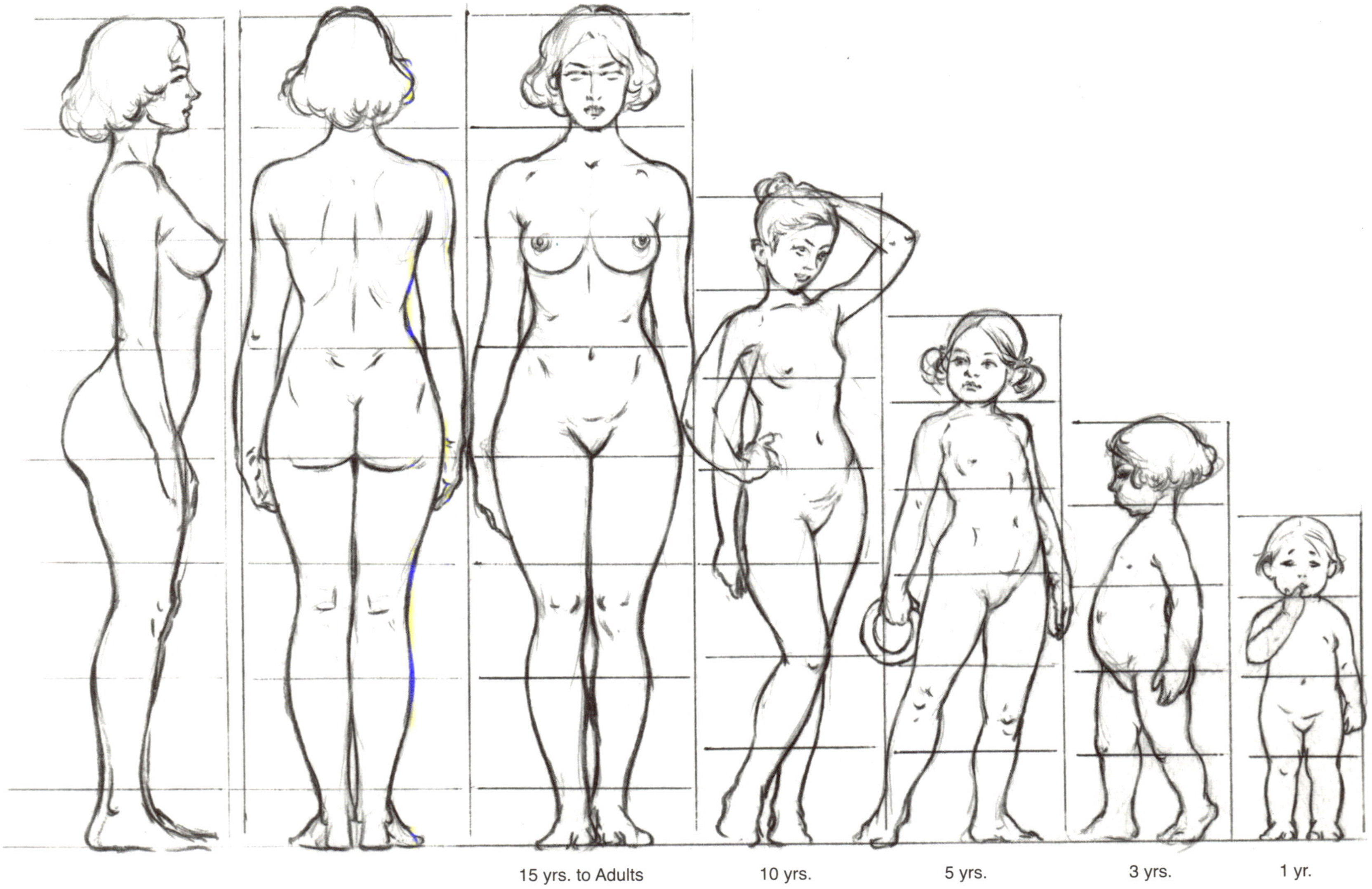

15 yrs. to Adults
10 yrs.
5 yrs.
3 yrs.
1 yr.

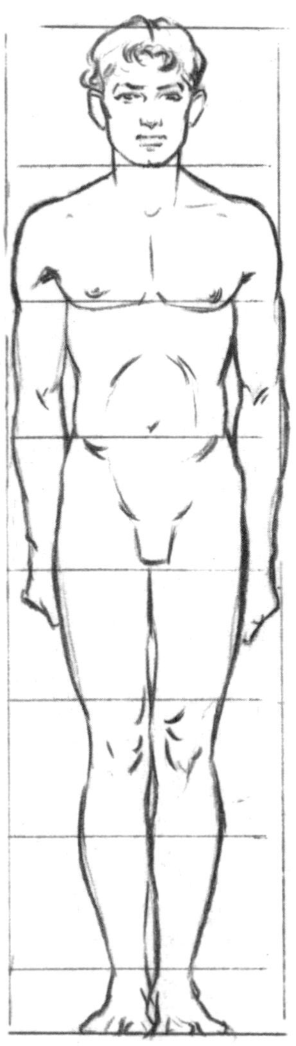

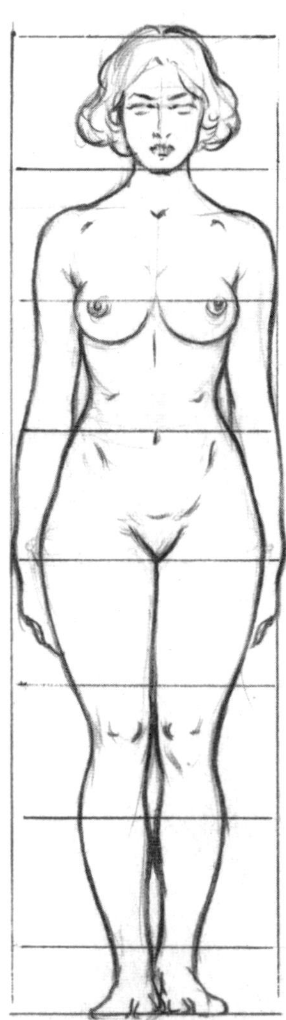

The male figure is approximately two heads broader at the widest point than the female figure. The nipples are slightly higher in the male than in the female. The female waistline measures one head unit across while the front of the thighs is slightly wider than the armpits and narrower at the back. Notice how the male navel is above or almost on line with the waistline while the female's is below it. The navel and nipples are always one head apart, but in the female figure, both are dropped below the head divisions. The elbow is above the navel. It is vital that you learn the various differences in the male and female forms.

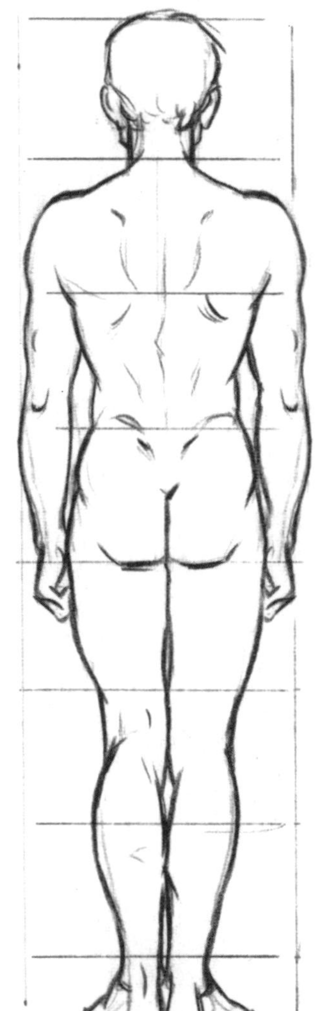

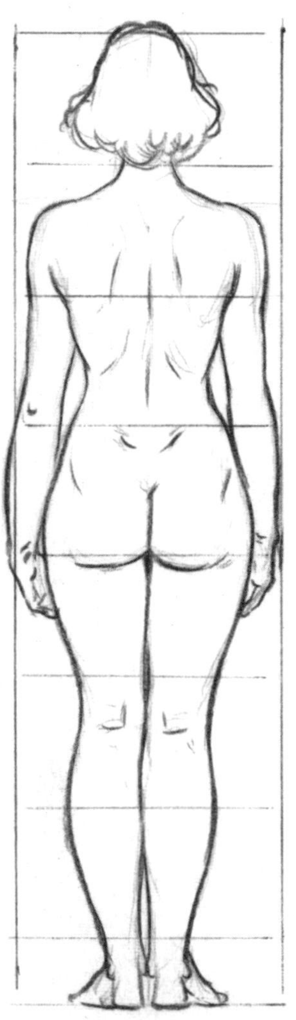

Although the number and kinds of bones and muscles are the same in males and females, there is a difference in the relative size of the bones in both sex. For example, there is a reversal of relationships with regards to the chest and pelvic bones: in a women, the chest cage is small and the pelvic bone is larger, while in a man, the chest cage is large and the pelvis bone is small.

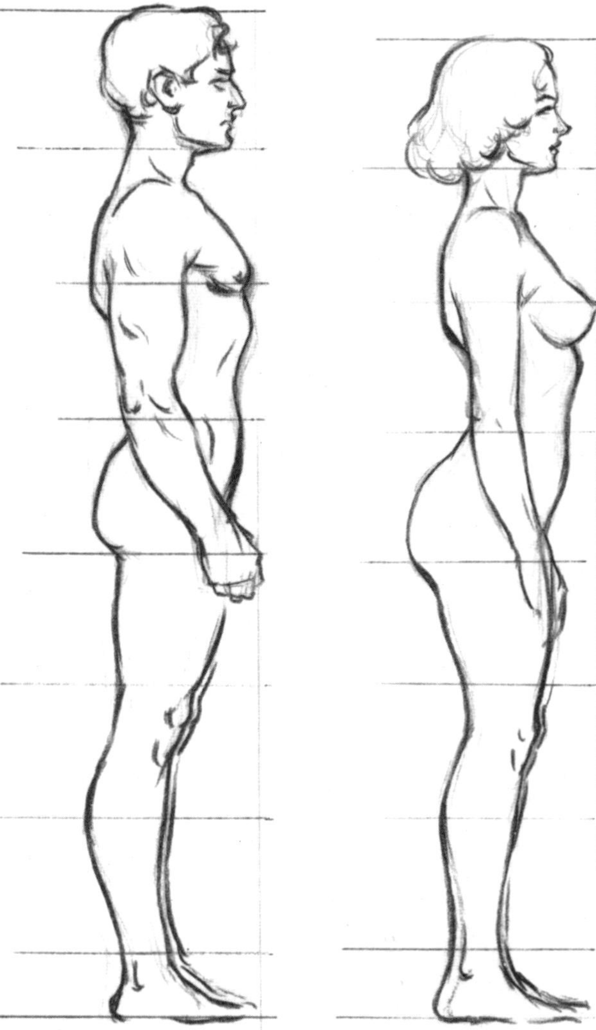

The muscular development in males and females is distributed differently. The male usually has broad shoulders and narrow hips. His upper torso and arms are more muscular and his arms hang down in a straight line. A female on the other hand, has narrower shoulders and wider hips, with larger thigh muscles. Due to her narrower shoulders, her elbows are closer to the body, making the forearm swing out. The skin of the female is smoother than that of the male while the female neck is longer and thinner as compared to a shorter and thicker male neck. The hands and feet of a female are more delicate and small while a male's are broad and bigger in proportion to the figure.

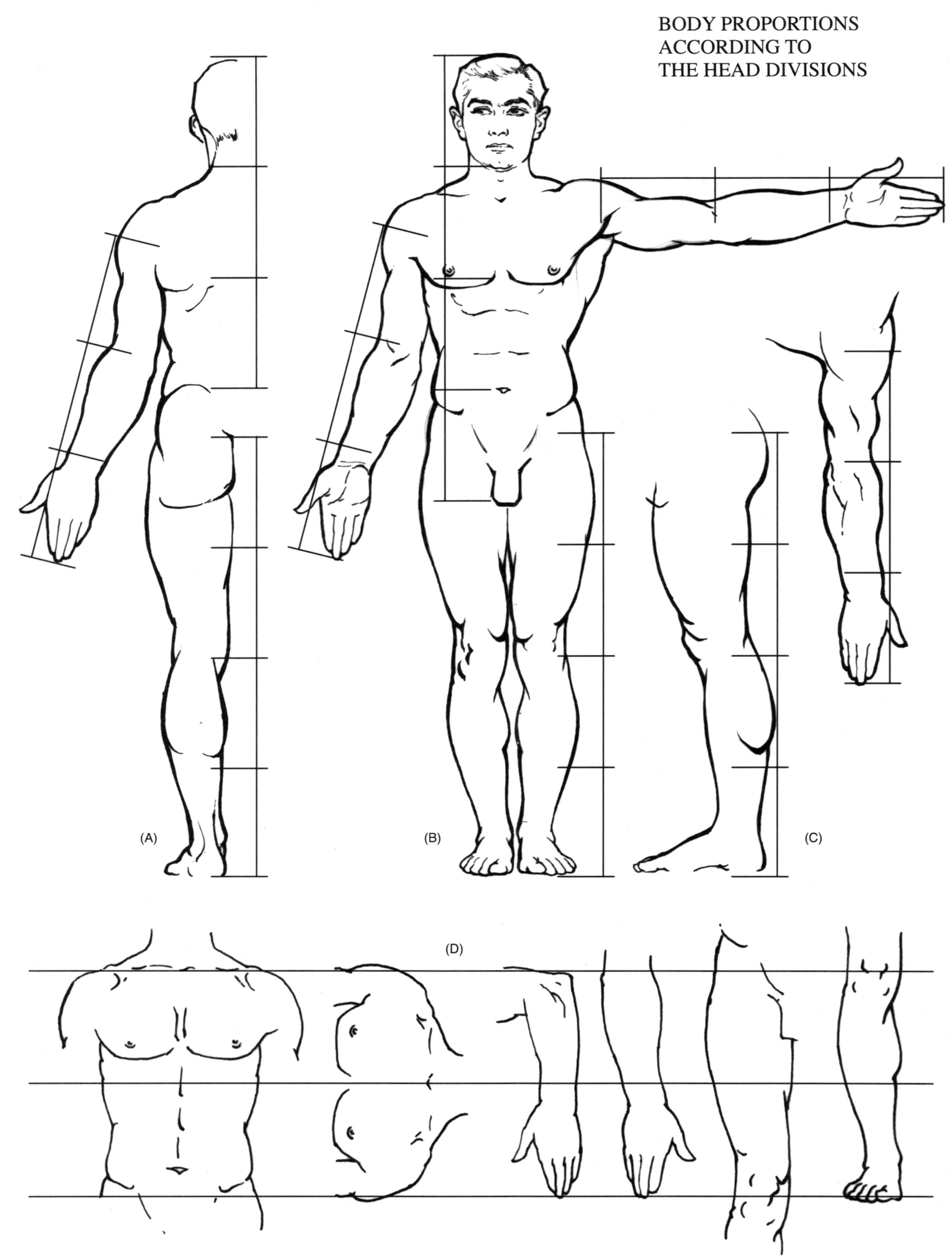
BODY PROPORTIONS
ACCORDING TO
THE HEAD DIVISIONS
(A)
(B)
(C)
(D)

SIMPLIFYING HUMAN SKELETON

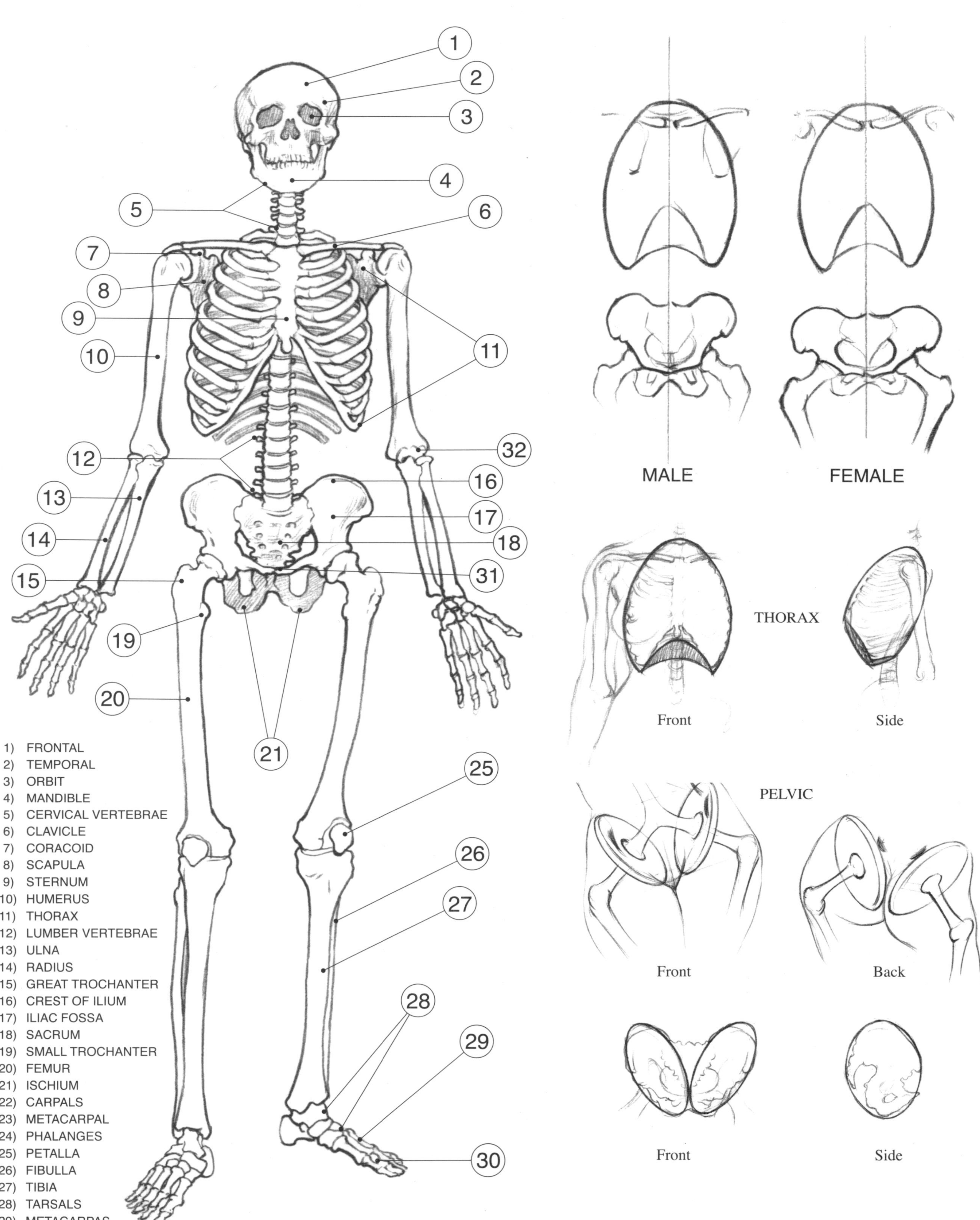

1) FRONTAL
2) TEMPORAL
3) ORBIT
4) MANDIBLE
5) CERVICAL VERTEBRAE
6) CLAVICLE
7) CORACOID
8) SCAPULA
9) STERNUM
10) HUMERUS
11) THORAX
12) LUMBER VERTEBRAE
13) ULNA
14) RADIUS
15) GREAT TROCHANTER
16) CREST OF ILIUM
17) ILIAC FOSSA
18) SACRUM
19) SMALL TROCHANTER
20) FEMUR
21) ISCHIUM
22) CARPALS
23) METACARPAL
24) PHALANGES
25) PETALLA
26) FIBULLA
27) TIBIA
28) TARSALS
29) METACARPAS
30) PHALANGES
31) PUBIS
32) TROCHLEA

The labeled illustrations of human skeleton. Try to remember the names, it will help you in referring. This simplified skeleton diagram will help you in sketching figures in various poses.

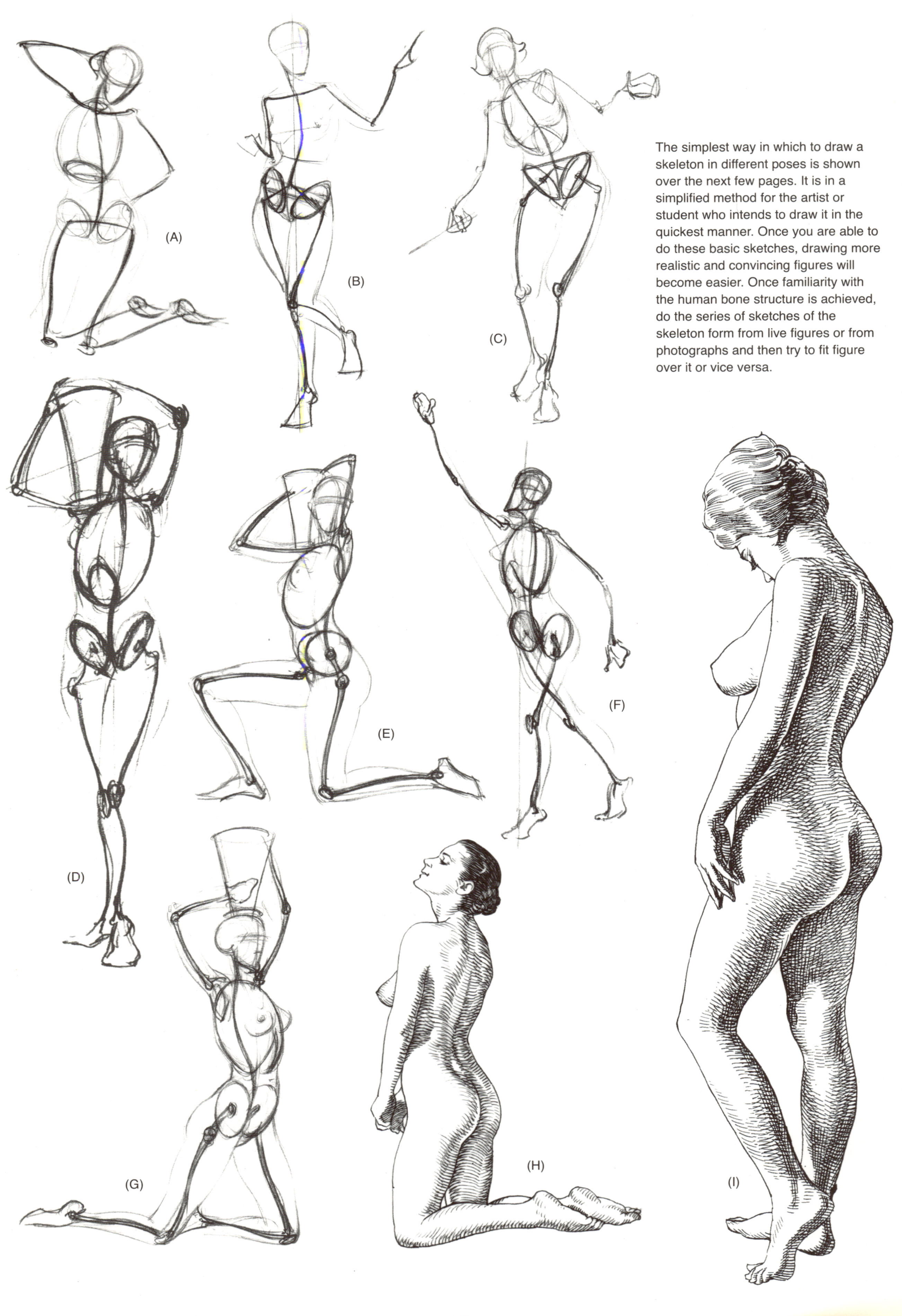

The simplest way in which to draw a skeleton in different poses is shown over the next few pages. It is in a simplified method for the artist or student who intends to draw it in the quickest manner. Once you are able to do these basic sketches, drawing more realistic and convincing figures will become easier. Once familiarity with the human bone structure is achieved, do the series of sketches of the skeleton form from live figures or from photographs and then try to fit figure over it or vice versa.

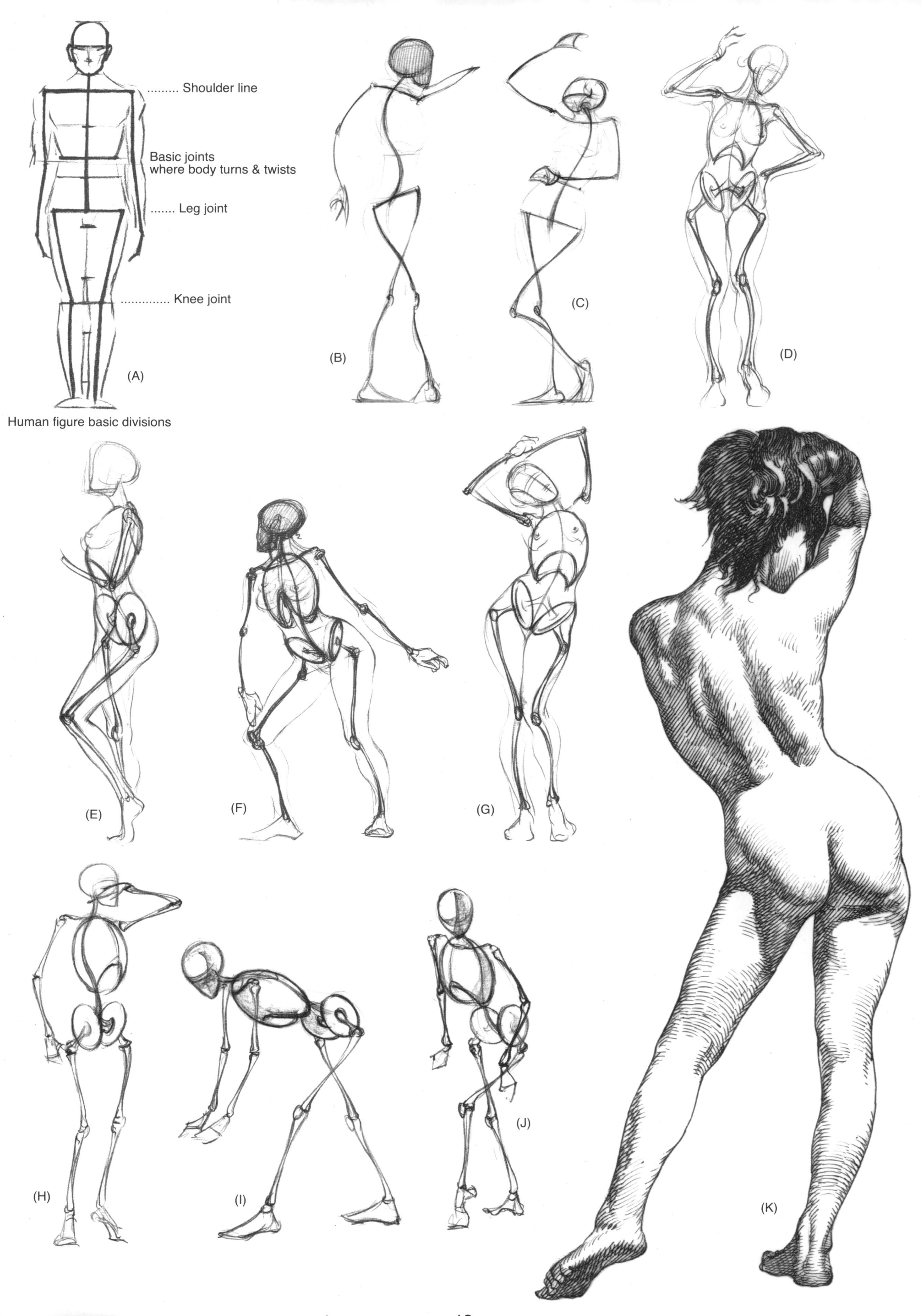

Human figure basic divisions

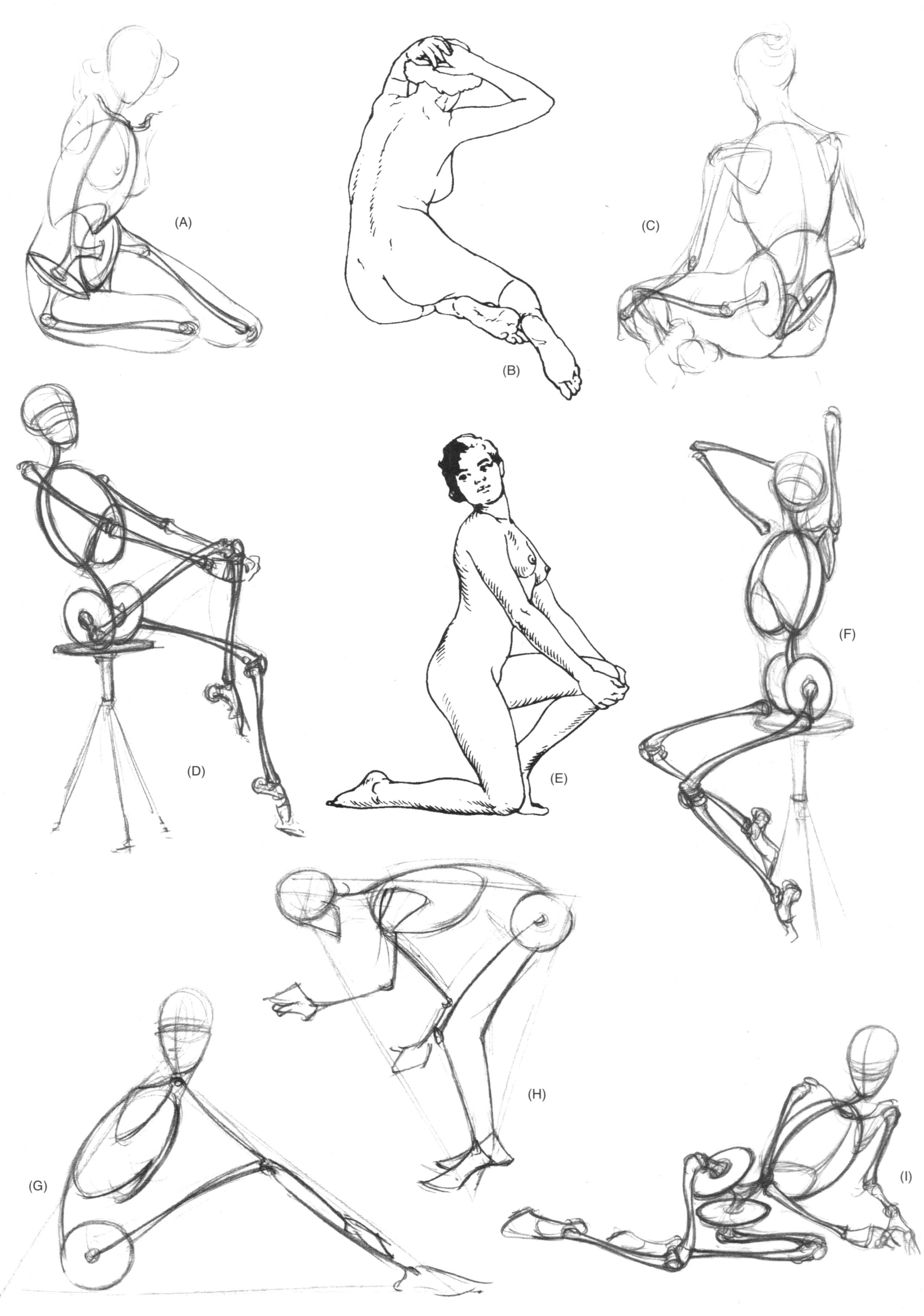
(A)
(B)
(C)
(D)
(E)
(F)
(H)
(G)
(I)

HEAD

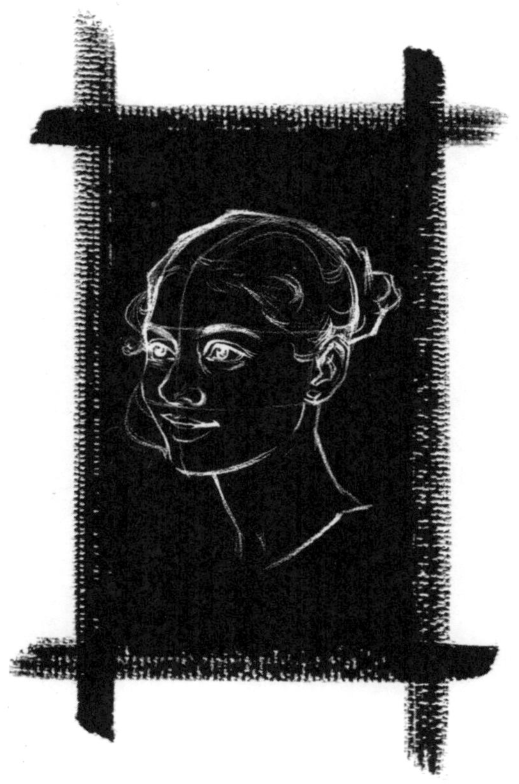

In the over all human figure, head and face are the main focal point of attention and their vivid expressions are the means of communication. The eyes are the main center of attraction , they express more emotions and different moods than words, which suggests the inner feeling of the drawn character. Next comes the eye brows which plays great role in complementing the expression of eyes. Nose gives a character to the face, its slightest change in planes can change the entire look of the face, so take special care while portraying some one. Ear has got the most complex form as compared to any other body part, so it requires practice to draw it properly. The lips are the second most important feature in expressing emotions, the shape of it is not so difficult to draw but needs to be given proper attention, the shape of the lips are just like the petals of rose, so needs to be rendered softly. Chin and the jaw line are the final features of the face to study, males usually have a prominent jaw line and females have round and curvy out line.

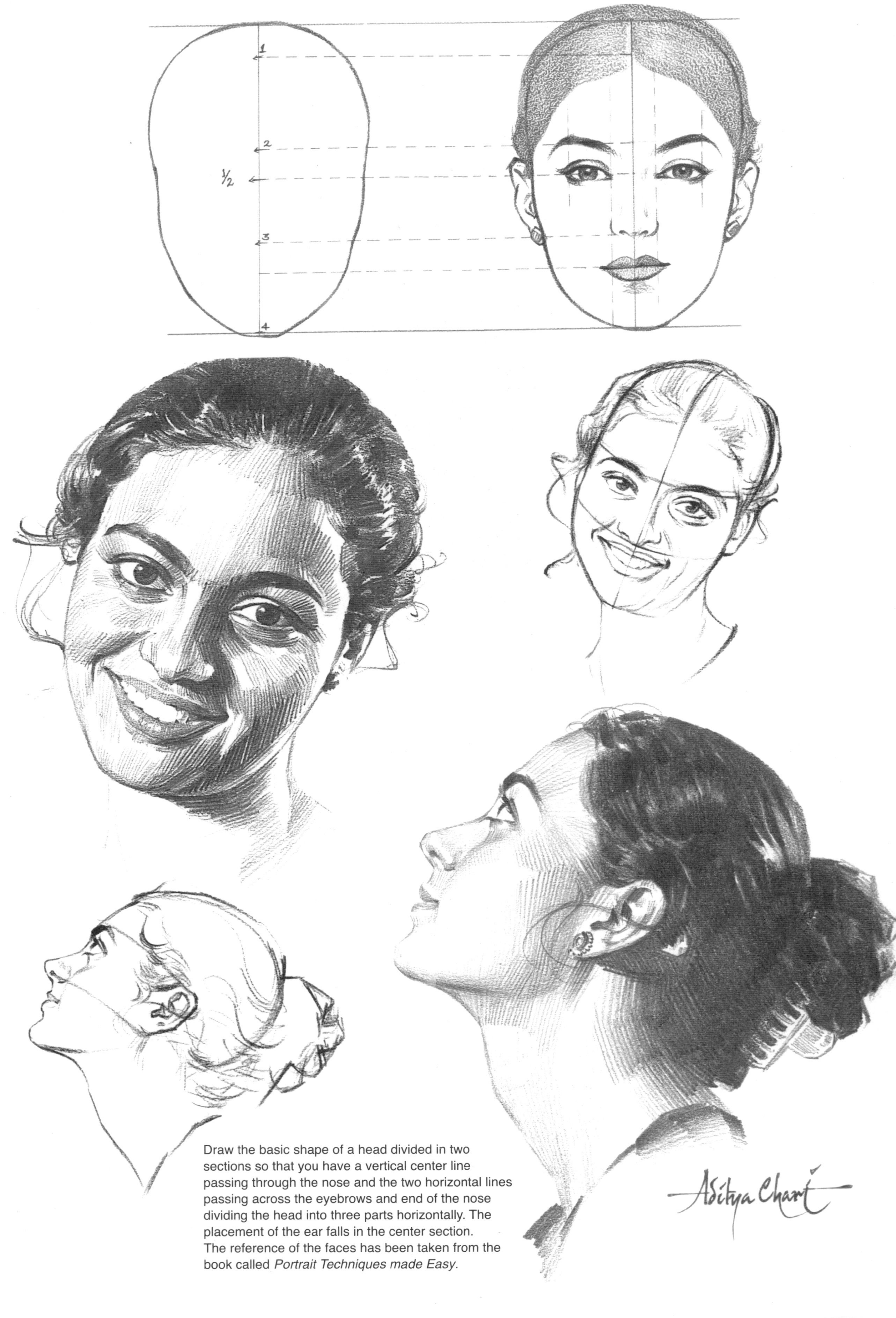

Draw the basic shape of a head divided in two sections so that you have a vertical center line passing through the nose and the two horizontal lines passing across the eyebrows and end of the nose dividing the head into three parts horizontally. The placement of the ear falls in the center section. The reference of the faces has been taken from the book called *Portrait Techniques made Easy*.

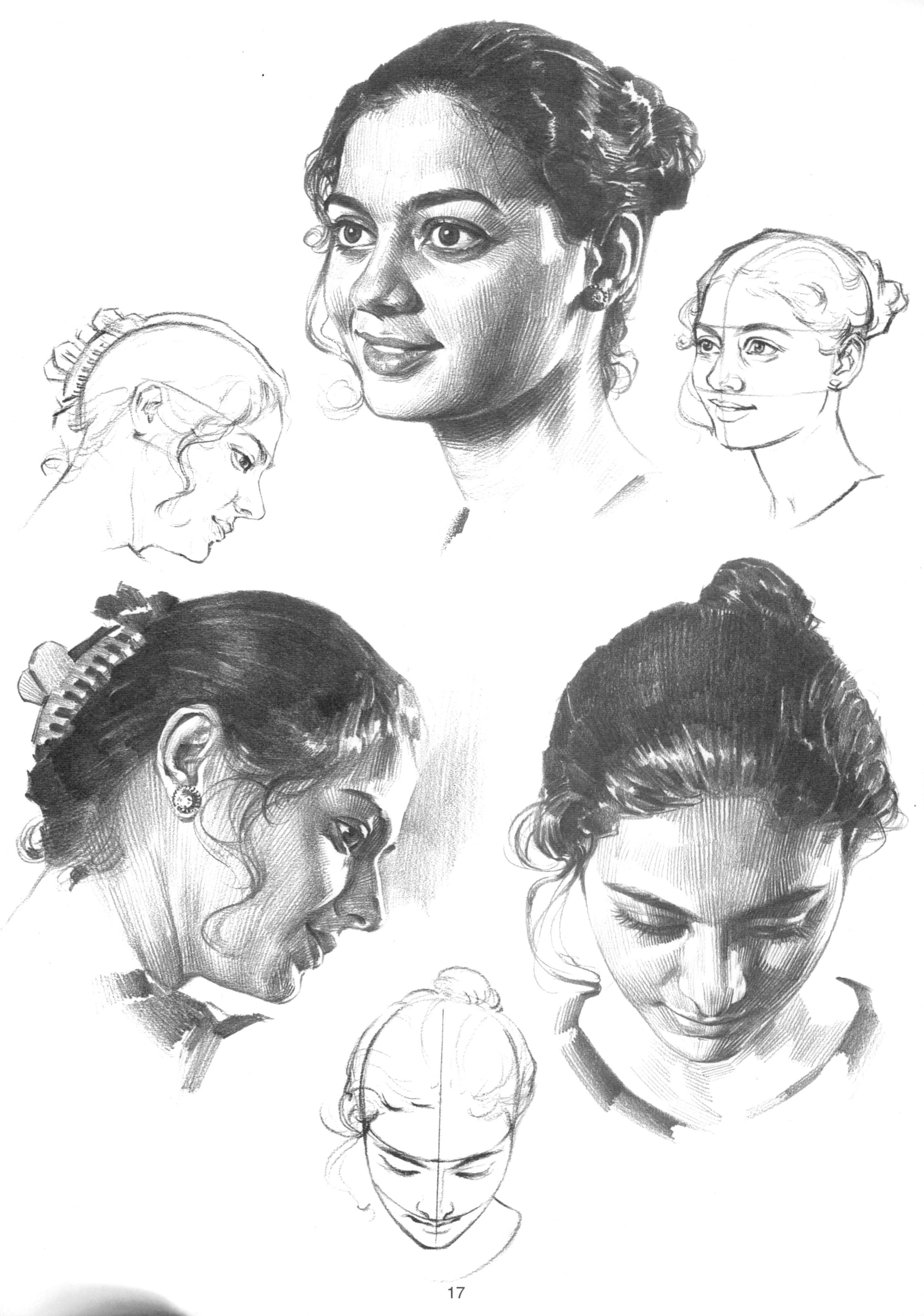

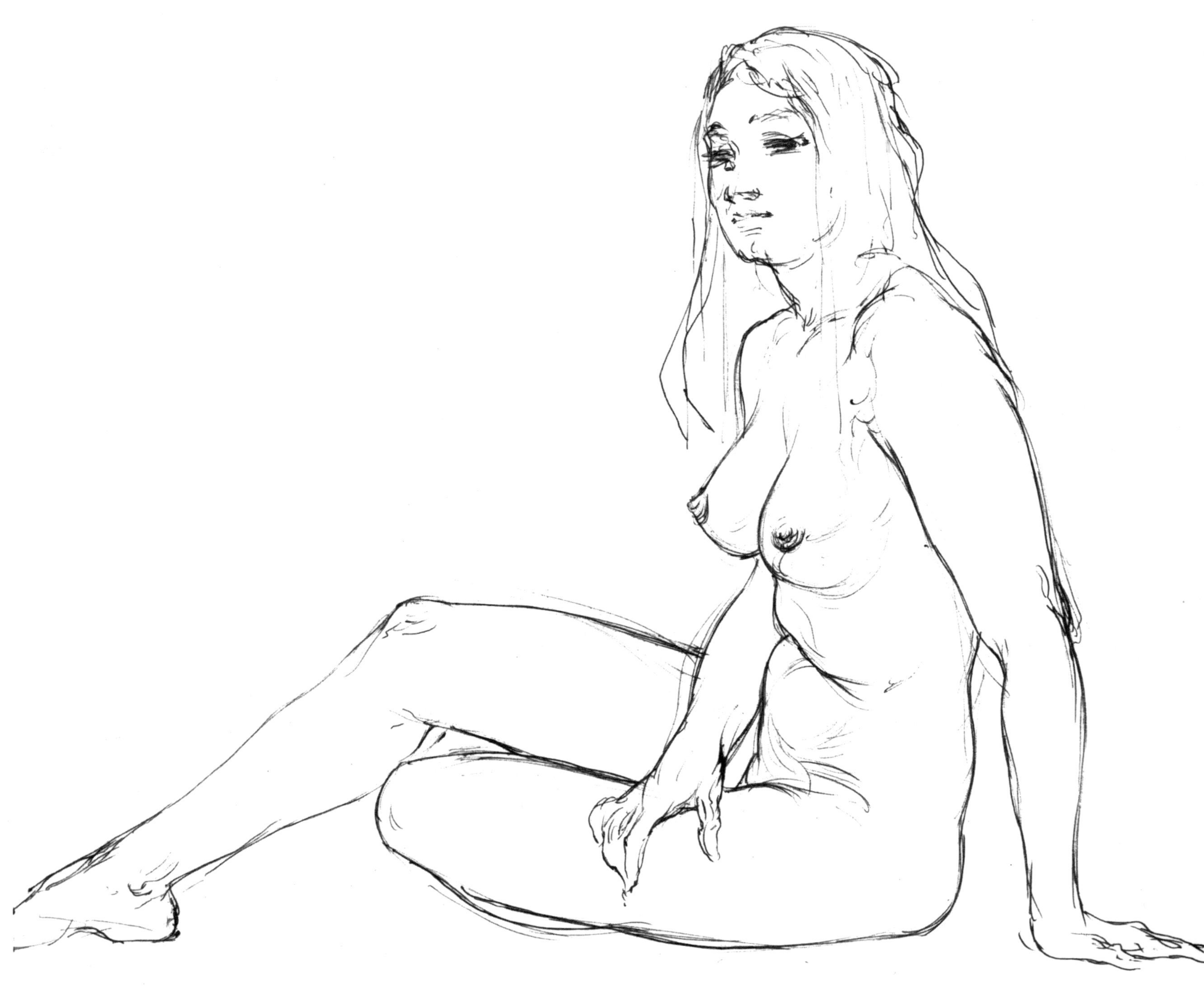

ROTATION IN ARCS

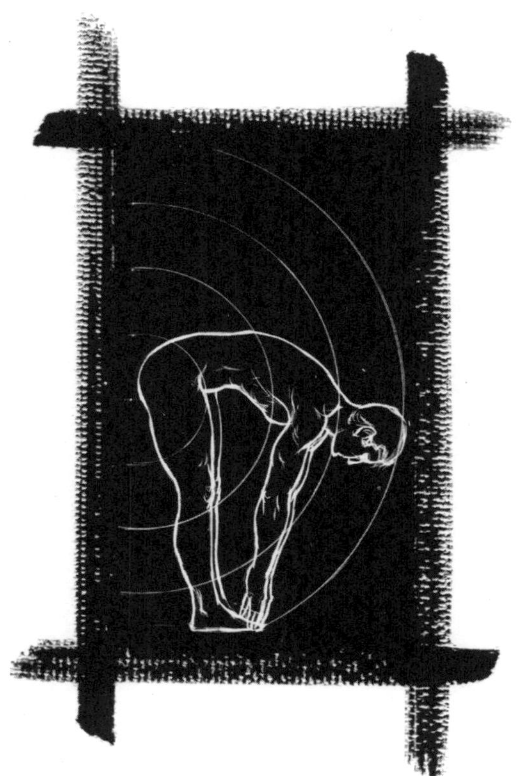

There are three categories of skeletal joints in the human body namely: ball and socket, hinge and Irregular. It is because of these joints that a human is able to move a particular body part in a certain direction. All this movement occurs within an arc, without distorting or losing its proportion.

The ball-and-socket joints, allow roughly 95 percent movement of action and provide the adjacent limbs the ability to extend in an almost 360 degree circle rotation. The only disadvantage of this range of motion is that, without the large muscles in the body that surround them, these joints would be relatively unstable.

The hinge joints such as the knee or elbow bend only in one direction and are less flexible. However, they are more rigid and stronger than the ball and socket joints. The knee has the hinge joint to enable it to maintain the balance of the body, give it stability and more importantly, to give the body support while performing any action of movement. It is due to these joints that all body parts move in an arc. These joints move on their own fixed axis (do not dislocate from their joints) and hence they ensure perfect arcs.

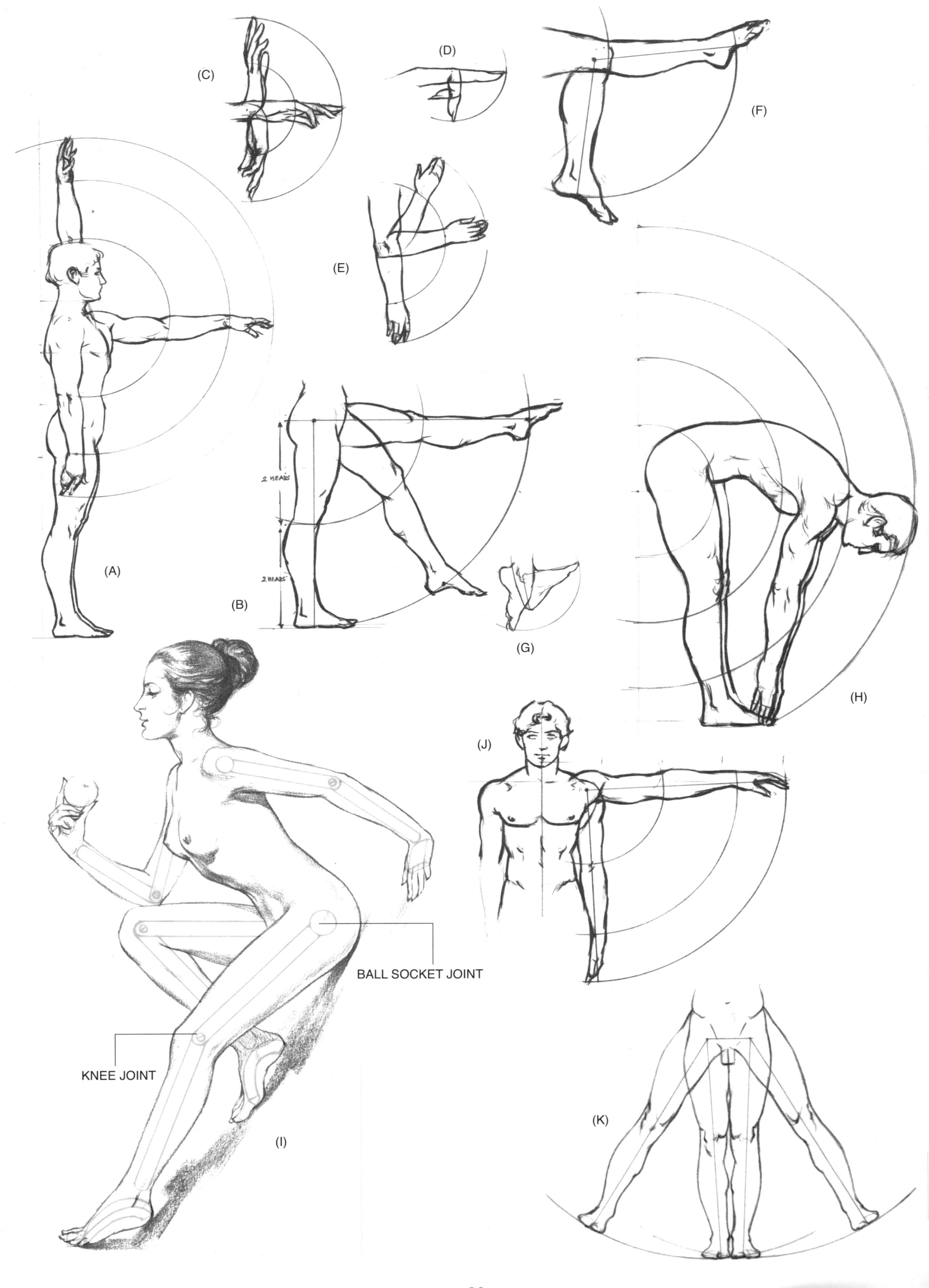
(C)
(D)
(F)
(E)
2 HEADS
2 HEADS
(A)
(B)
(G)
(H)
(J)
BALL SOCKET JOINT
KNEE JOINT
(I)
(K)

KEY LINE

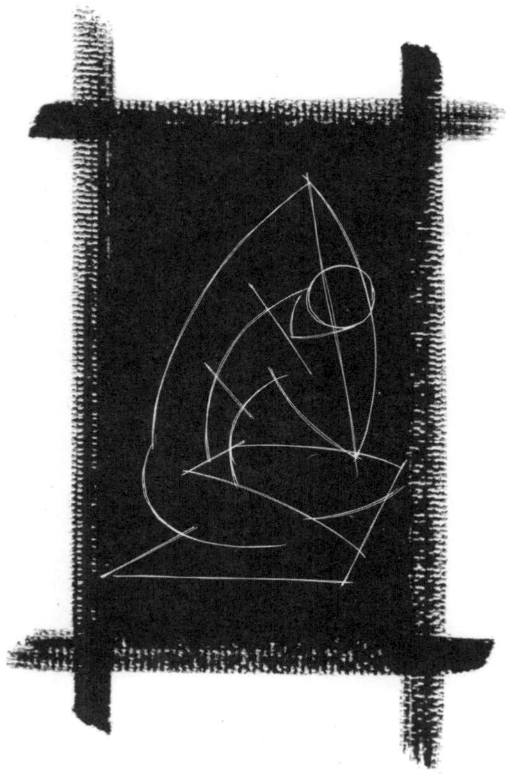

Key lines are lines that are used for Structural Division. However, these lines also give a feeling of speed and movement to the figure. In key lining, one has to observe and inspect the inter-relationships of the figure and all its parts and then insert KEY lines connecting these parts. (In this case, KEY simply means main or important lines).

While inserting key lines, it is important to look at two parts of the model at once and co-ordinate their positions. For instance, while observing the head of the model, you may also have to look at the foot or hand as well. While doing this, you will have to observe how the head is placed in reference to that of foot or hand. In this way, there has to be a continual occurrence of 'co-relating' body parts. These key lines can be curved or straight, depending on the pose or position of the model.

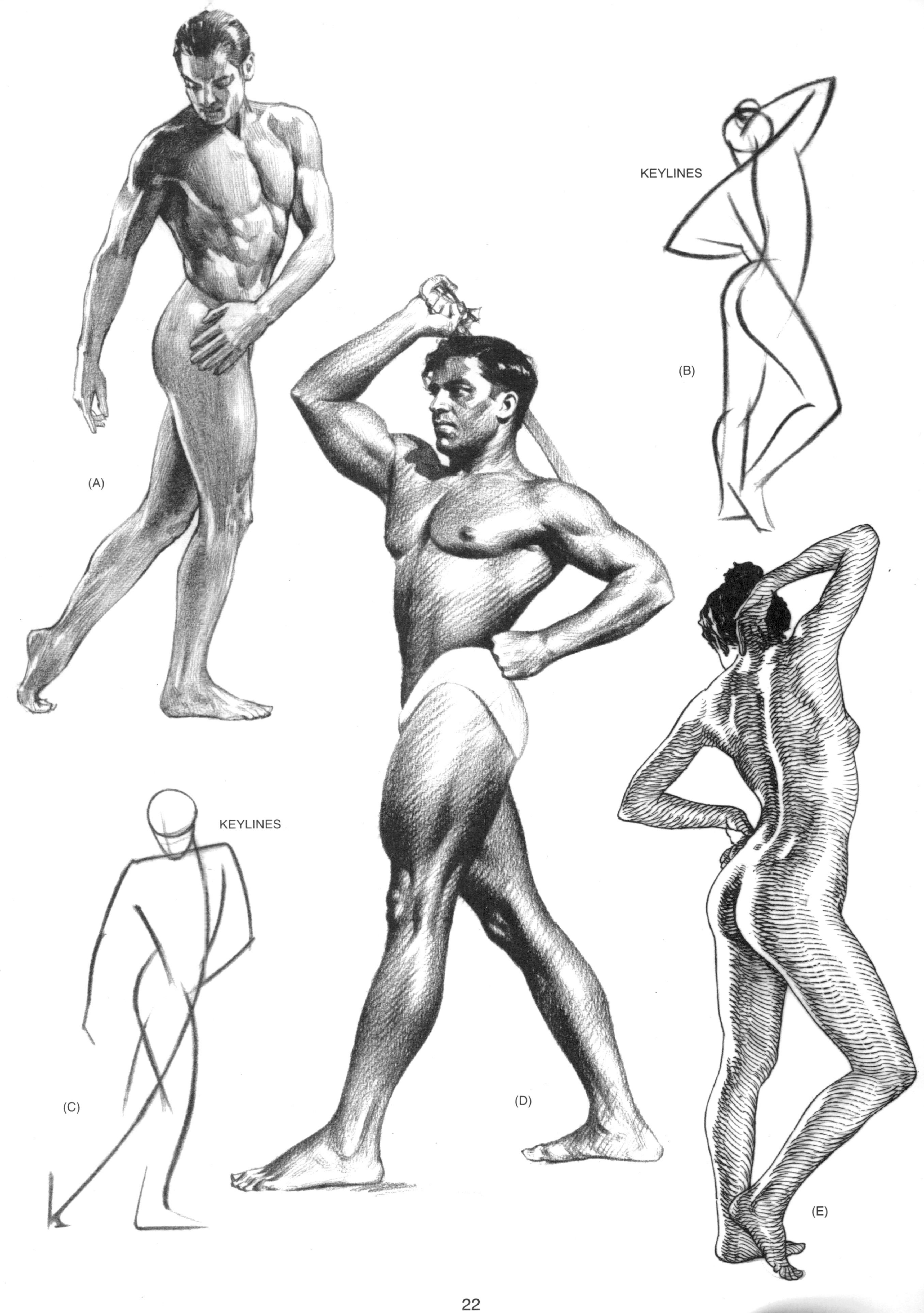
KEYLINES
(A)
(B)
KEYLINES
(C)
(D)
(E)

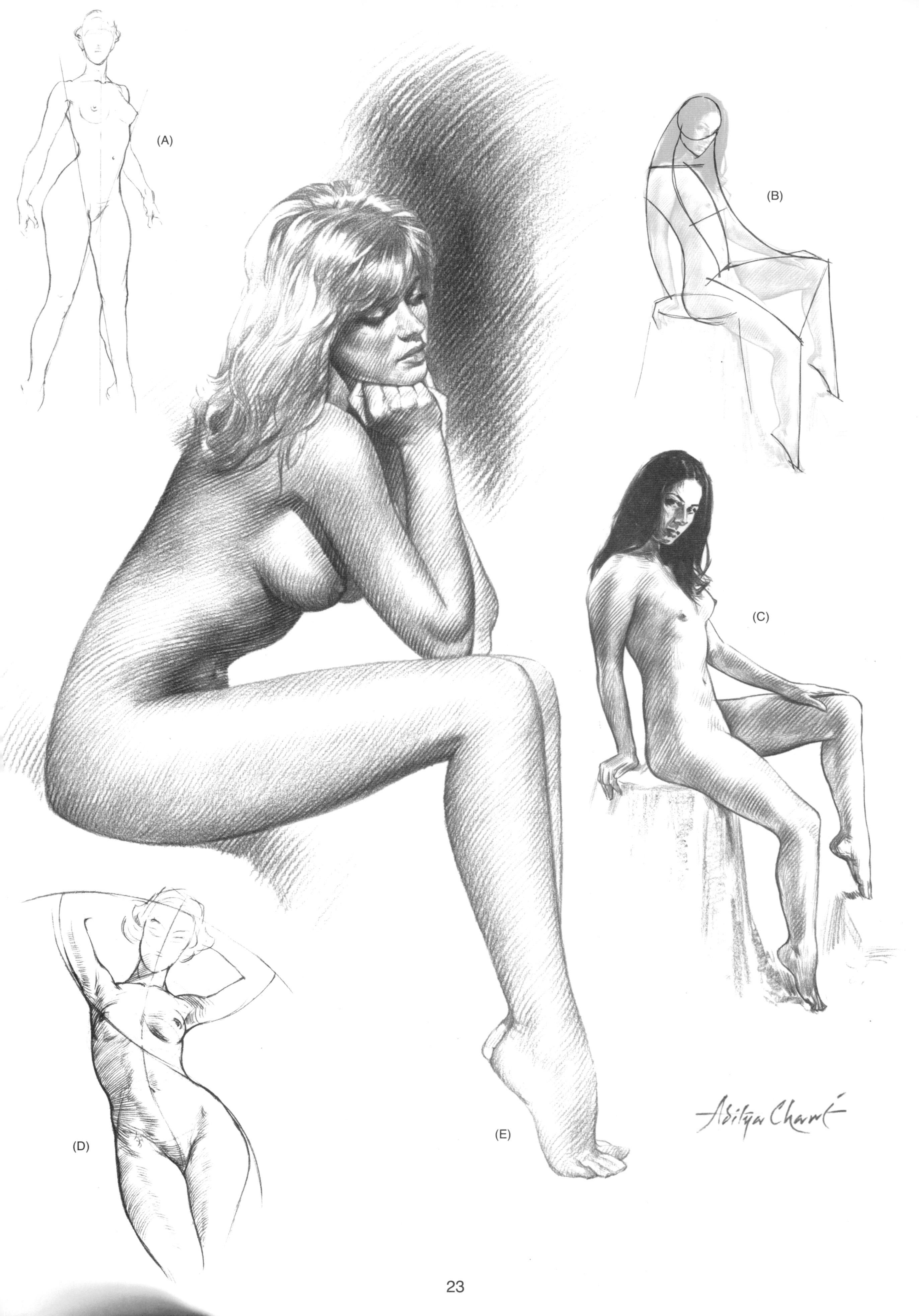
(A)
(B)
(C)
(D)
(E)
Aditya Chari

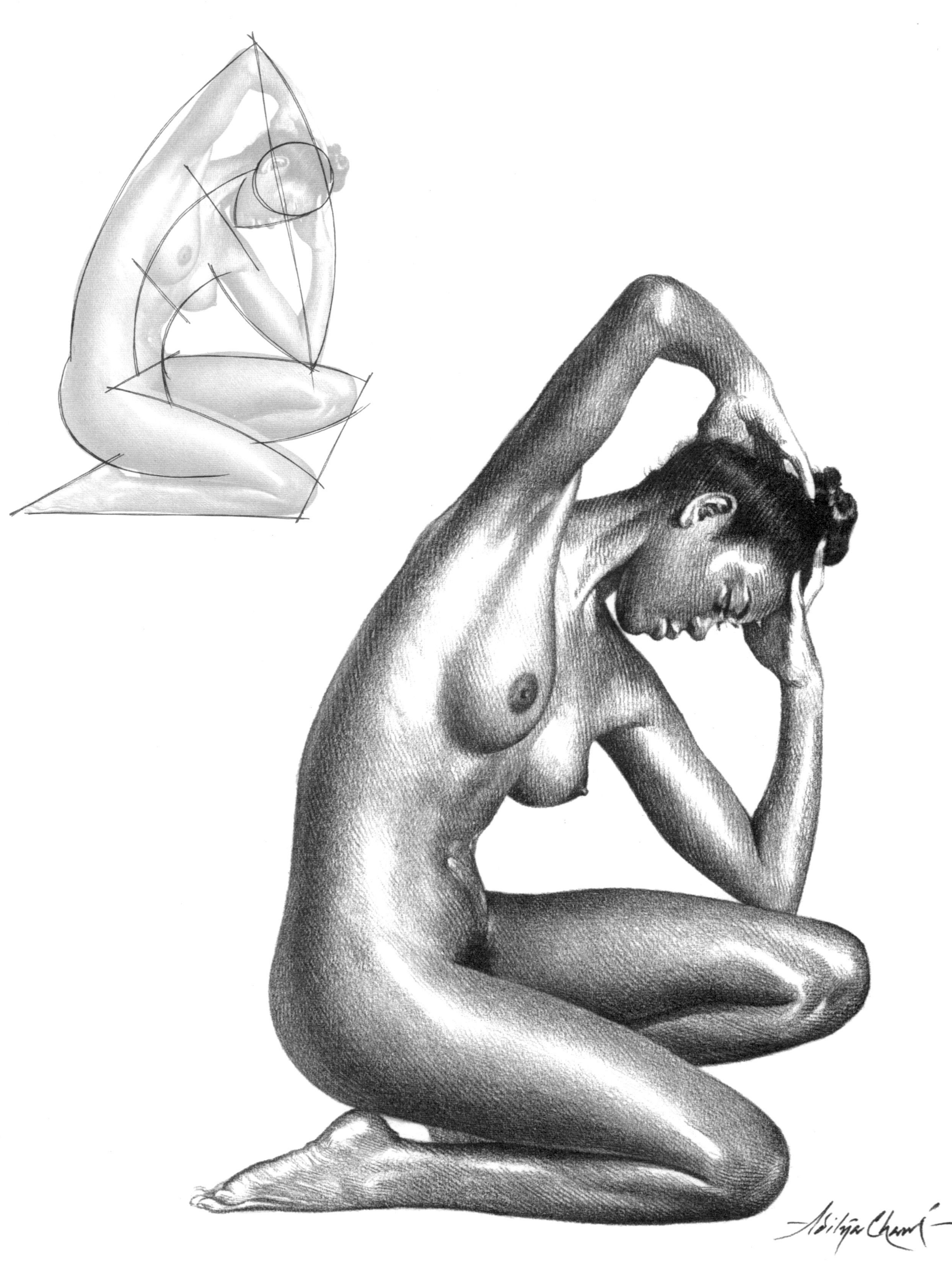

PERSPECTIVE

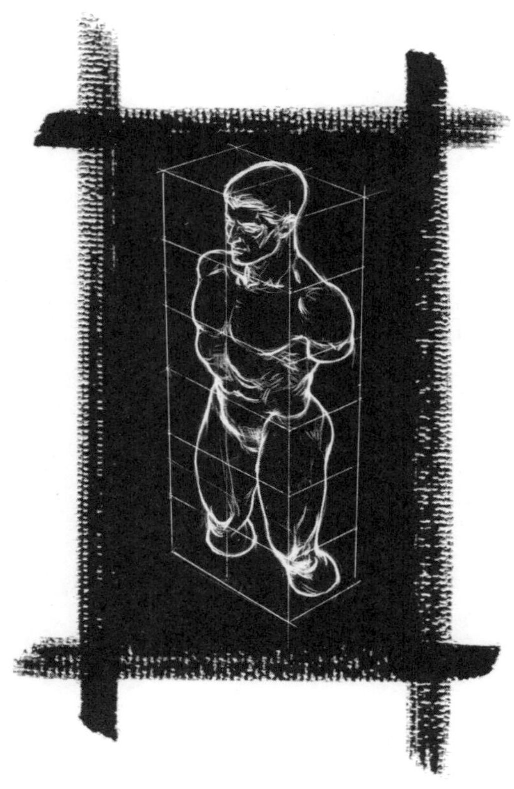

You may know a lot on the anatomy and the structure of the human Figure, but you still will not be able to draw realistic figures from memory until you can relate the various parts of the figure to the eye level or to the horizon. This relationship is referred to as Perspective.

Perspective is not a guide on how to draw the figure. However, you will never be able to draw a figure without the proper perspective. Perspective in the figure actually means that all the parts of the figure are related to a particular eye level. The perspective of the same figure will change as per the level at which you view it – i.e from above, from below etc. Perspective is all about visualizing every object as fitted into a block and that block into planes and vanishing points.

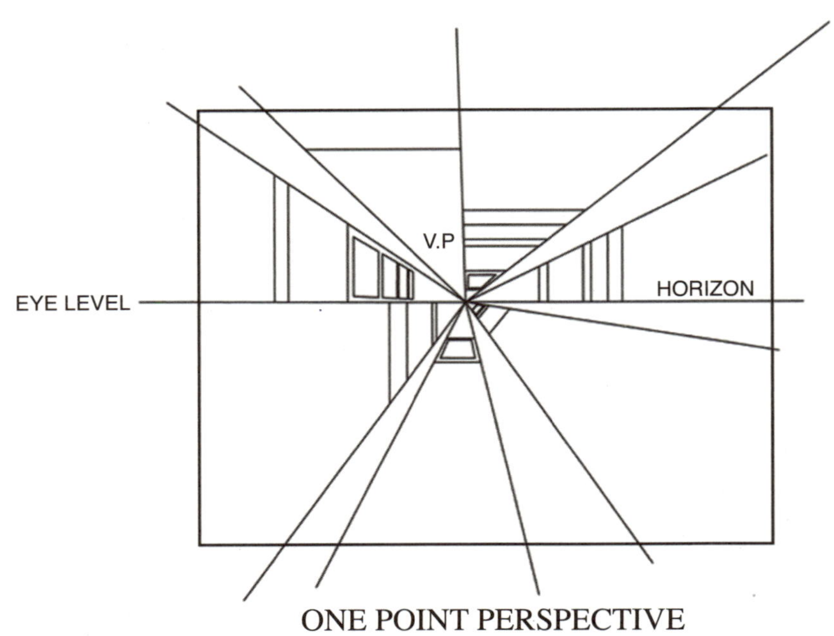

ONE POINT PERSPECTIVE

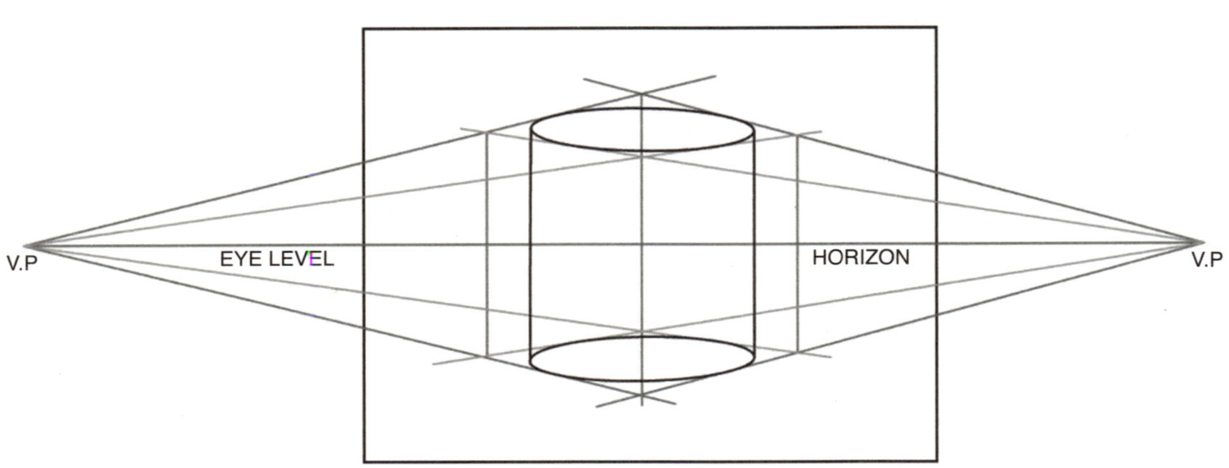

TWO POINT PERSPECTIVE

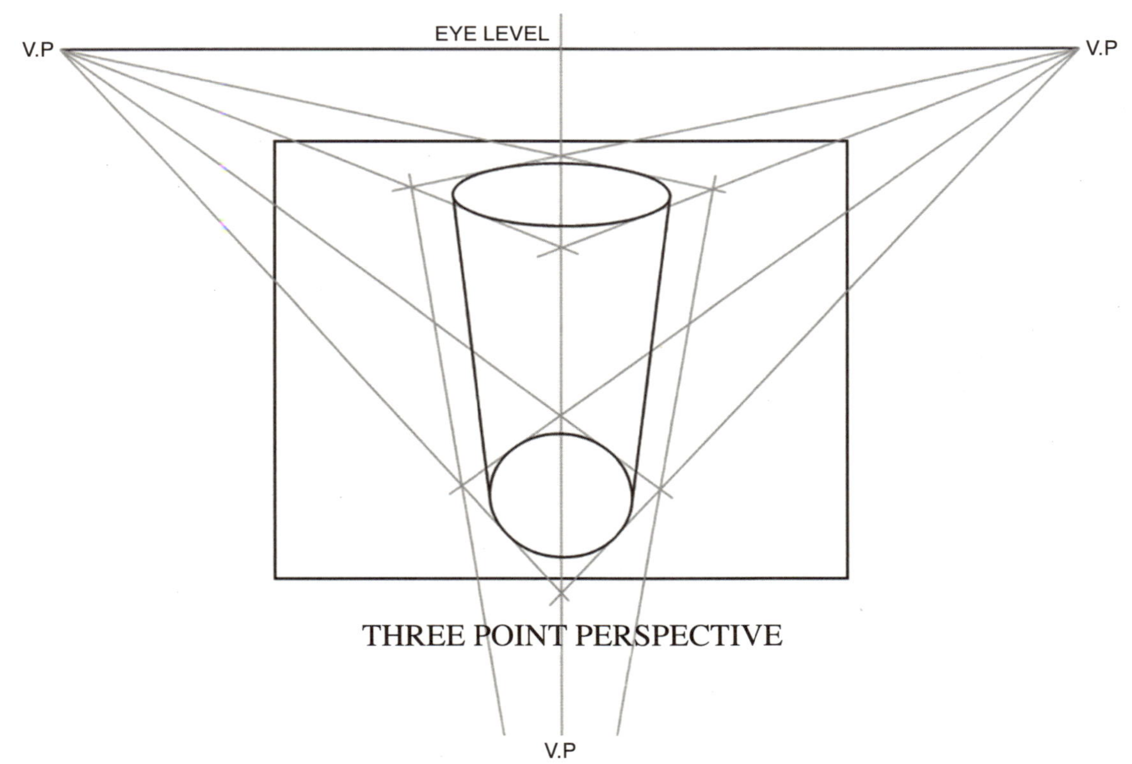

THREE POINT PERSPECTIVE

Perspective is another way to create drawings with the depth and the feeling of the actually existing object in space. Drawing in perspective allows you to establish object on a foreground, middle ground, and background.

One point perspective:
In one point perspective , there is only one vanishing point. This means that if you draw lines extending the edges of the objects that are parallel to each other, they will converge at this one point on the horizon line. The vanishing point is always located in the drawing itself, never out side the panel. The extensions of all lines that are neither horizontal nor vertical converge at the single vanishing point.

Two point perspective:
Here there are two vanishing points instead of one, and they are on the same horizon line, opposite to one another. Not a single more point will locate inside the panel. Extensions of the edges of all parallel objects that are neither horizontal nor vertical will converge at one of these two points. The closer the two vanishing points are to each other, the more exaggerated the perspective of the drawing.

Three point perspective:
Here the two vanishing points will be on the horizon, but the third vanishing point will be either high above or far below the horizon line, depending upon whether you want the viewer to be looking up or down at the objects in the drawing. The closer the third point is to the horizon line, the more exaggerated the perspective will appear. Horizon is always on the eye level.

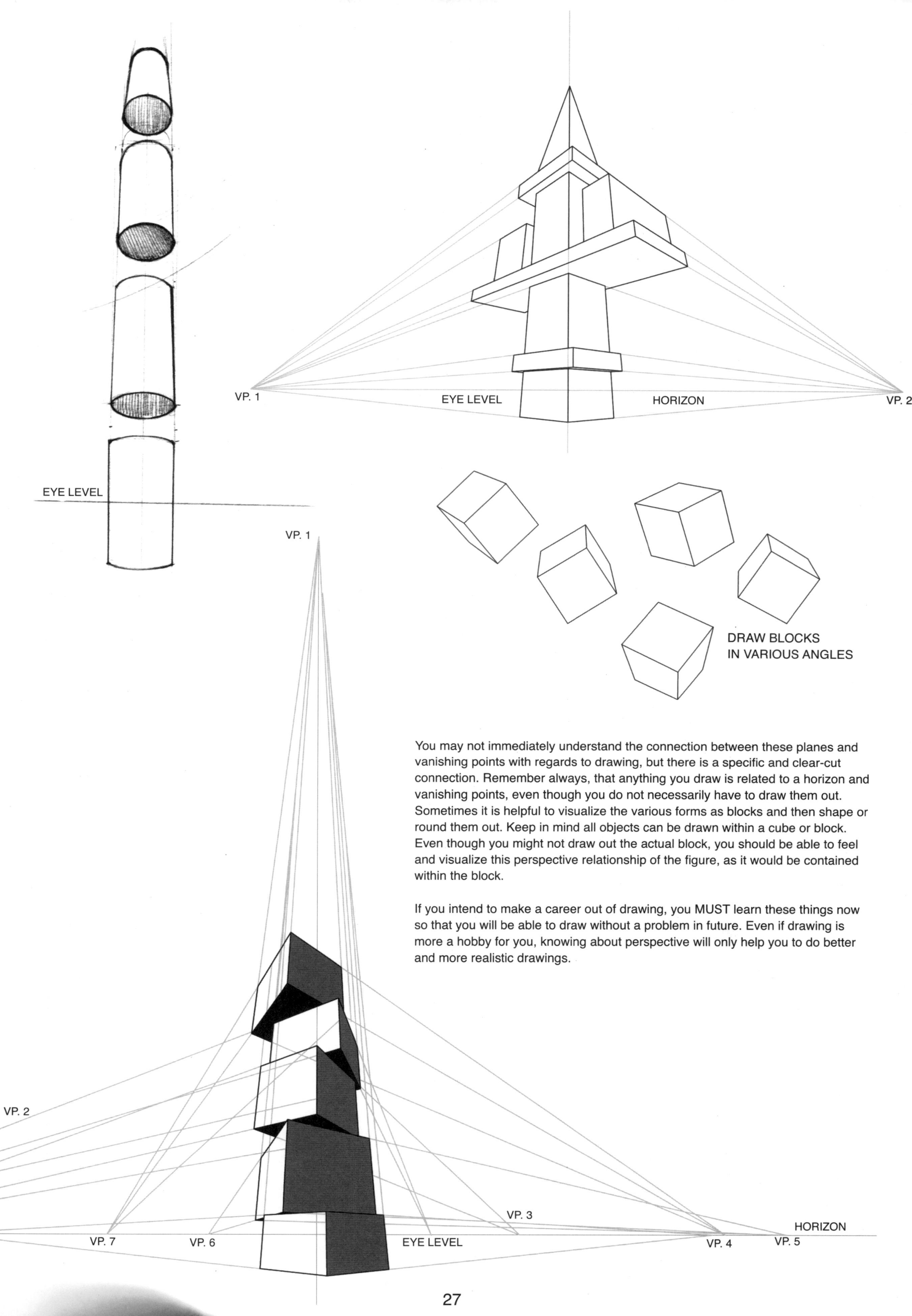

You may not immediately understand the connection between these planes and vanishing points with regards to drawing, but there is a specific and clear-cut connection. Remember always, that anything you draw is related to a horizon and vanishing points, even though you do not necessarily have to draw them out. Sometimes it is helpful to visualize the various forms as blocks and then shape or round them out. Keep in mind all objects can be drawn within a cube or block. Even though you might not draw out the actual block, you should be able to feel and visualize this perspective relationship of the figure, as it would be contained within the block.

If you intend to make a career out of drawing, you MUST learn these things now so that you will be able to draw without a problem in future. Even if drawing is more a hobby for you, knowing about perspective will only help you to do better and more realistic drawings.

Foreshortening applies linear perspective to the drawing and creates depth to it. In the example at the upper right of this page, we are looking down on the figure from above. You can notice the differences in the size of elements, for example, the left foot is noticeably smaller then the left hand. So too are the arms portrayed as much larger than the legs.

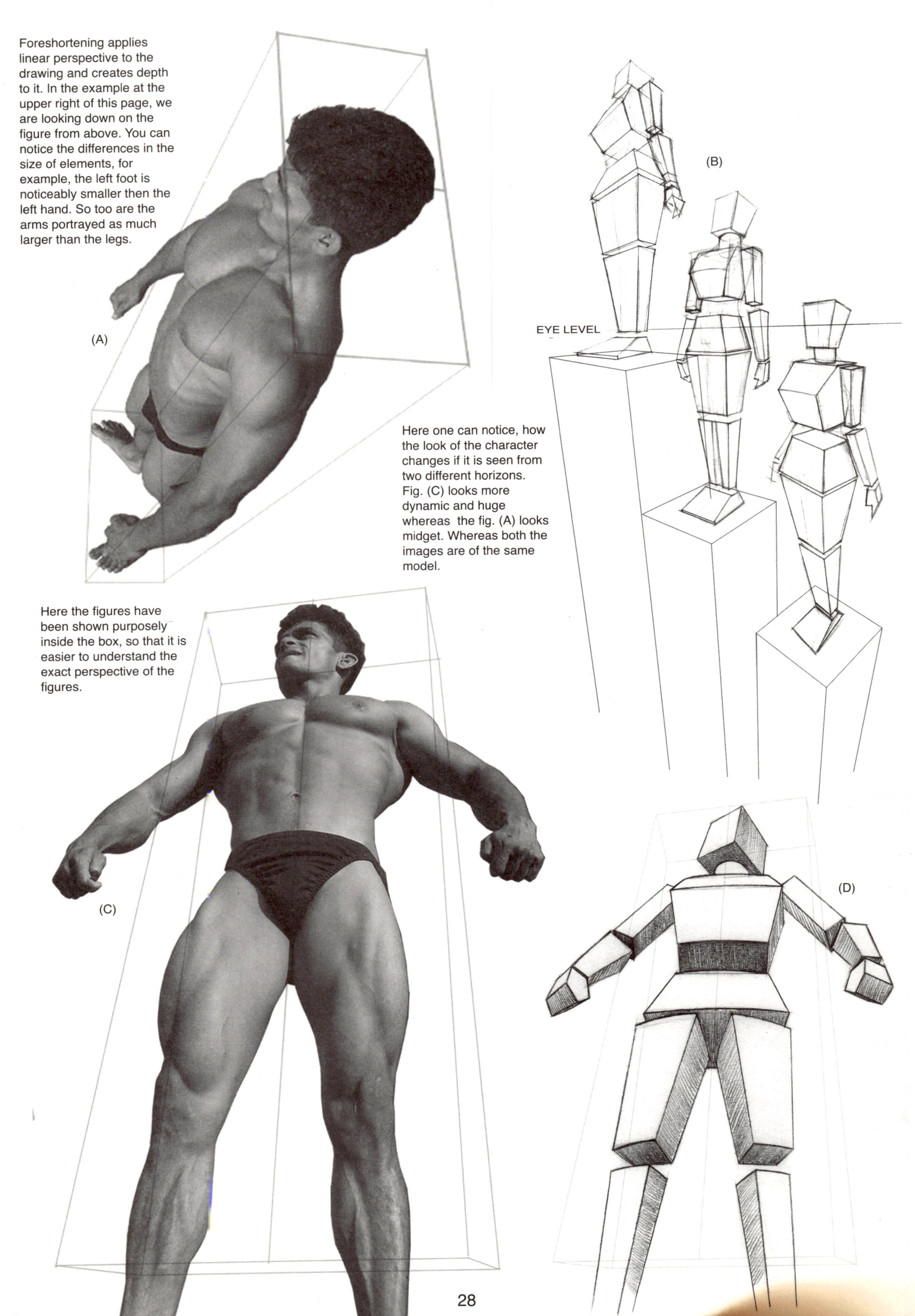

Here one can notice, how the look of the character changes if it is seen from two different horizons. Fig. (C) looks more dynamic and huge whereas the fig. (A) looks midget. Whereas both the images are of the same model.

Here the figures have been shown purposely inside the box, so that it is easier to understand the exact perspective of the figures.

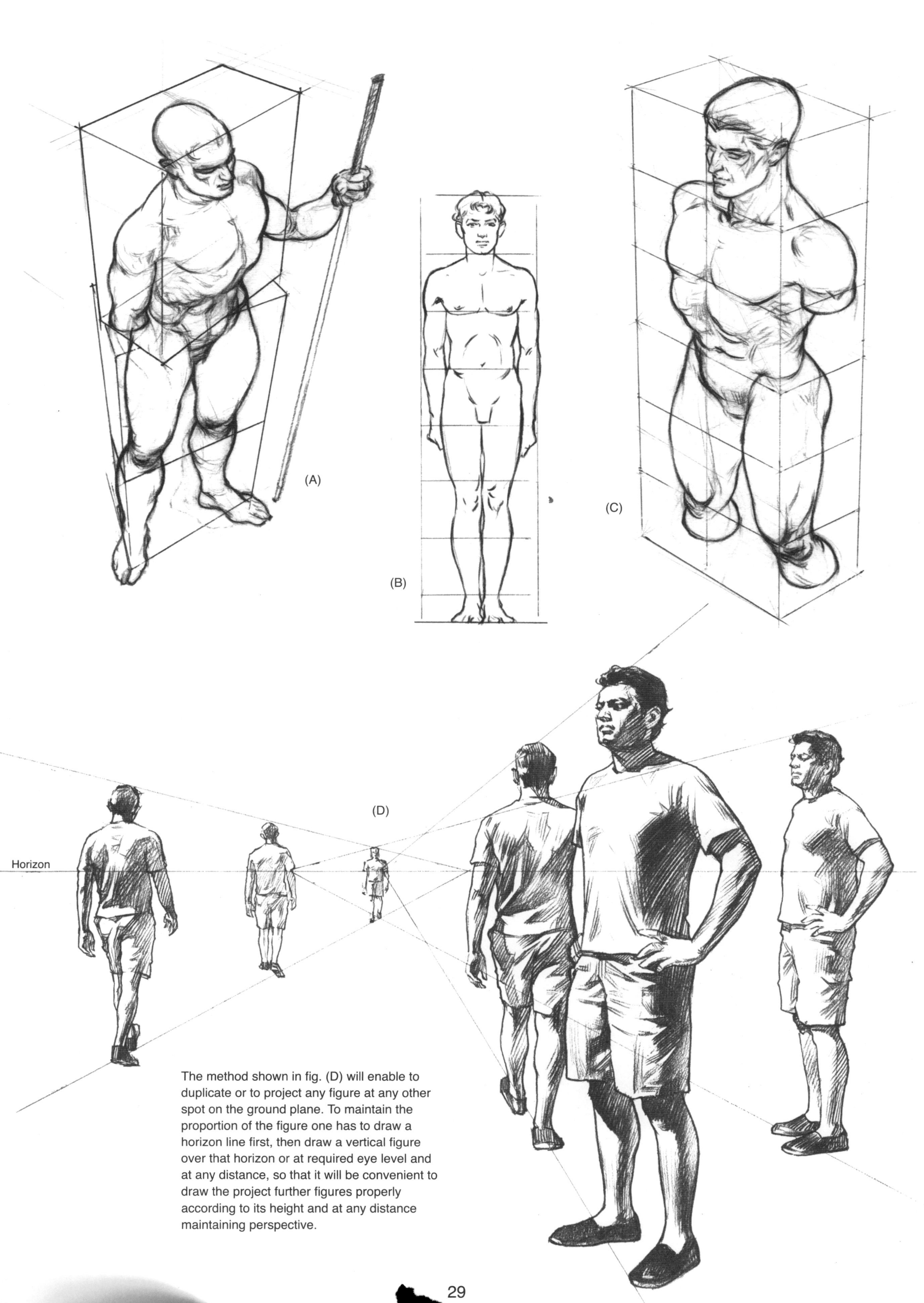

The method shown in fig. (D) will enable to duplicate or to project any figure at any other spot on the ground plane. To maintain the proportion of the figure one has to draw a horizon line first, then draw a vertical figure over that horizon or at required eye level and at any distance, so that it will be convenient to draw the project further figures properly according to its height and at any distance maintaining perspective.

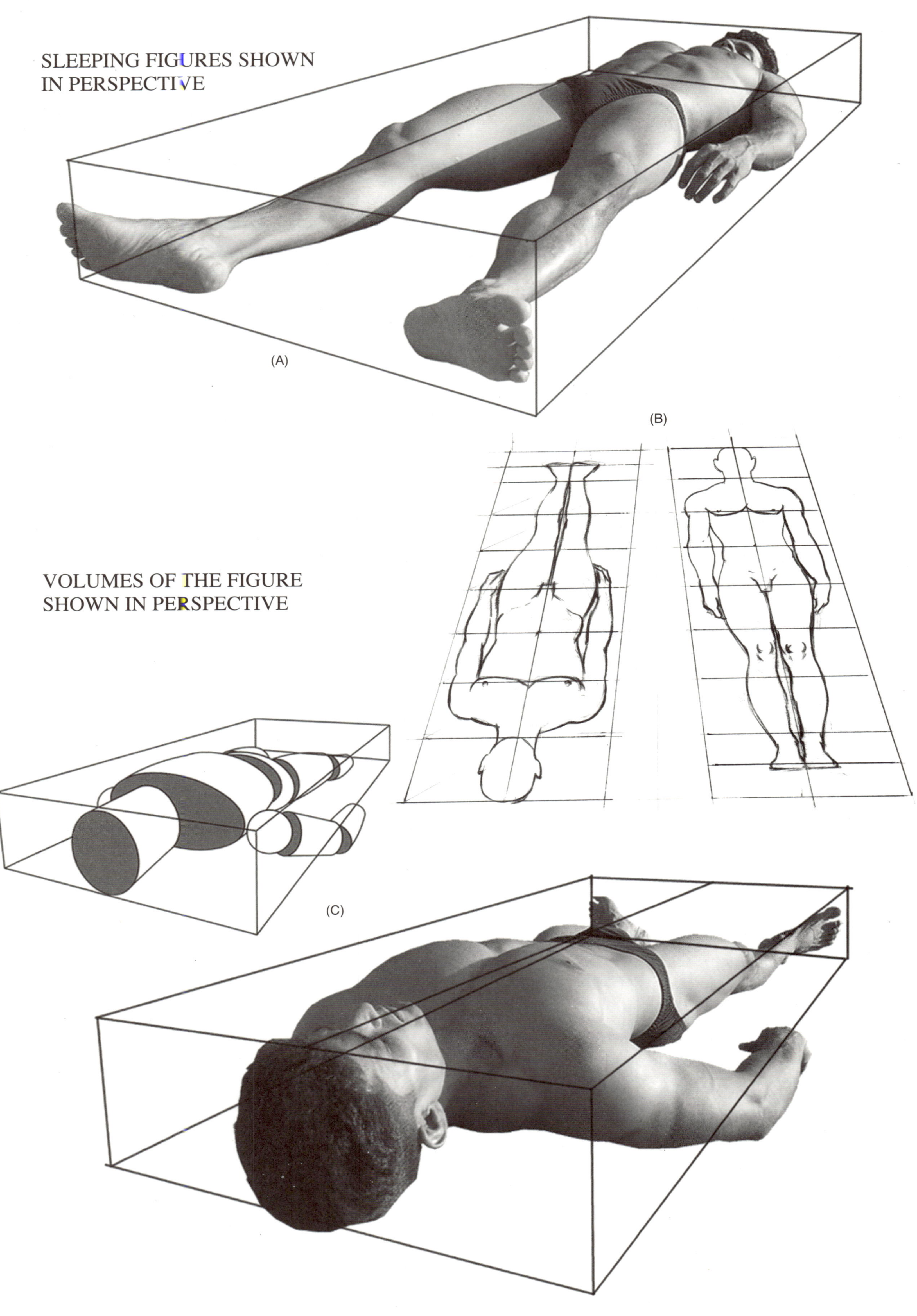
SLEEPING FIGURES SHOWN
IN PERSPECTIVE
(A)
(B)
VOLUMES OF THE FIGURE
SHOWN IN PERSPECTIVE
(C)

MANNEQUIN

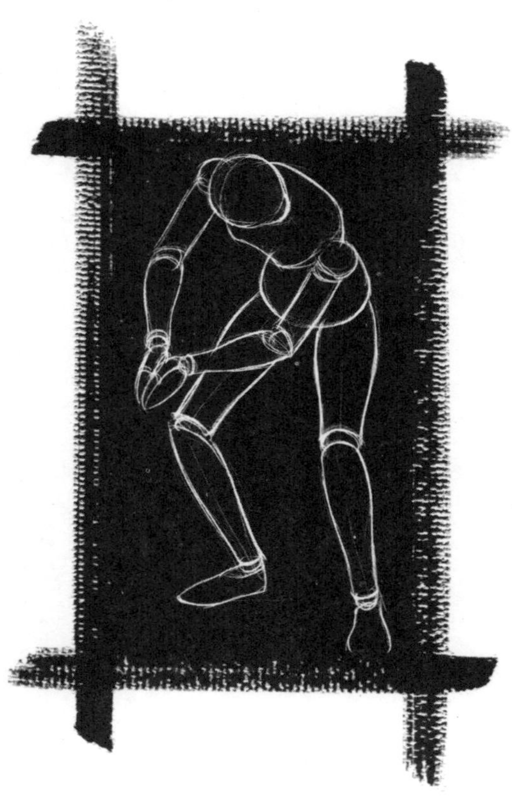

A mannequin is an extremely useful aide in figure drawing. What is a mannequin, you may ask? It is a small wooden construction of the human body, but in its basic, simple form of cylinders, ellipsoids, complete with joints at the neck, shoulders, elbows, wrists, waist, hips, knees and ankles. One of the key features of the mannequin is that it can be conformed to any human posture. This helps when you may not find a model to pose for you or to even hold a pose indefinitely. While sketching with a mannequin as a model, you should sit with the proper illustration of the human anatomy in front of you so that you can use it for reference in your drawing.

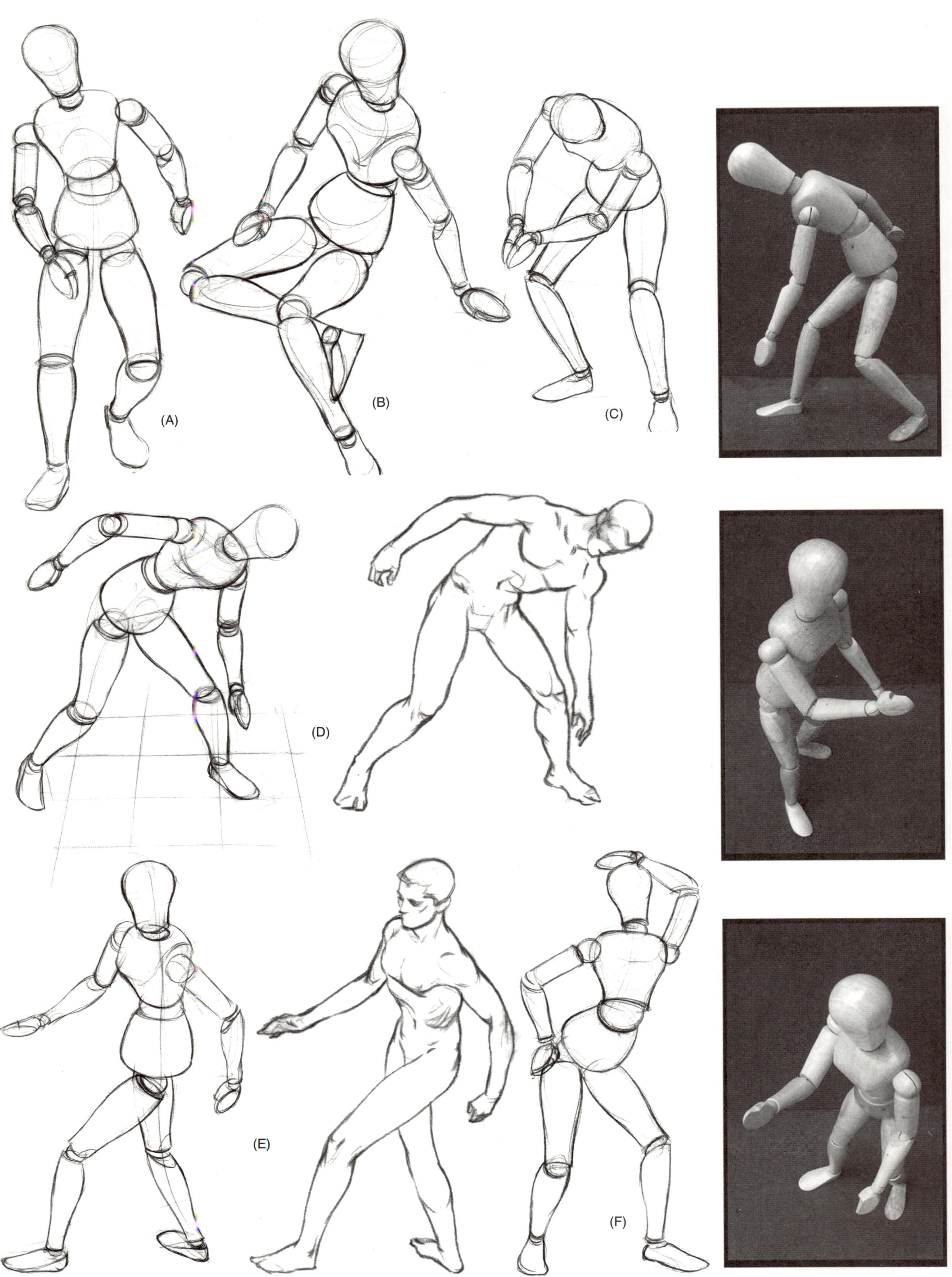

You can start doing gesture sketches of the mannequin in various poses and postures. This will help you gain confidence in sketching any kind of posture. As you progress and gain experience, you can use the anatomical references in front of you and sketch out the pose of the mannequin and add the corresponding muscles (from your reference) suitable to that posture.

It is good to draw the ground planes before drawing the mannequin, so that the drawing will get the perfect base and will not look suspended. It helps to know the exact perspective.

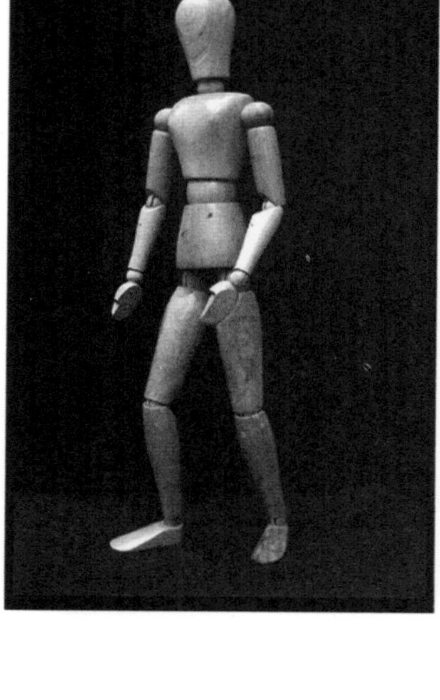

(A)

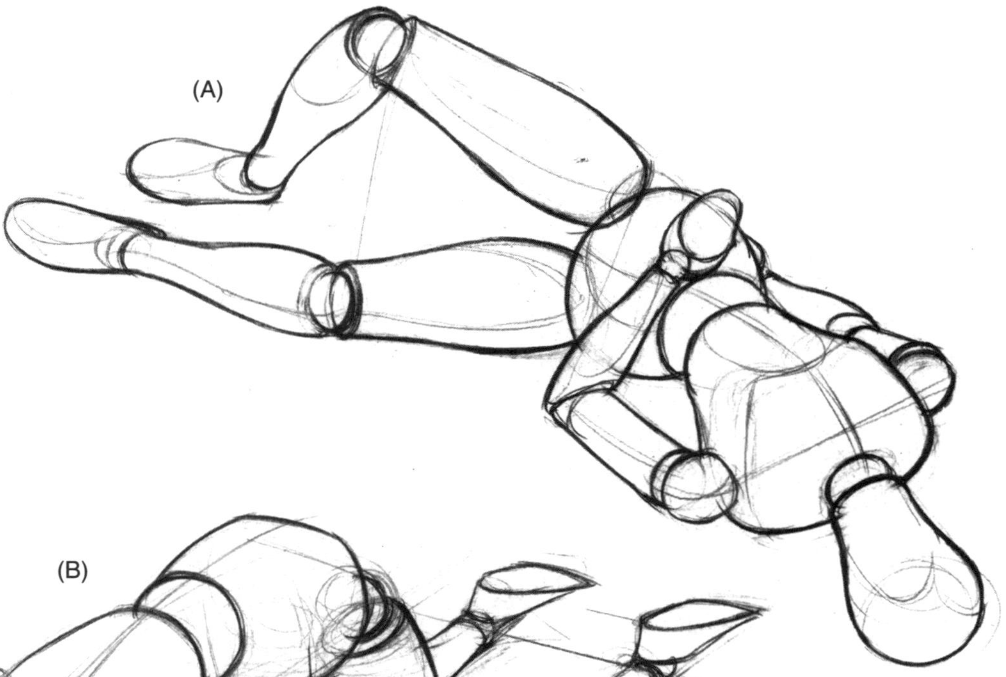

(B)

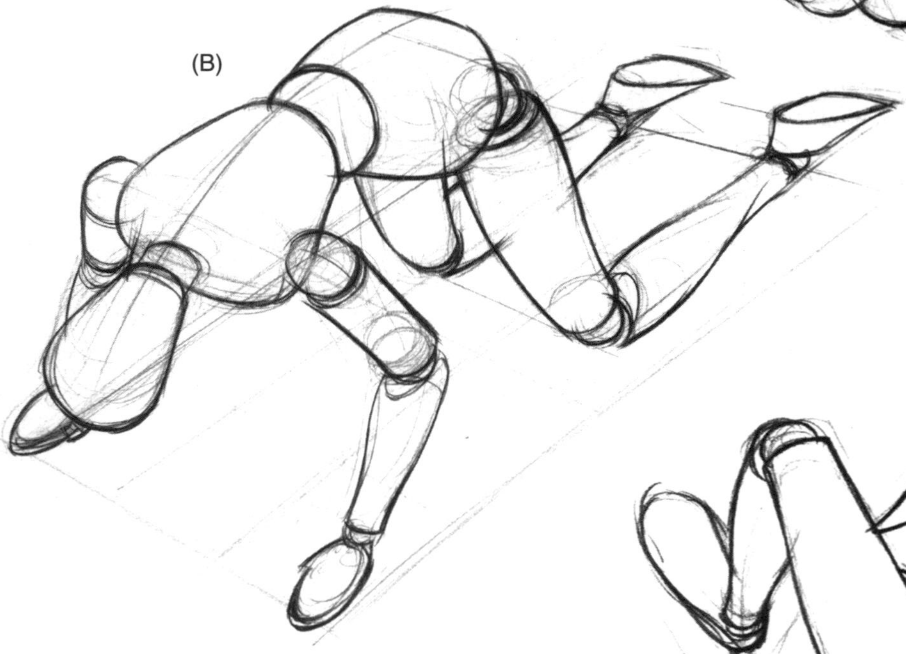

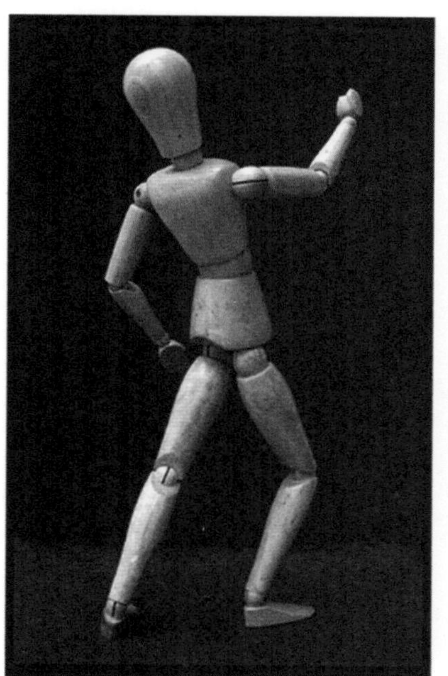

(C)

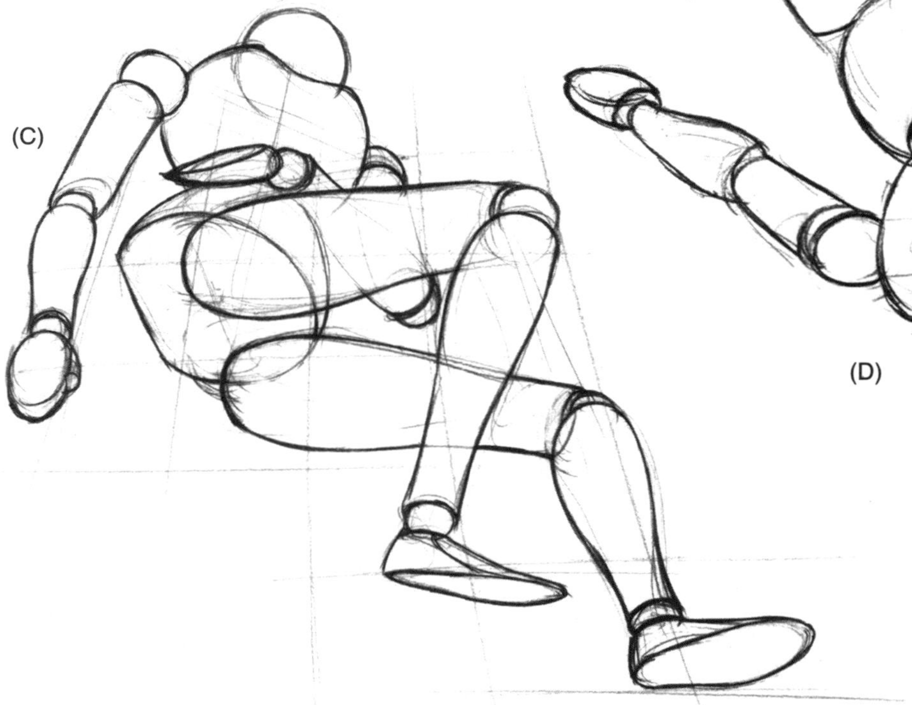

(D)

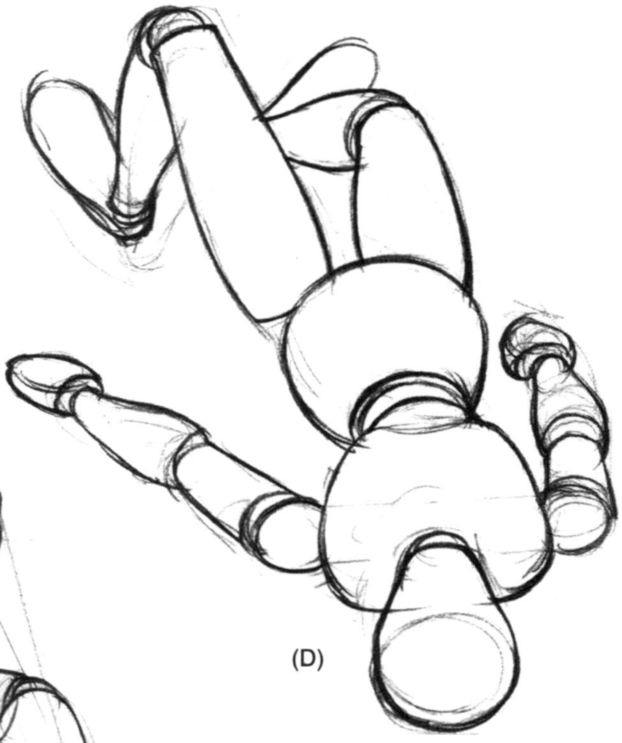

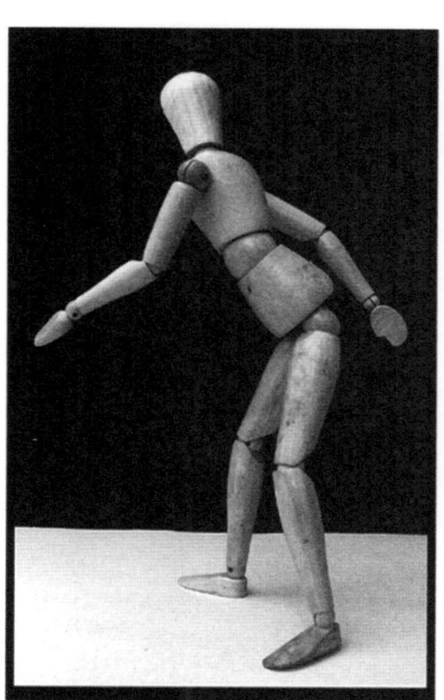

The function of the mannequin is only to help you gain experience in the study of action and nothing else. (You must study the line of action in each pose). This practice is extremely useful especially in loosening your drawing in the gestured drawing exercise. One of the most important features of a mannequin is that it can be used in still poses that no live model could hold.

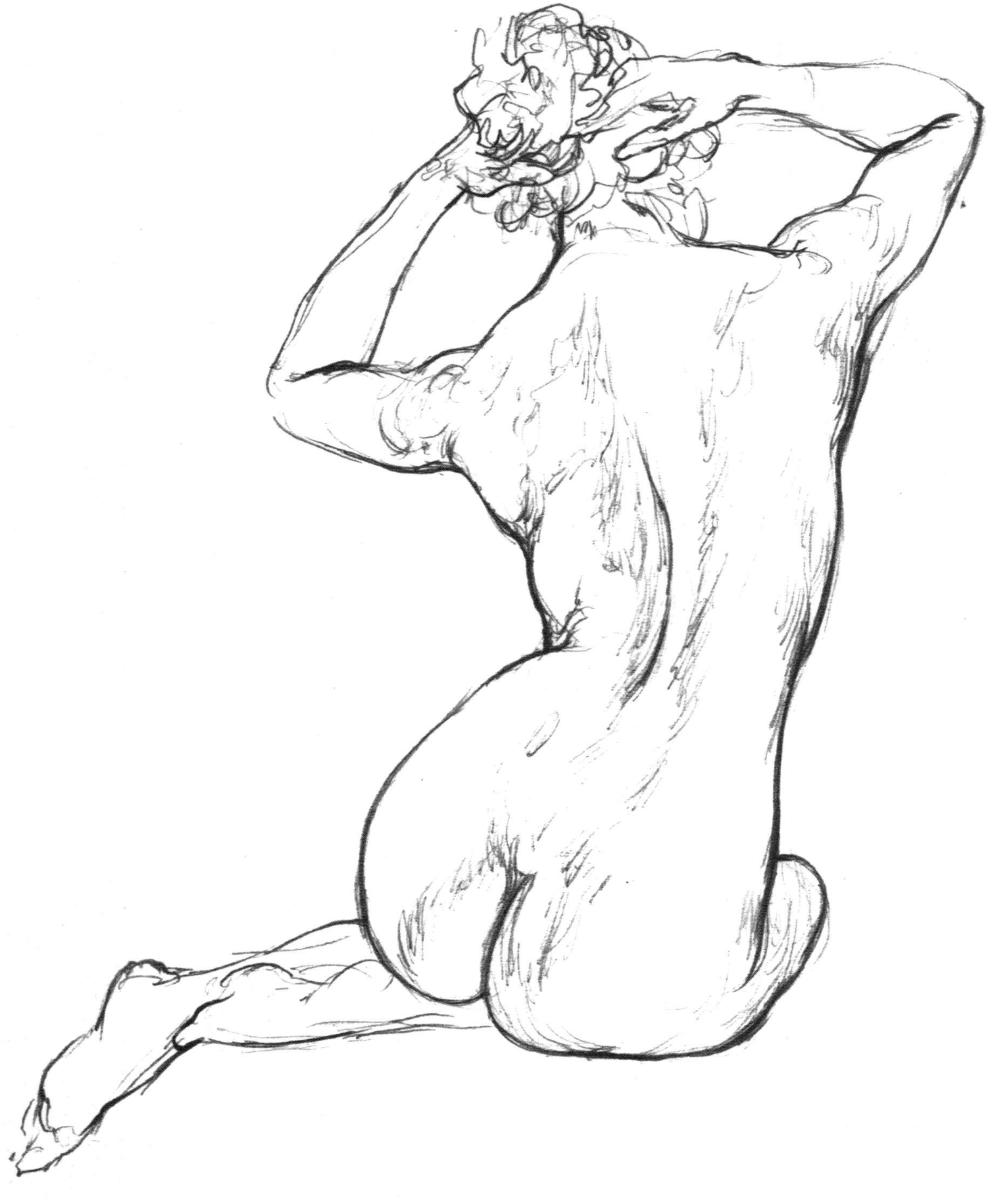

VOLUME CONSTRUCTION

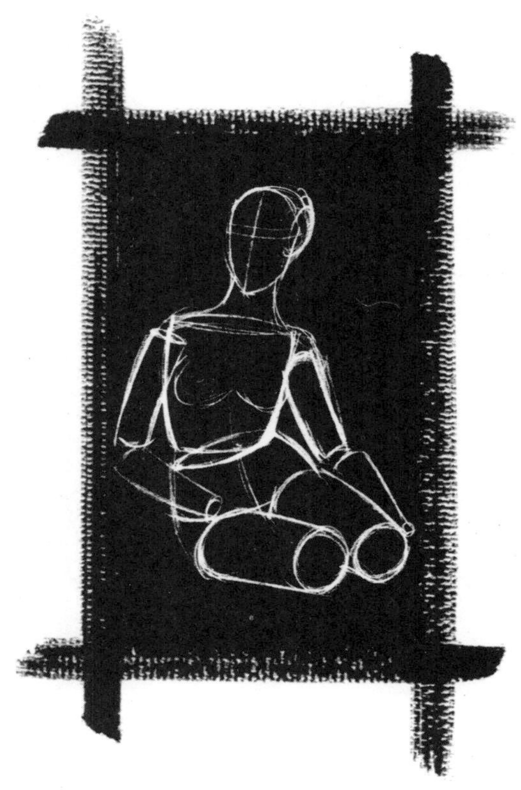

The sphere, the cube, and the cone are the three fundamental or basic forms in nature. All other forms like the cylinder, for example, are derived from these three basic forms. You should be able to see, recognize and relate these shapes to the human form in the large areas, for example the torso, as well as the smaller areas, for example the fingers and toes of the human form.

Once you get comfortable with the various body parts as translated into these shapes, you should then start to practice drawing the human form, with these geometrical shapes, in various positions. This is the basic guide to figure modeling or construction. Sketching these will give you an excellent and solid foundation of good figure drawing.

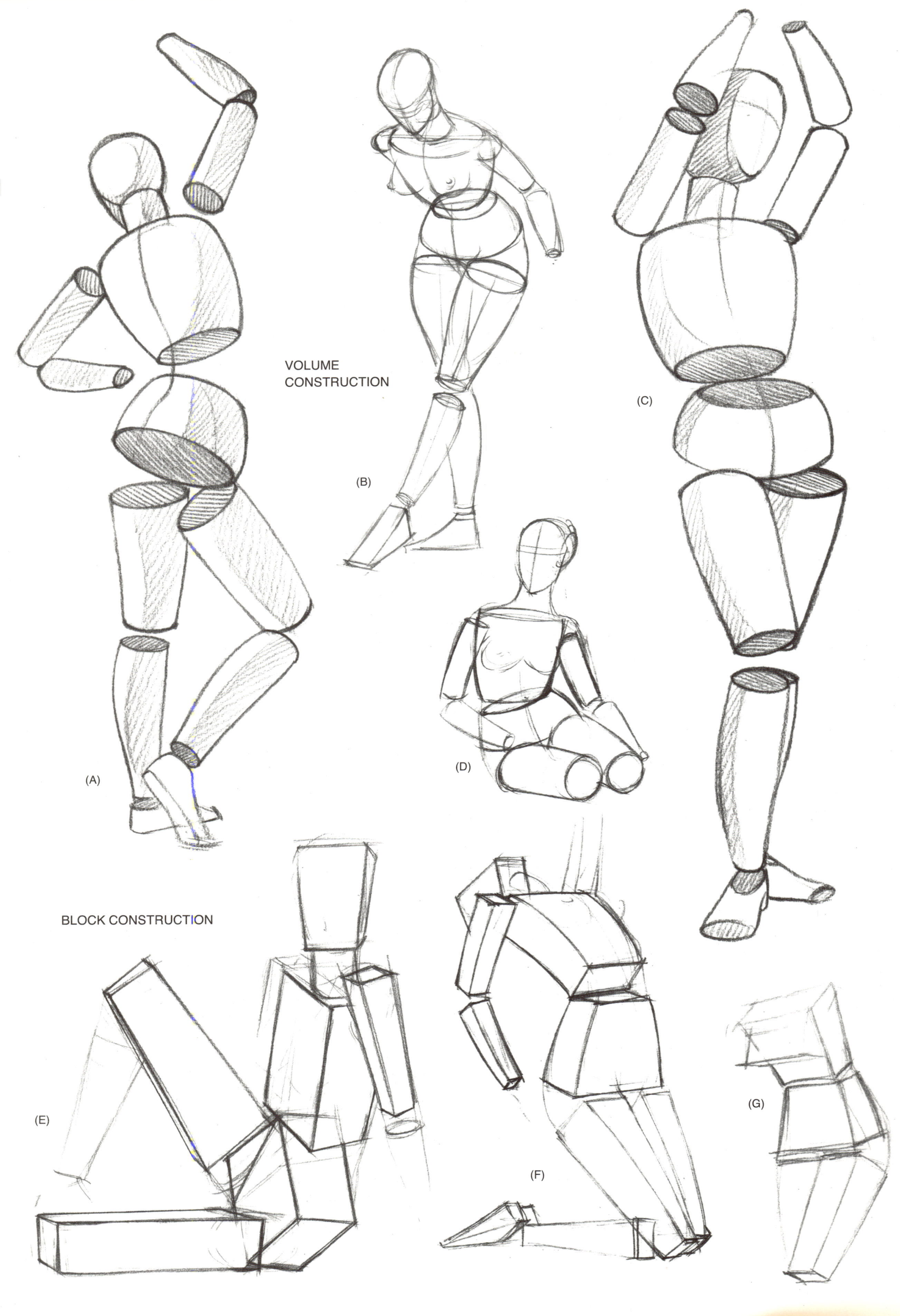
VOLUME
CONSTRUCTION
(A)
(B)
(C)
(D)
BLOCK CONSTRUCTION
(E)
(F)
(G)

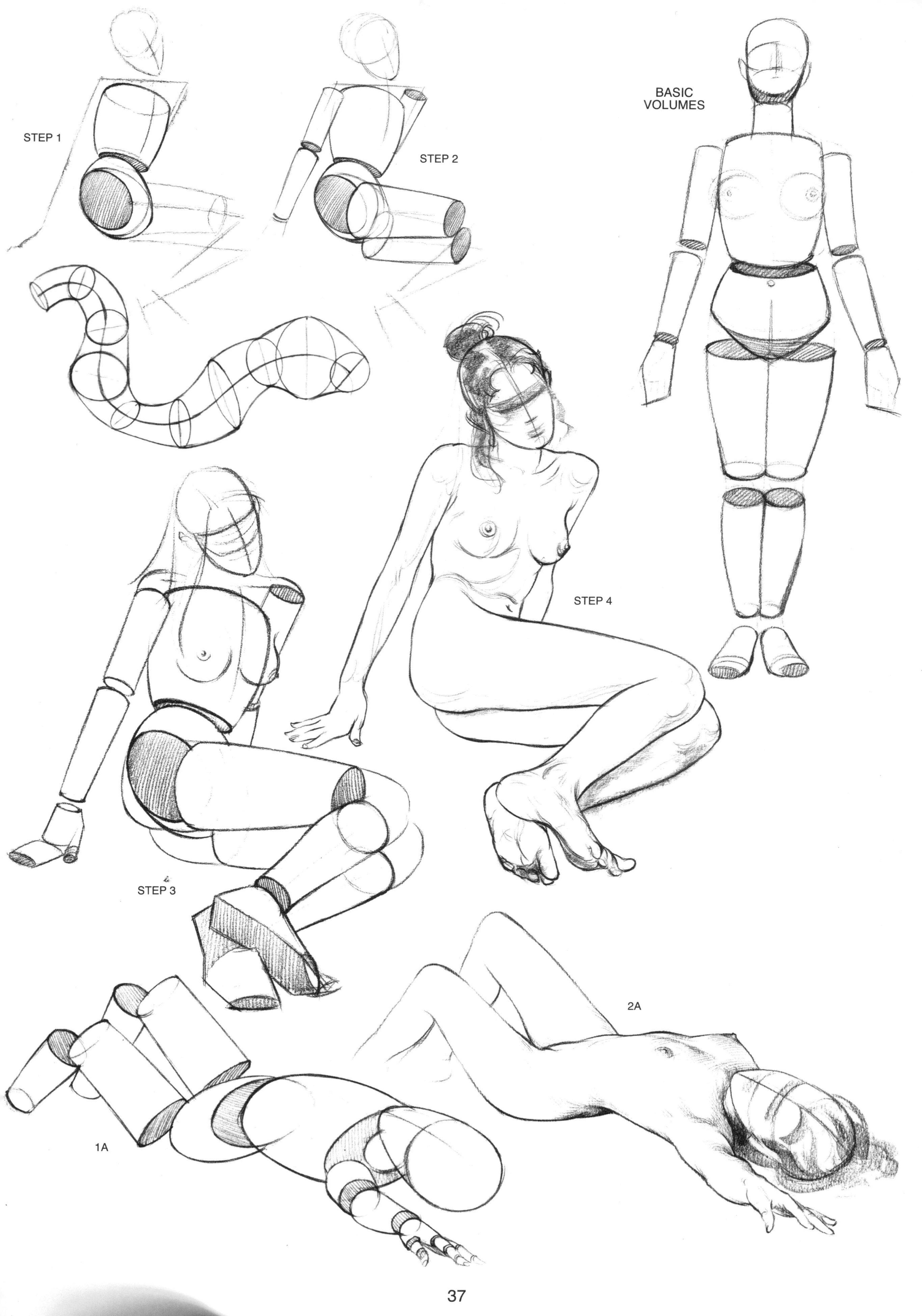
STEP 1
STEP 2
BASIC
VOLUMES
STEP 4
STEP 3
2A
1A

The twisting or bending that is involved in any action will result in some kind of twist or turn of the body. This is true in the case of even the smallest and simplest of actions. As the body twists, muscles on one side constrict or shorten, while those on the opposite side extend or lengthen.

Think of the trunk or torso as geometric shapes: namely, the torso box as an elongated cube and the waist box as a shorter cube. Now picture these cubes joined with a cord from behind the torso and the waist, which gives it flexibility and enables it to turn, twist, and bend as per the action you envision. This procedure helps especially when you are confused to draw certain angles in a foreshortening figure or if the figure is standing in some perspective angle.

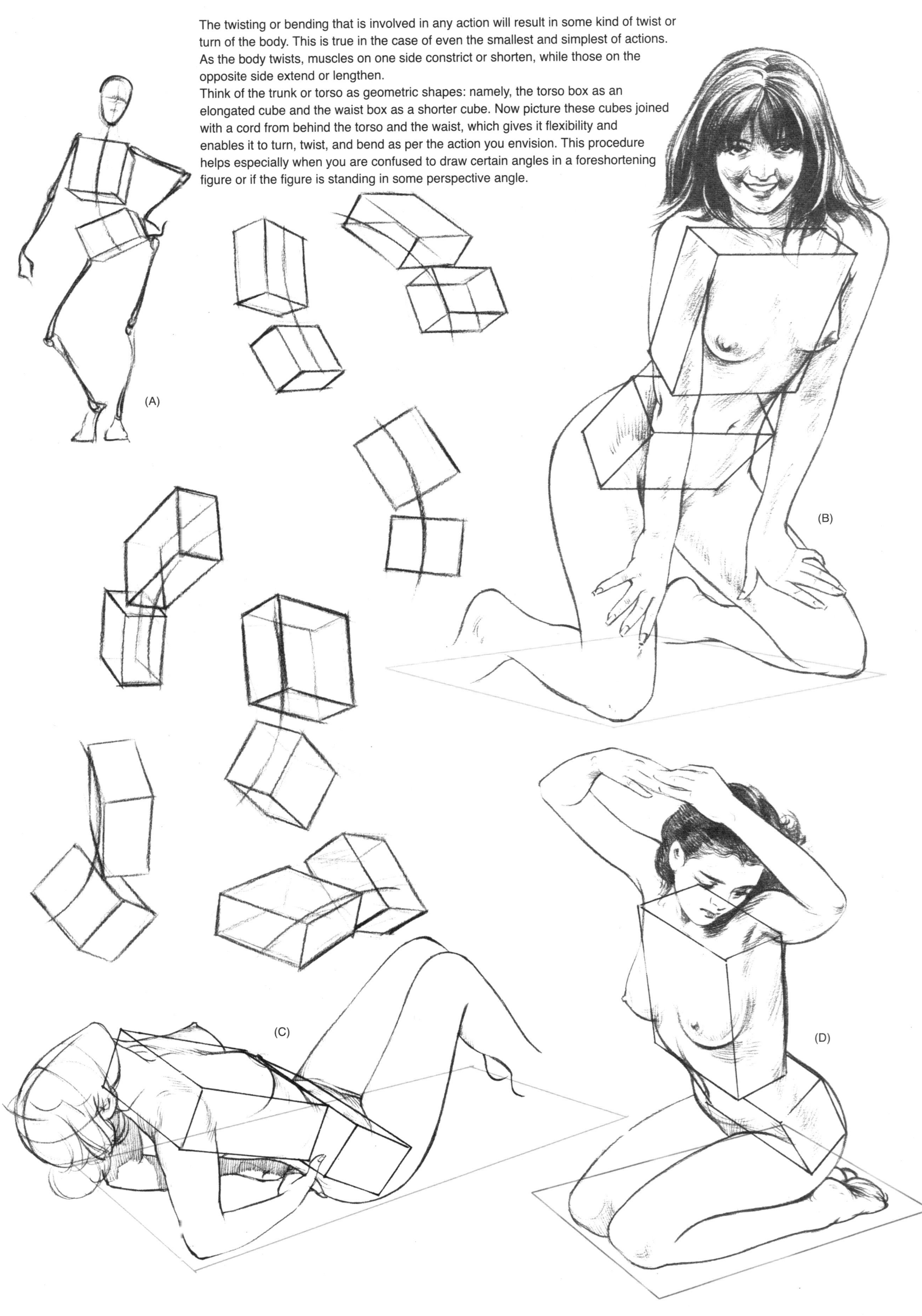

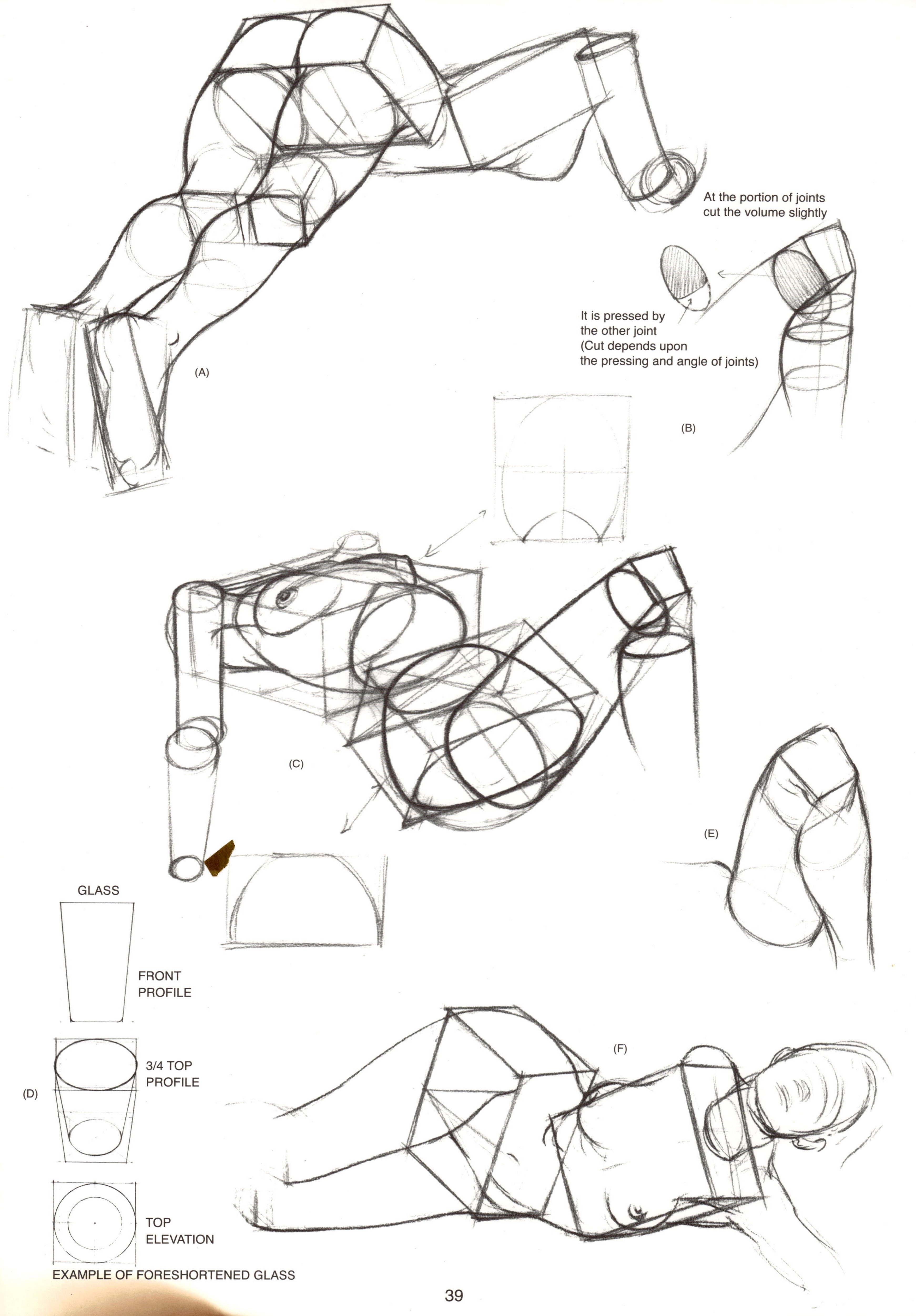

(A)
At the portion of joints
cut the volume slightly
It is pressed by
the other joint
(Cut depends upon
the pressing and angle of joints)
(B)
(C)
(E)
GLASS
FRONT
PROFILE
3/4 TOP
PROFILE
(D)
TOP
ELEVATION
EXAMPLE OF FORESHORTENED GLASS
(F)

STUDY OF LEG JOINTS

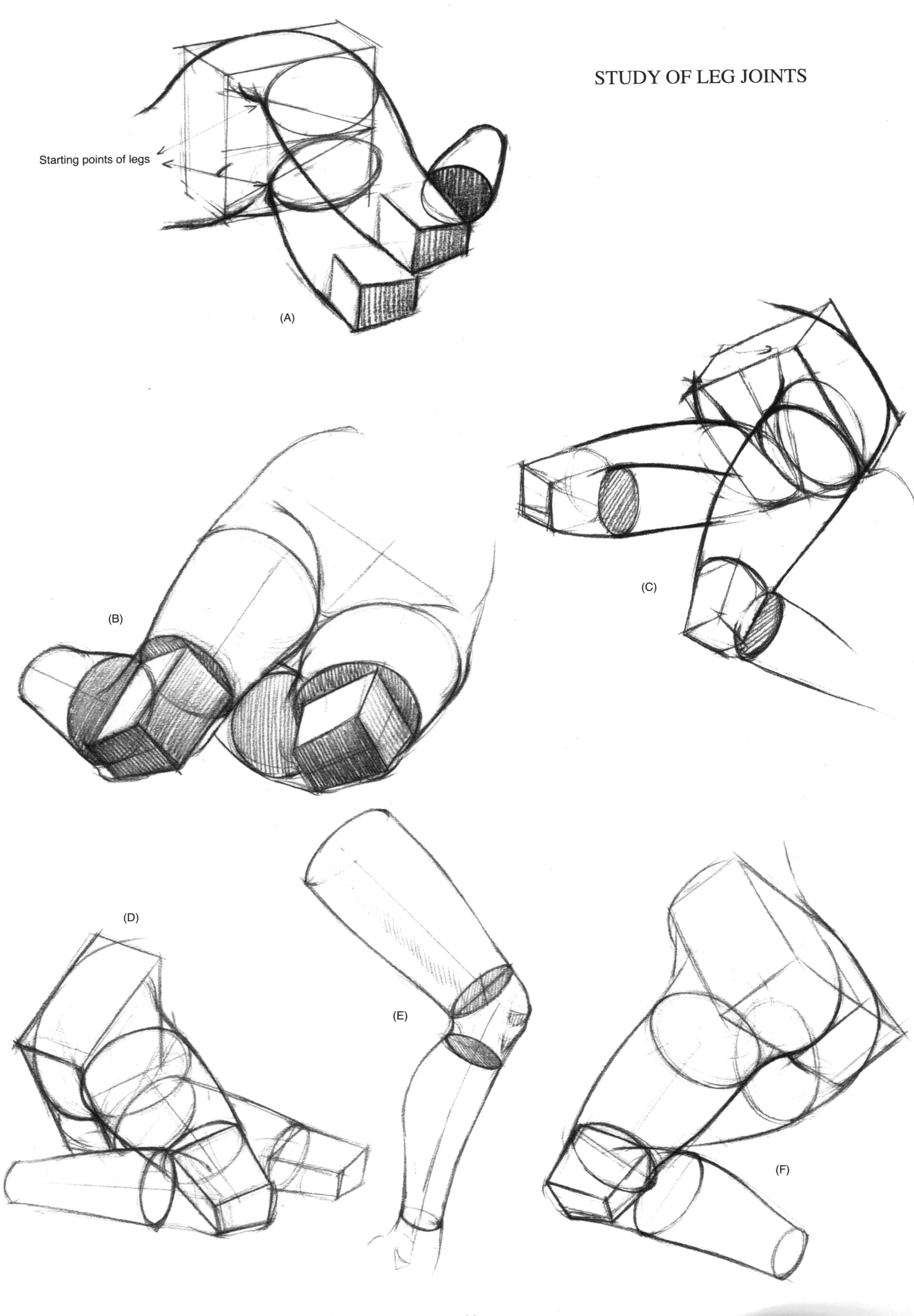

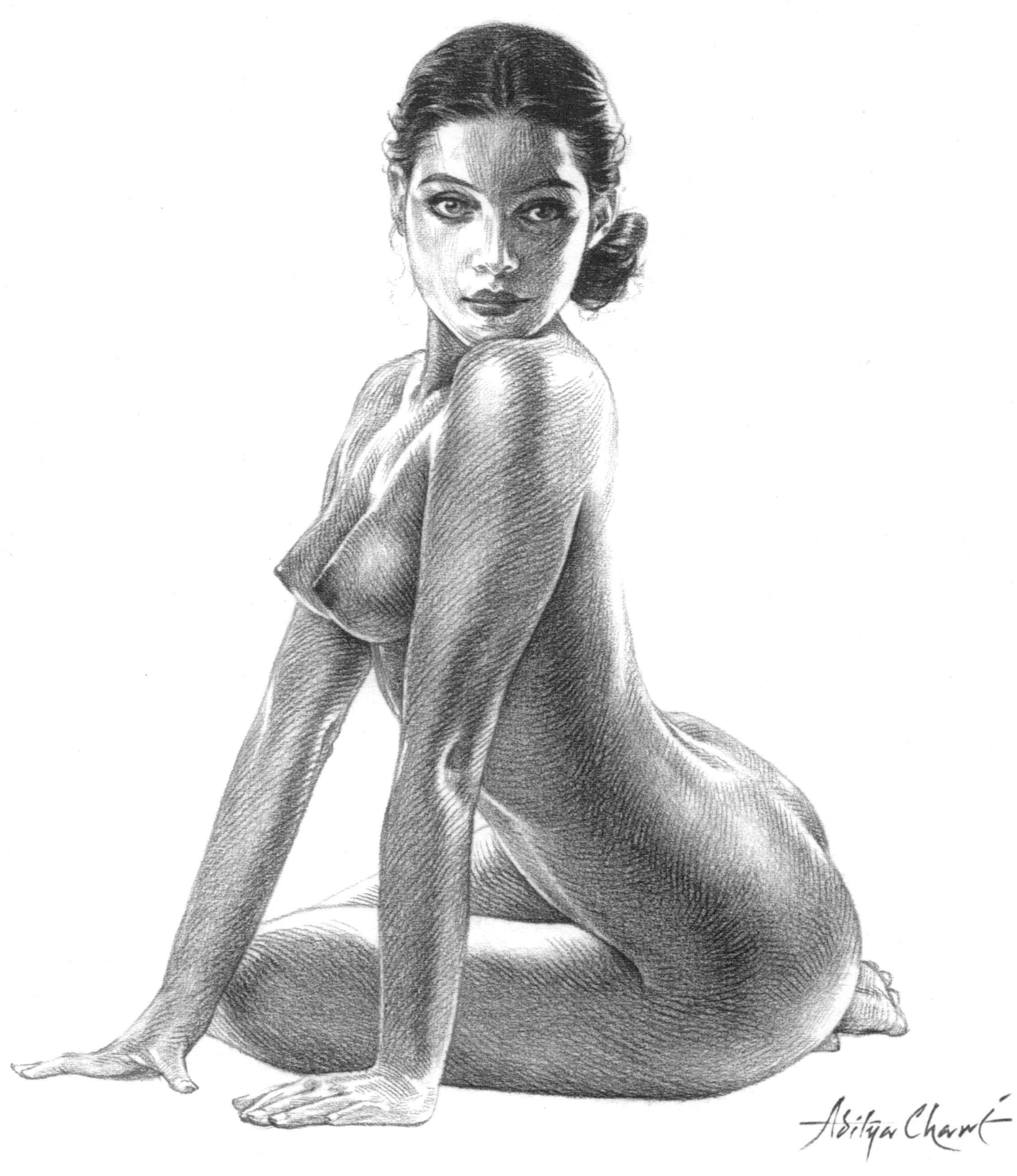

The drawings on the page no. 37, shows the human body simplified with basic individual parts which, when taken together, collectively make up the whole body. (These are the head and neck; upper torso and lower torso; upper arms, lower arms and hands, upper legs, lower legs and feet.).

Notice how the cylindrical forms appear to get shorter when foreshortened but maintain their width. Keep in mind that every form has three dimensions and that it occupies a specific area. It would be easier if you visualize each form as being carved out from a solid block of stone. This method helps us to visualize and draw solid, three-dimensional figures.

You can use an ordinary drinking glass to aid you in visualizing how the ellipses of the cylinders change as they are foreshortened (refer to page 39). You should continuously visualize all the parts of the human body in its simplest basic form, namely: cylinder, cube, and sphere.

1. At the very first stage try to look at figure in a simple box forms, as if the whole figure is wrapped inside the box, to understand the basic perspective angle of the figure.
2. Now define each body parts in cubes and oblongs, maintaining perspective.
3. Curve out the cubes and oblongs into cylindrical forms.
4. Now it becomes more easier to dress up these forms with flesh.

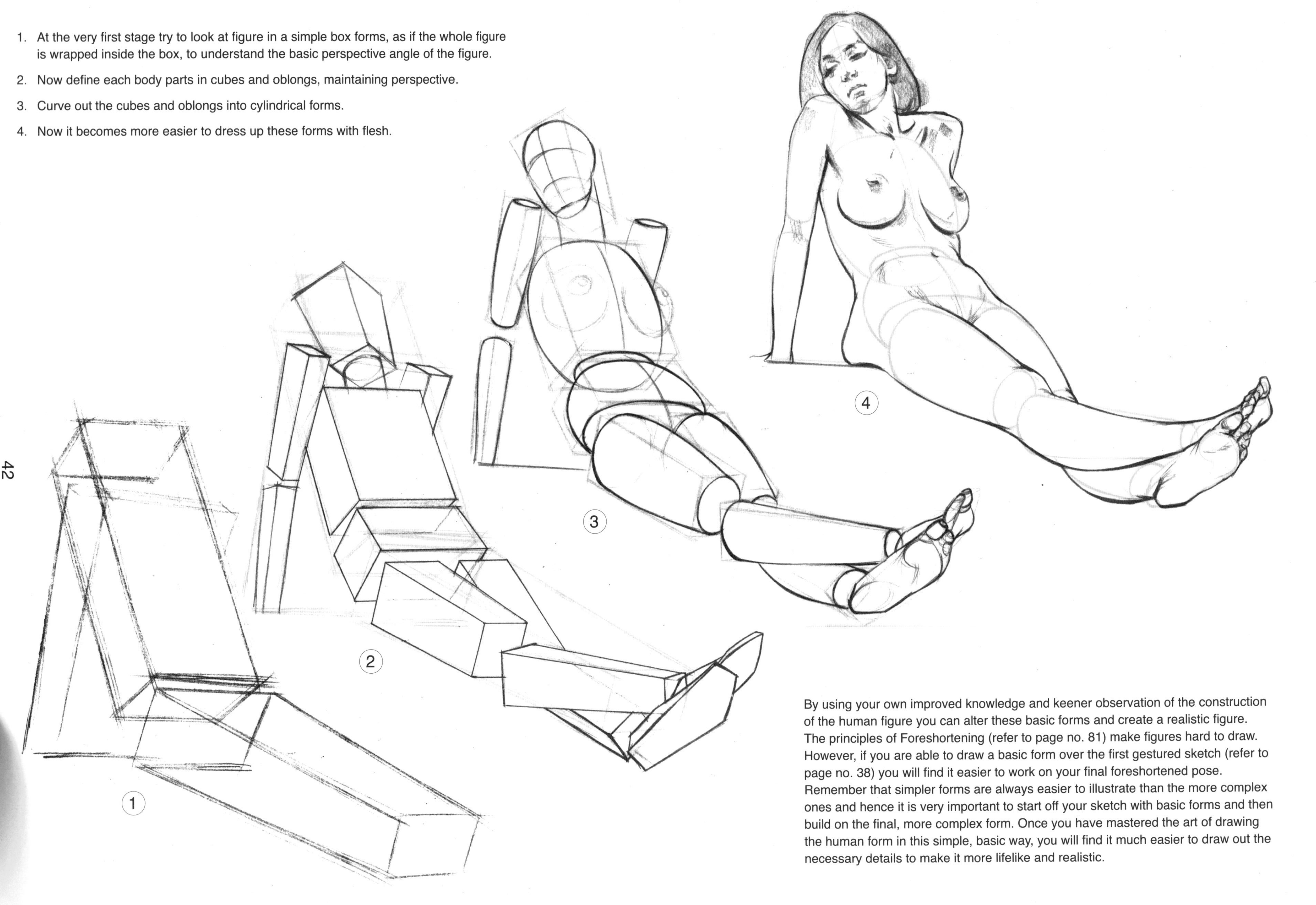

By using your own improved knowledge and keener observation of the construction of the human figure you can alter these basic forms and create a realistic figure. The principles of Foreshortening (refer to page no. 81) make figures hard to draw. However, if you are able to draw a basic form over the first gestured sketch (refer to page no. 38) you will find it easier to work on your final foreshortened pose. Remember that simpler forms are always easier to illustrate than the more complex ones and hence it is very important to start off your sketch with basic forms and then build on the final, more complex form. Once you have mastered the art of drawing the human form in this simple, basic way, you will find it much easier to draw out the necessary details to make it more lifelike and realistic.

BALANCE

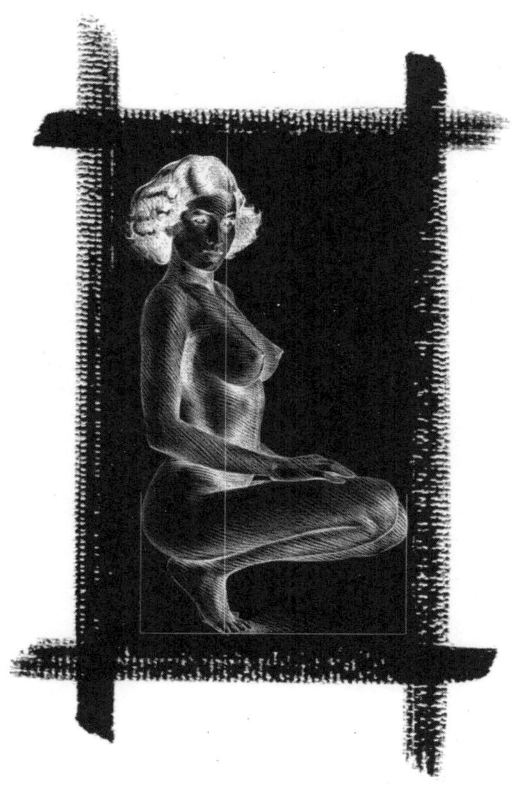

Balance enables the human being to keep from falling whether he is in motion or standing still. This occurs because the weight of an individual is equally distributed. However, the state of balance is constantly changing, depending on whether the body is stationary or in motion, and an artist must be attentive to study these momentary changes in balance. Drawings in which the figures are out of balance are always unsettling.

When several objects are balanced one above the other, at different angles, their centre of gravity is common. So too, in the case of a drawing, the sense of balance between the opposing or counteracting forces, irrespective of where the centreline may lie, has to be firmly established. This applies to any posture that may be illustrated. An upright, standing figure is motionless or stationary. The center of gravity, starting from the pit of the neck, passes through the supporting foot, or between the feet when they are supporting the weight uniformly.

Before you start your drawing you can draw out a light vertical line, which would act as a guide for placing the various body parts in their proper positions. This line is extremely useful for drawing the figure in any of its numerous poses (For example, running, walking, bending, crouching, etc.).

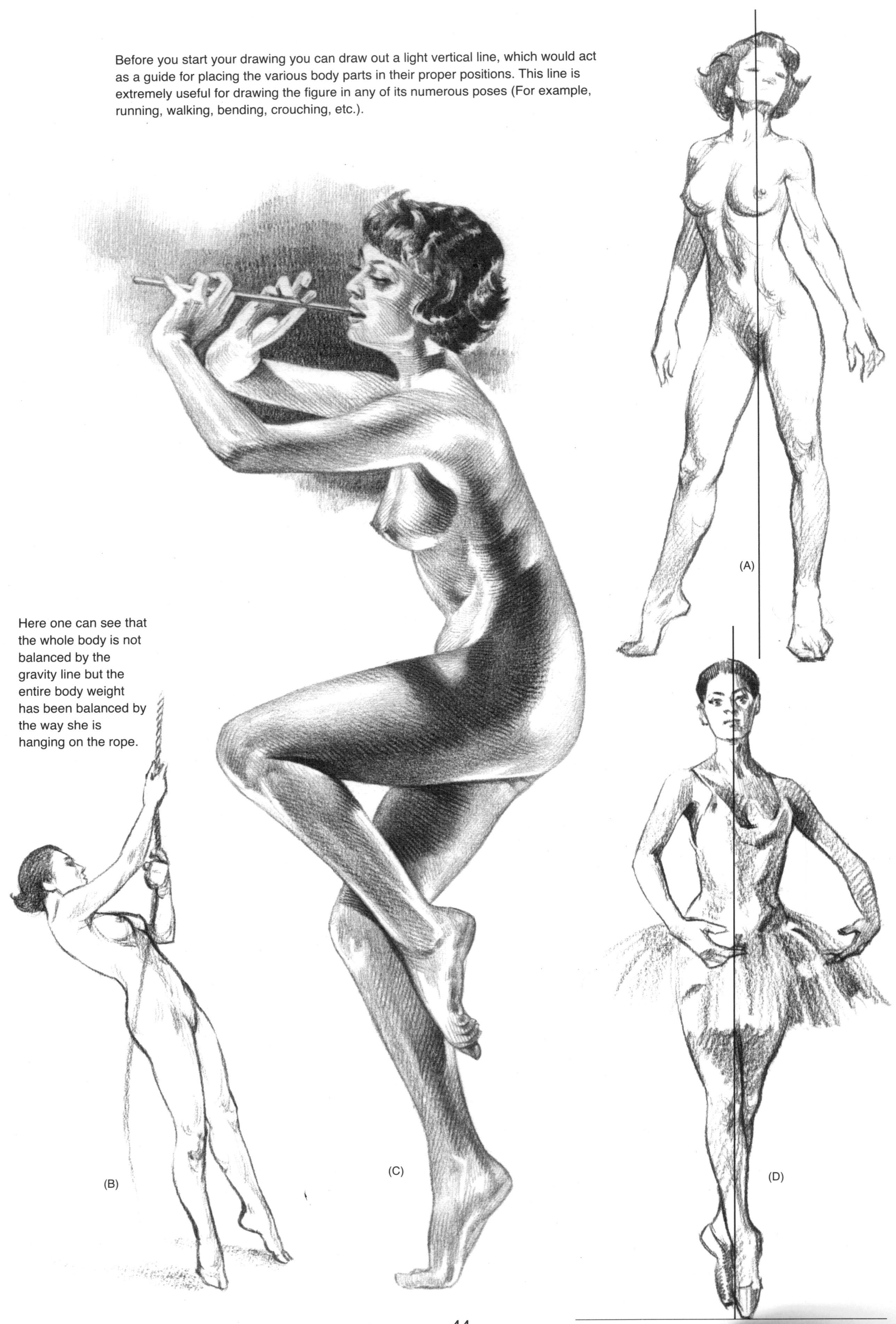

Here one can see that the whole body is not balanced by the gravity line but the entire body weight has been balanced by the way she is hanging on the rope.

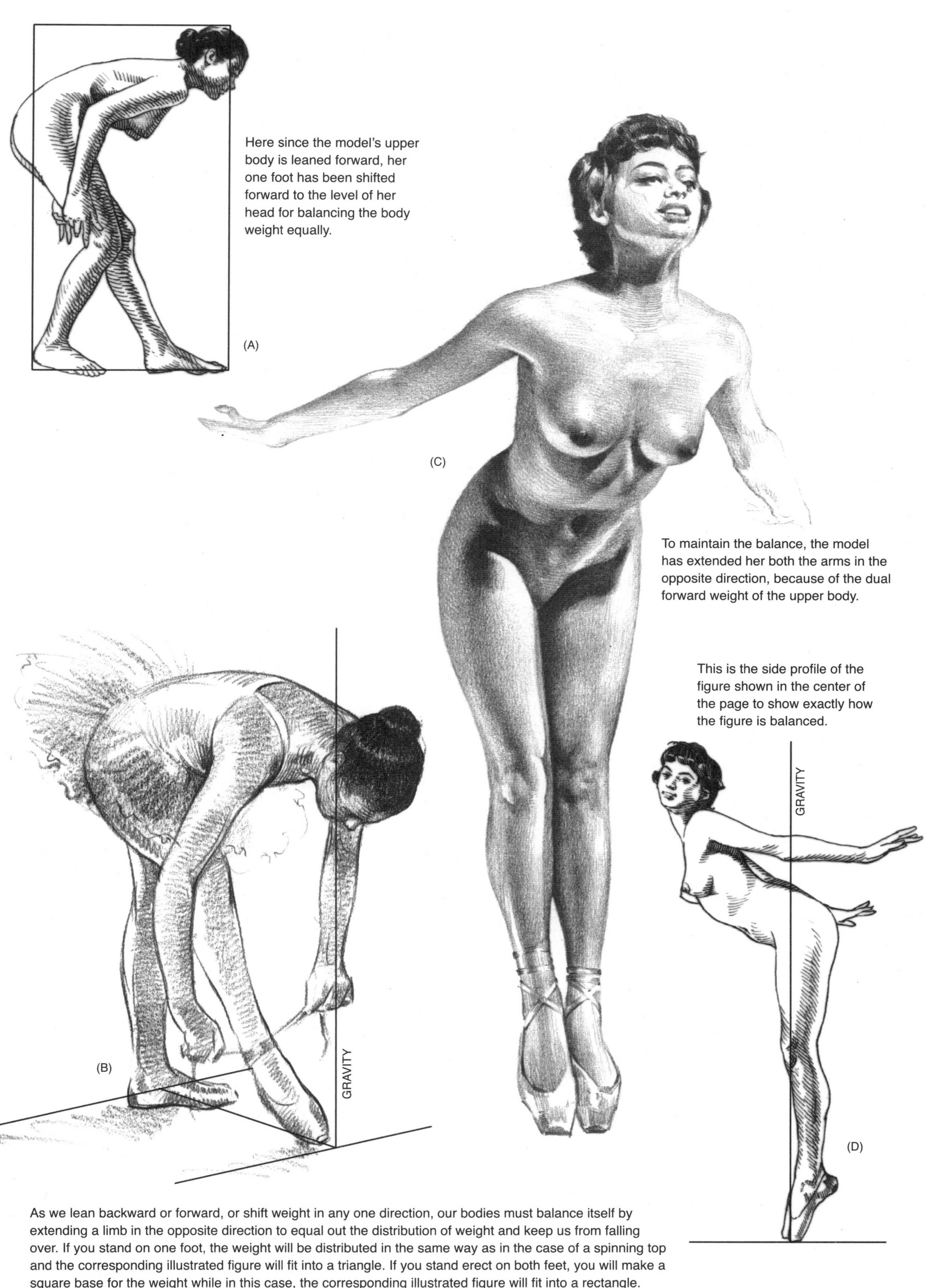

As we lean backward or forward, or shift weight in any one direction, our bodies must balance itself by extending a limb in the opposite direction to equal out the distribution of weight and keep us from falling over. If you stand on one foot, the weight will be distributed in the same way as in the case of a spinning top and the corresponding illustrated figure will fit into a triangle. If you stand erect on both feet, you will make a square base for the weight while in this case, the corresponding illustrated figure will fit into a rectangle.

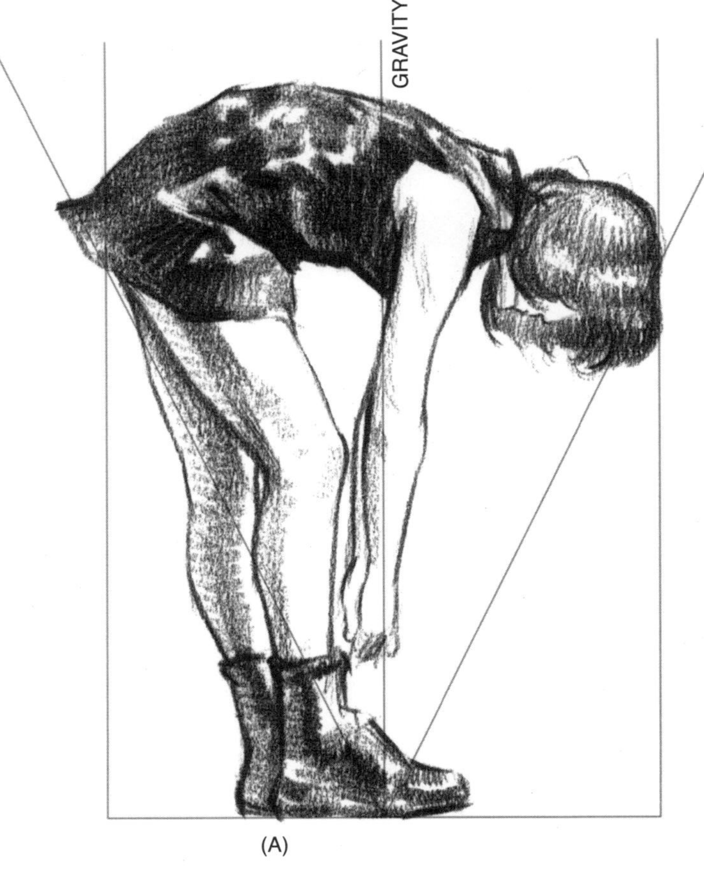

(A)

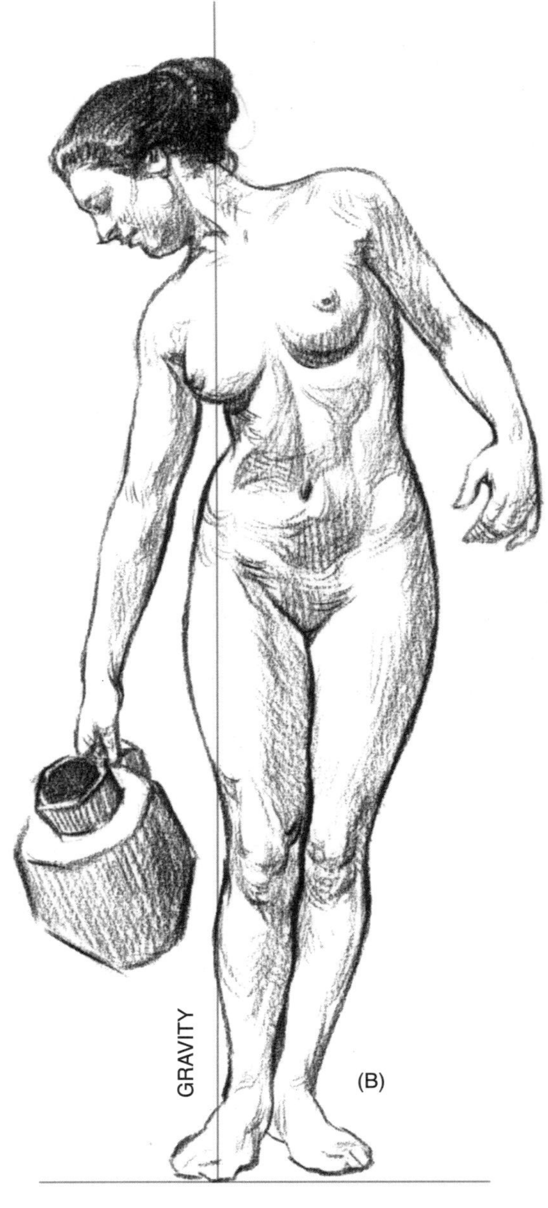

(B)

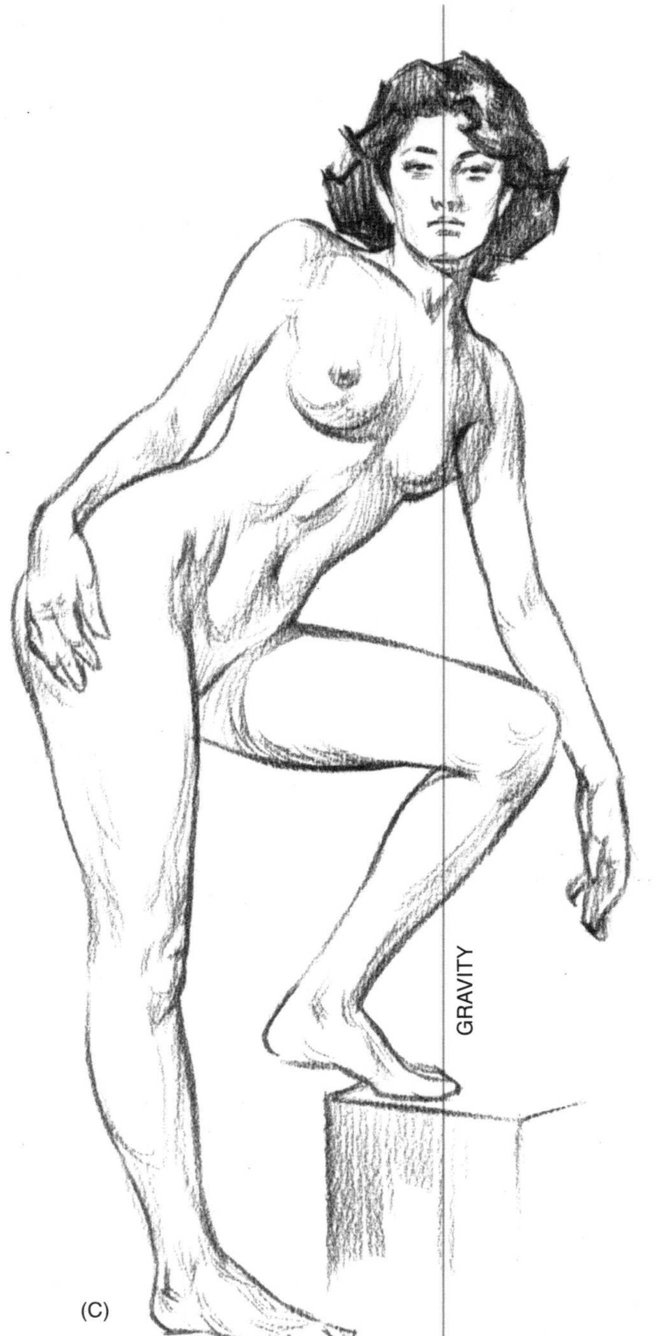

(C)

While bending to any one side, you will find that you naturally extend the arm on the other side to maintain your balance - you usually raise the heel of the other foot on the other side as well (like in the action of lifting a heavy object or reaching). This shows that you must place adequate weight on the opposite side to preserve your balance in every attitude and action. When the body bends, turns or twists, it tends to elongate on one side and proportionately shorten on the other.

A balanced figure is one that, no matter what action it is doing, its weight is equally distributed. Balance is an essential part of drawing any figure, and without it, a figure will look unnatural and awkward.

The key to the body's balance is the Spinal Column. Due to its flexibility, one is allowed to involuntarily adjust to changes in positions and shifts of weight. These changes, in turn affect the slant of the shoulders and hips as well as the turning and bending of the torso.

CENTER OF GRAVITY

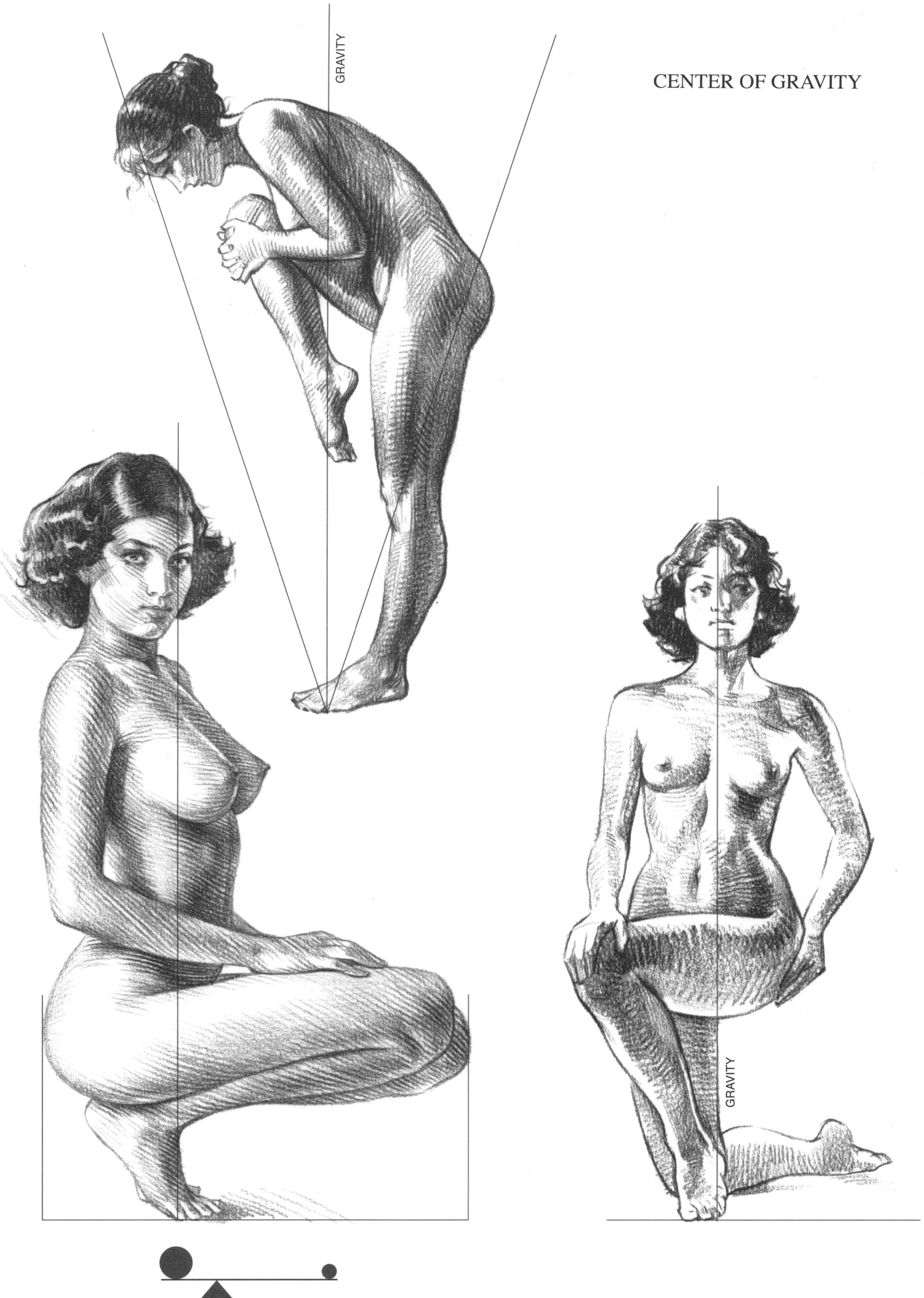

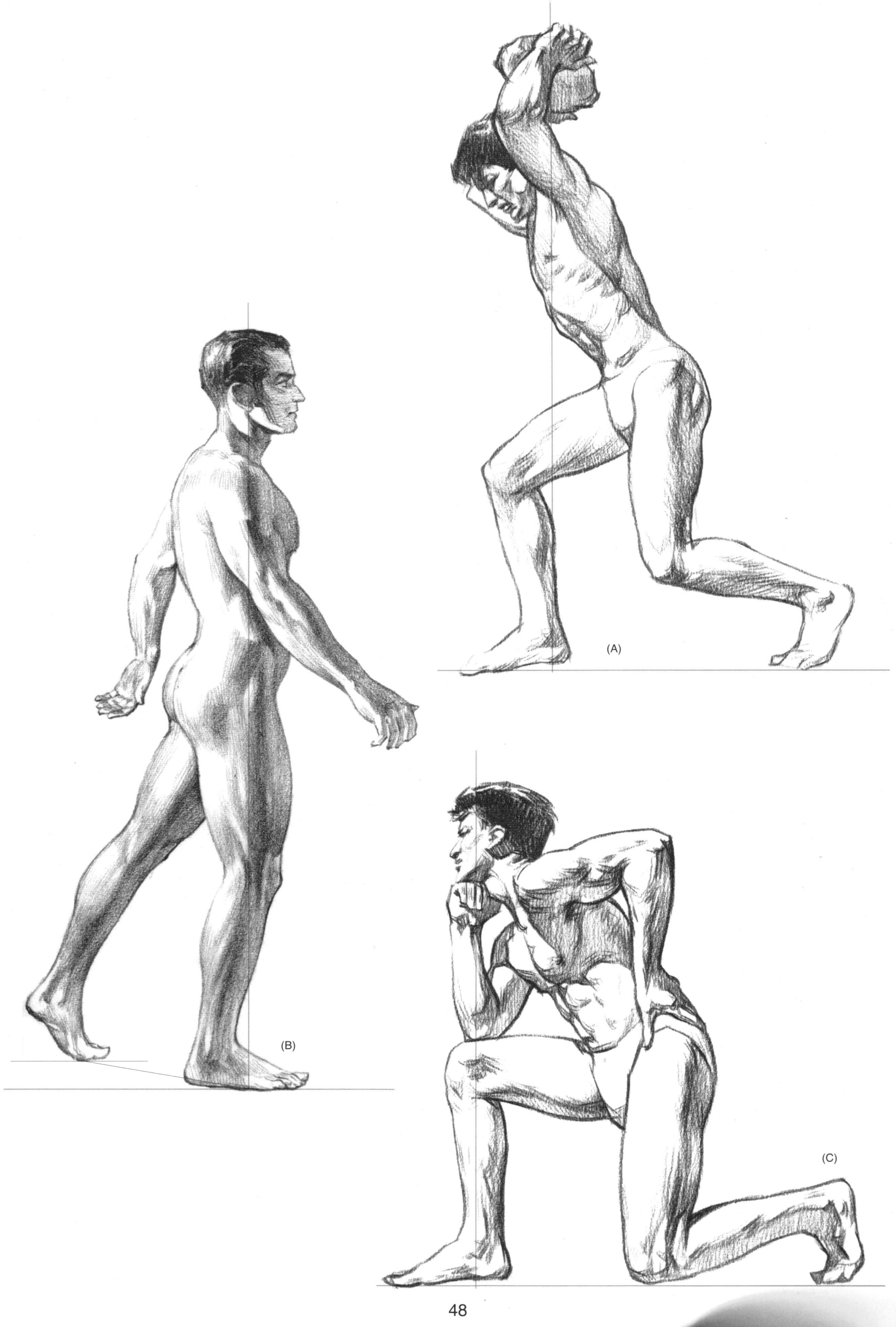
(A)
(B)
(C)

MUSCLES

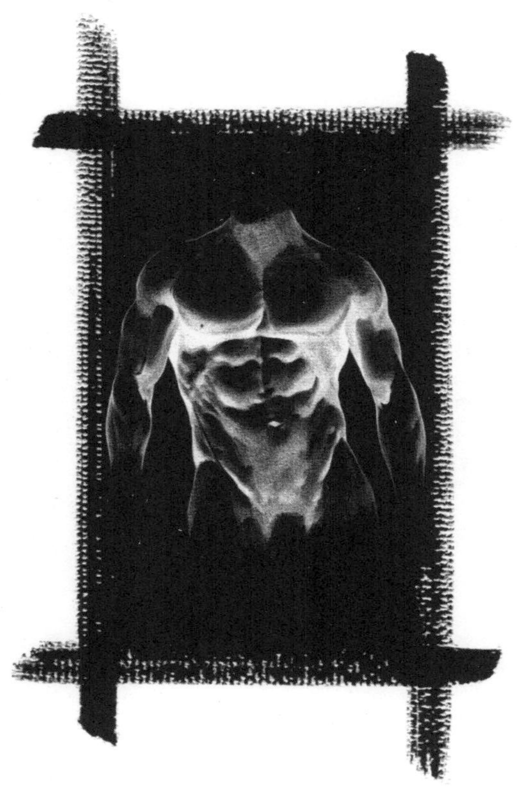

In this section, we deal with the various muscles that dress the skeleton. It is these muscles that give action, movement and solidity to the human figure. It is important that you learn the various outer surface muscles and a few important deeper, inner muscles in order to be able to draw various actions and poses accurately.
The following drawings show the differences in the male and female muscles. They will also explain why the surface forms of the muscles are different. Males and females have exactly the same muscles. However, the female muscles are smaller and are covered by a thicker layer of fat as compared to those of a male.
It is important to learn the size, position and action of the muscles groups. Knowledge of the muscles and their action will make it easier for you to understand what you observe in a real model or a photo. Try to learn the names of all these muscles, as it will be an added plus point for you. However, it is more important to know what these muscles are, where they start and end, and their various functions. Along with the muscle diagrams I have lightly drawn the supporting appearance of the figure i.e. the actual body, which will help you to understand the surface over each muscle area and to understand the appearance over the entire figure. These are to be used only as a reference. When you draw the figure, you should know more about the anatomy than what merely appears on the surface. As an example, you will find that there will be a greater amount to draw in terms of muscle, when you draw the figure of a body builder or athlete, as compared to that of a teenager or a man who does not work out.

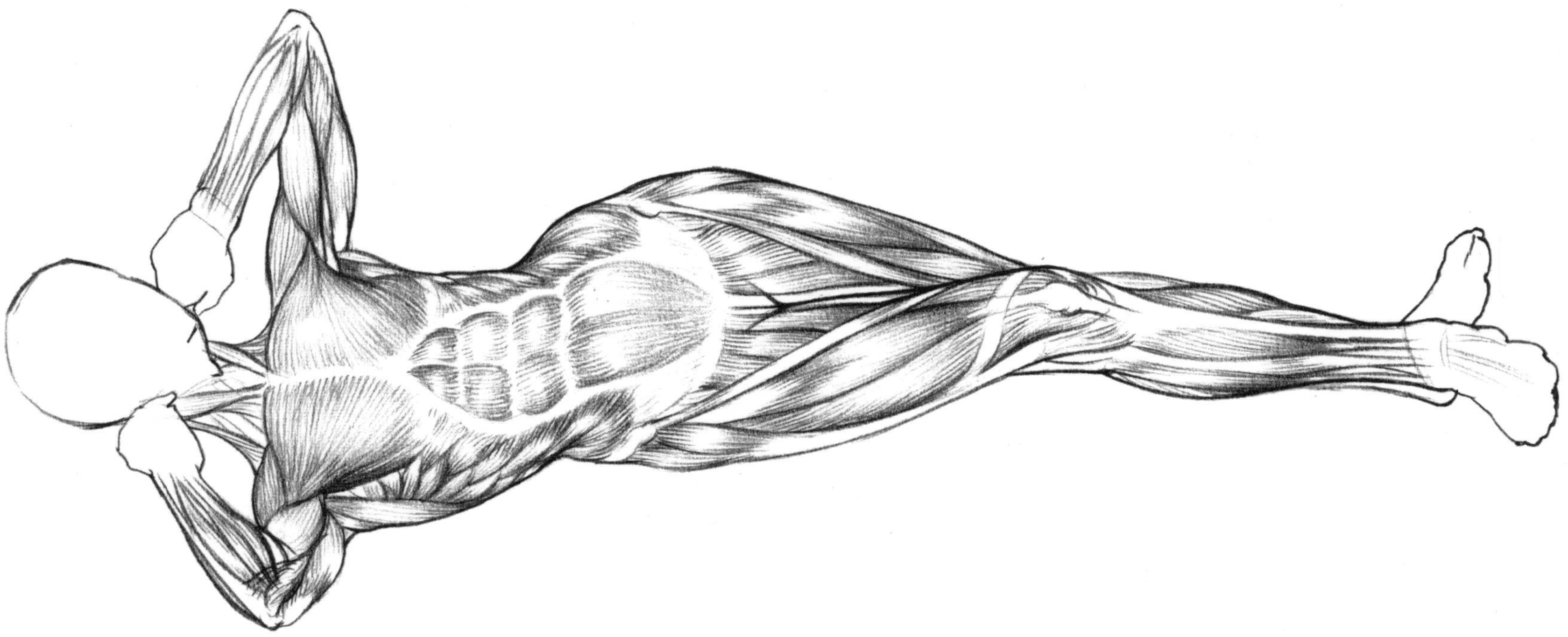

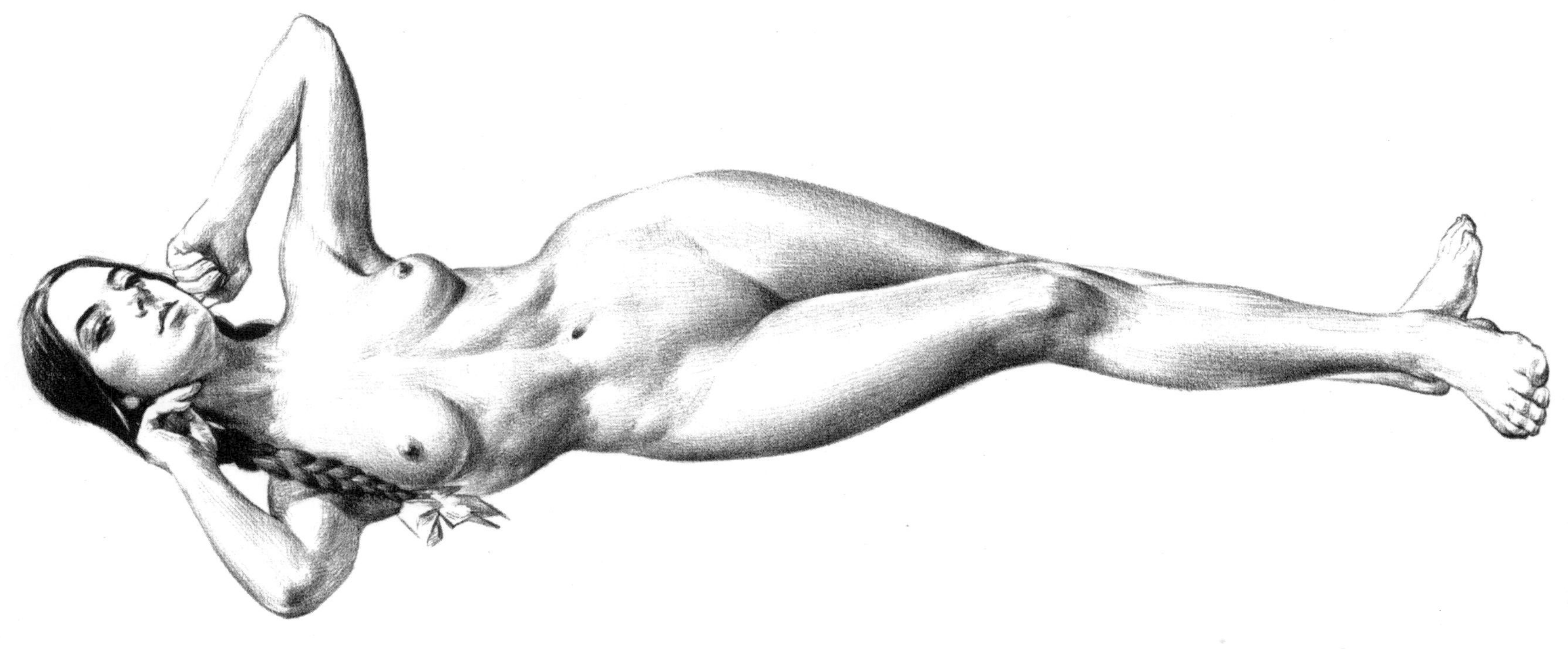

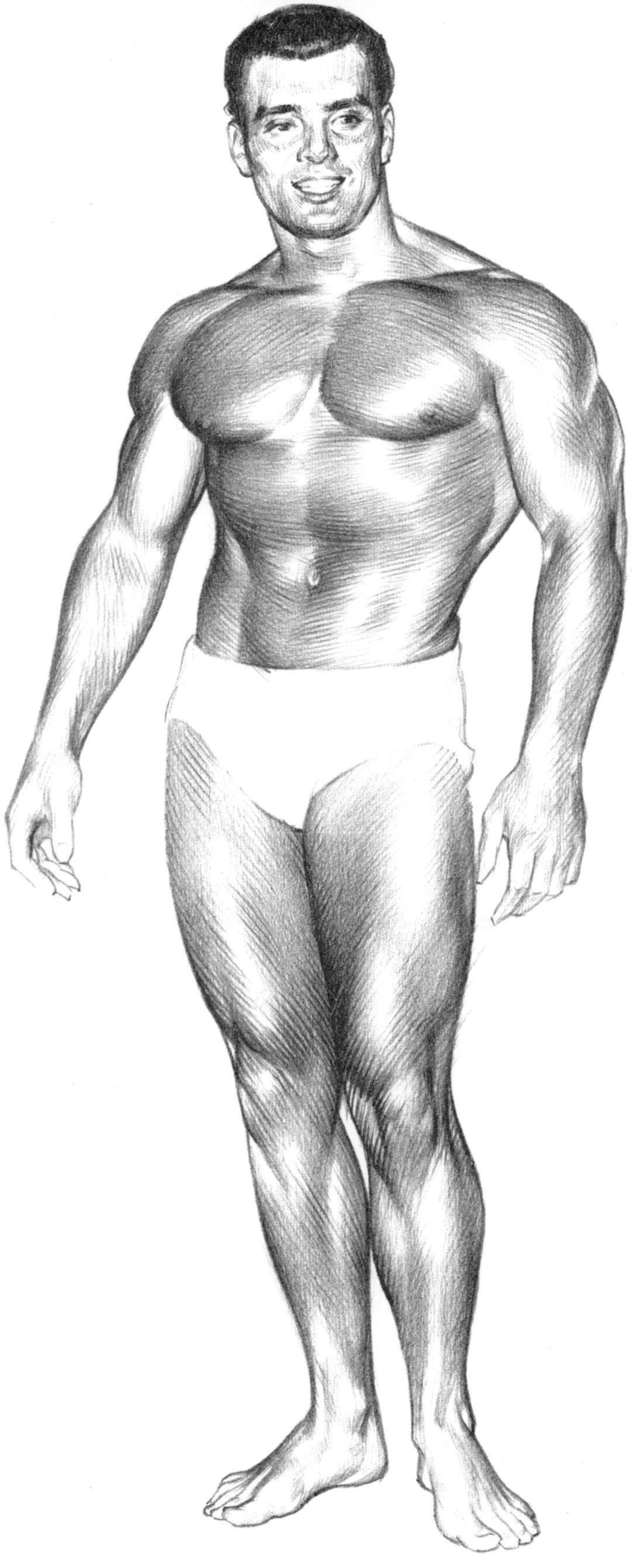

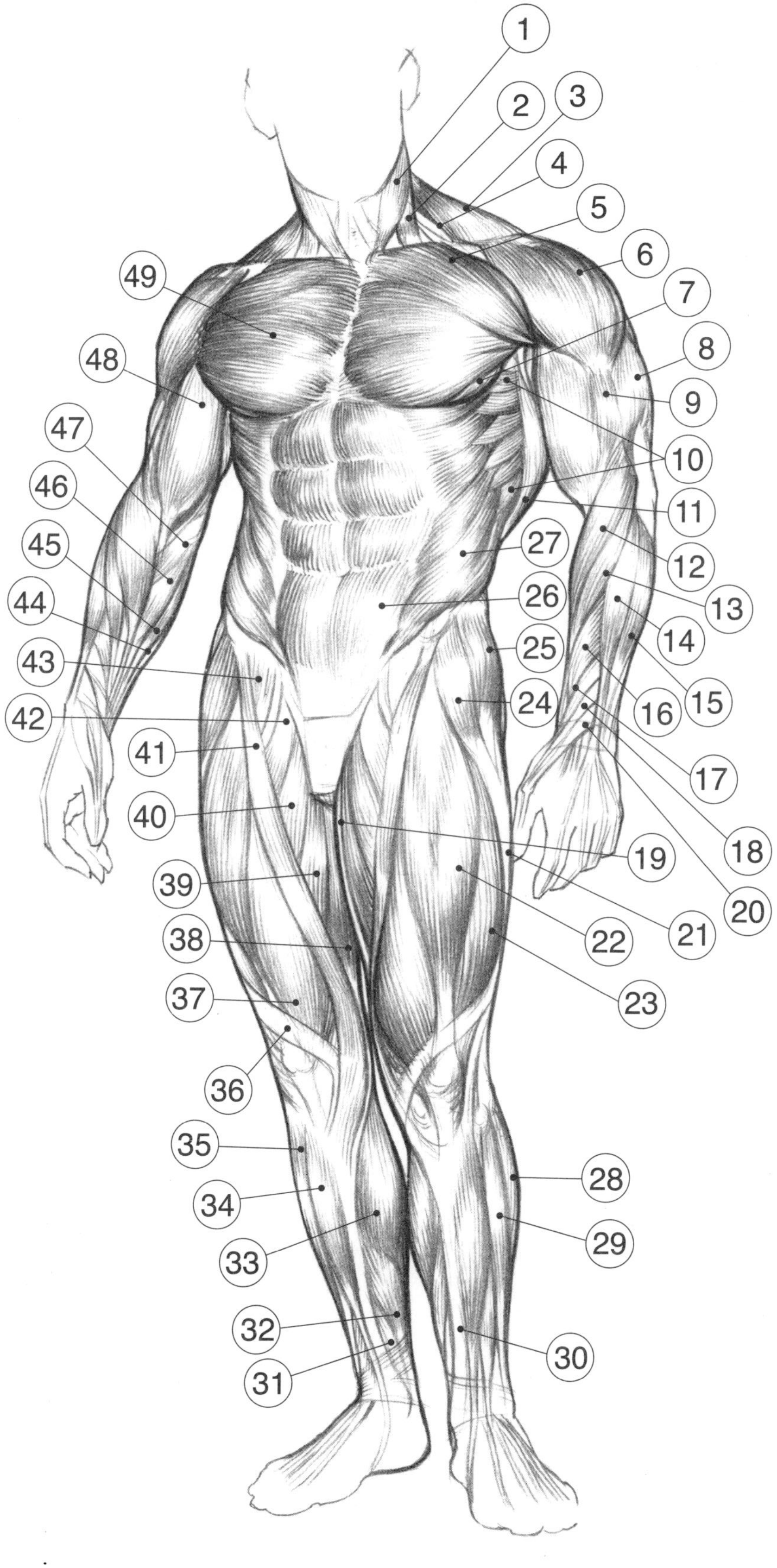

1) STERNOCLIEIDOMASTOID
2) STERNOCLIEIDOMASTOID
3) TRAPEZIUS
4) OMOHYOID
5) PECTORALIS MAJOR
6) DELTOID
7) PECTORALIS MINOR
8) TRICEPS
9) BRACHIALIS ANTICUS
10) SERRATUS ANTERIOR
11) LATISSIMUS DORSI
12) BRACHIORADIALIS
13) EXTENSOR CAPRI RADIALUS LONGUS
14) EXTENSOR COMMUNIS DIGITORUM
15) EXTENSOR DIGITI MINIMI
16) EXTENSOR CAPRI RADIALUS BREVIS
17) ABDUSTOR POLLICIS LONGUS
18) EXTENSOR POLLICIS BREVIS
19) GRACILIS
20) EXTENSOR POLLICIS LONGUS
21) ILIOTIBIAL TRACT
22) RECTUS FEMORIS
23) VASTUS LATERAL
24) TENSOR FASCIAE FEMORIS
25) GLUTEUS MEDIUS
26) RECTUS ABDOMINIS
27) EXTERNAL ABDOMINAL OBLIQUE
28) GASTRONEMIUS
29) PERONEUS LONGUS
30) LONG EXTENSOR OF TOE
31) TIBIALIS POSTICUS
32) SOLEUS
33) GASTRONEMIUS
34) TIBIALIS ANTICUS
35) PERONEUS LONGUS
36) RICHER'S LIGAMENT
37) VASTUS MEDIALIS
38) GRACILIS
39) ADDUCTOR MAGNUS
40) ADDUCTOR LONGUS
41) SARTORIUS
42) PECTINEUS
43) PSOAS LLIACUS
44) FLEXOR CAPRI ULNARIS
45) PALMARIS LONGUS
46) FLEXOR CAPRI RADIALIS
47) PRONATOR TERES
48) BICEPS
49) PECTORALIS MAJOR

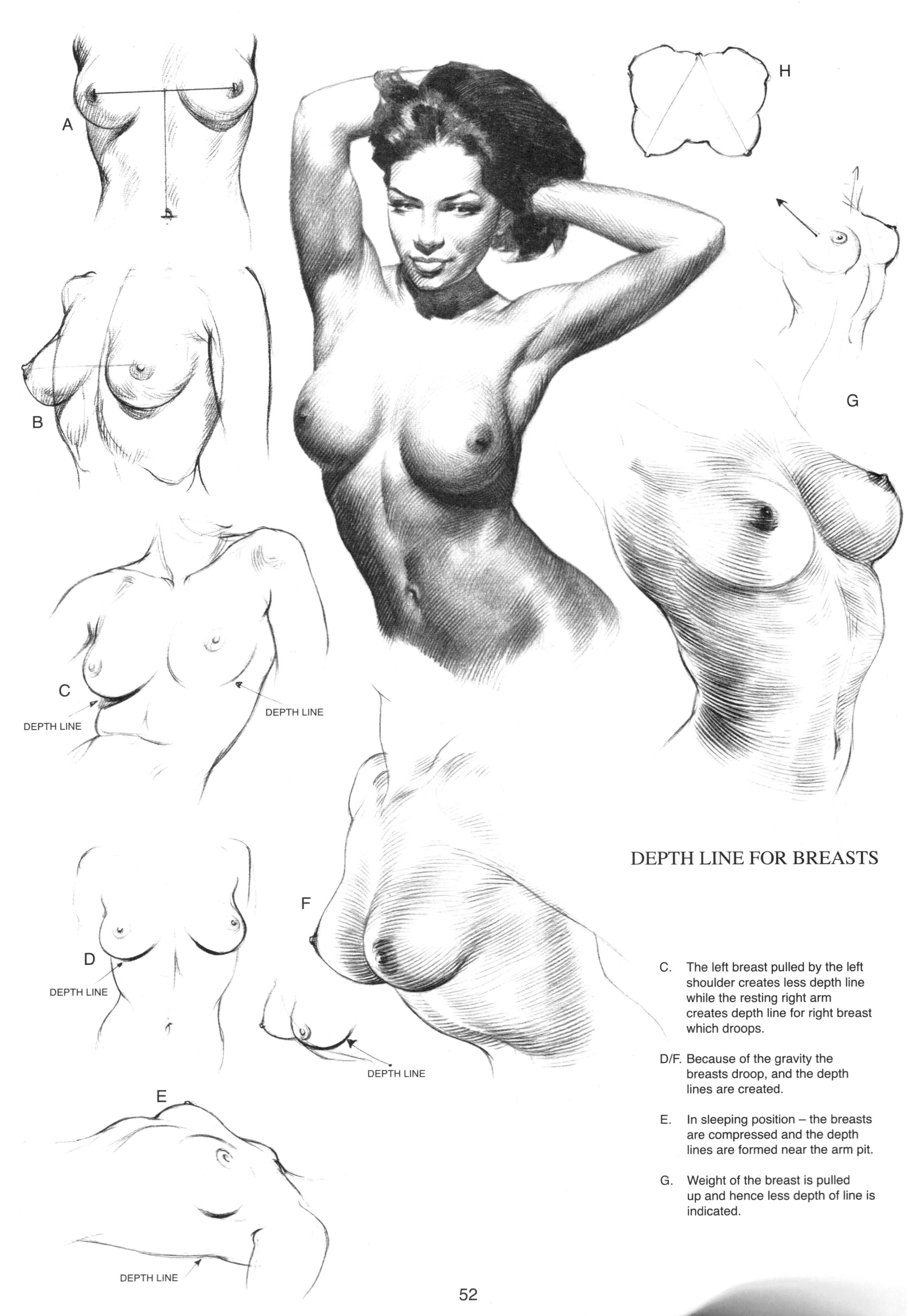

DEPTH LINE FOR BREASTS

C. The left breast pulled by the left shoulder creates less depth line while the resting right arm creates depth line for right breast which droops.

D/F. Because of the gravity the breasts droop, and the depth lines are created.

E. In sleeping position – the breasts are compressed and the depth lines are formed near the arm pit.

G. Weight of the breast is pulled up and hence less depth of line is indicated.

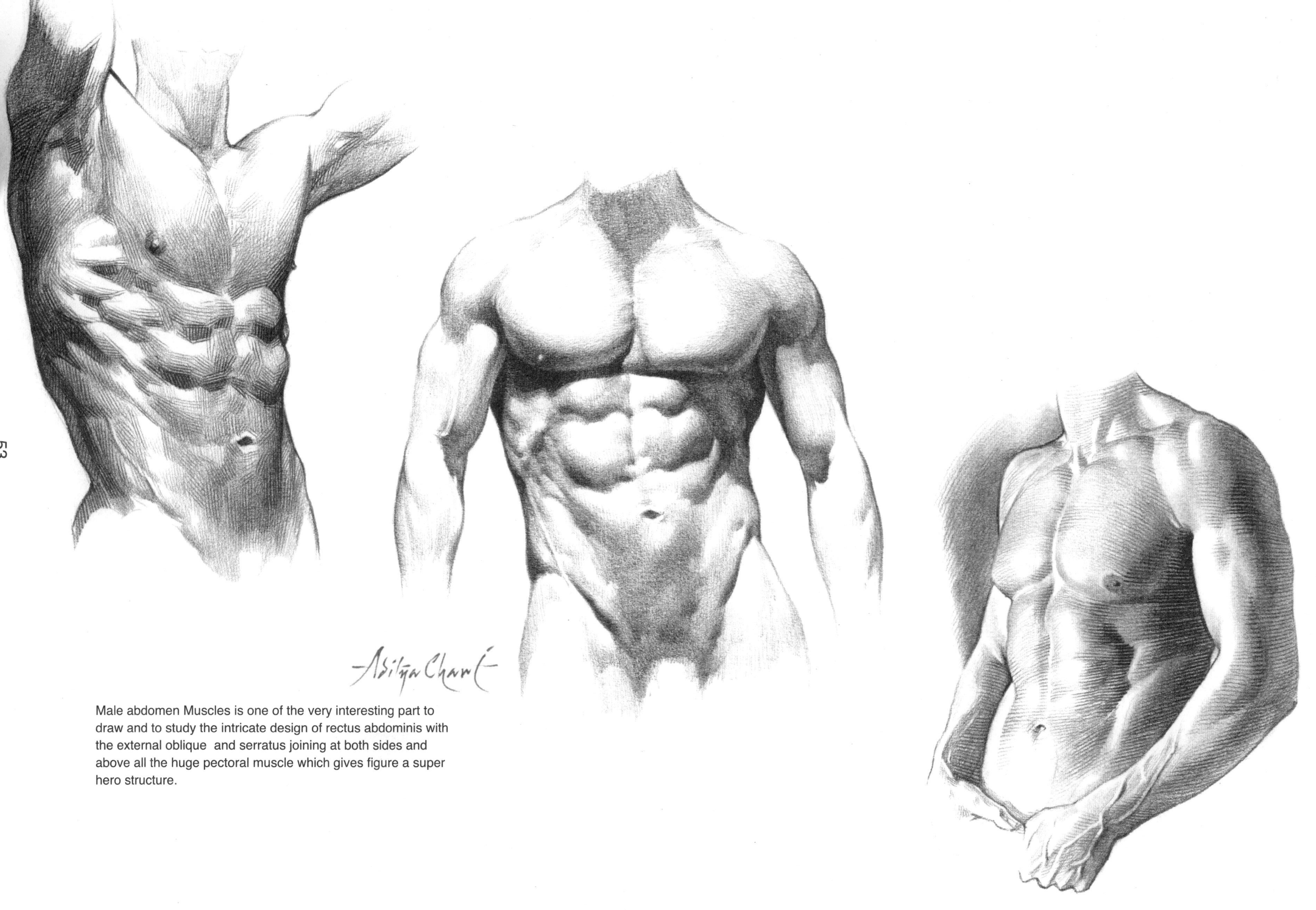

Male abdomen Muscles is one of the very interesting part to draw and to study the intricate design of rectus abdominis with the external oblique and serratus joining at both sides and above all the huge pectoral muscle which gives figure a super hero structure.

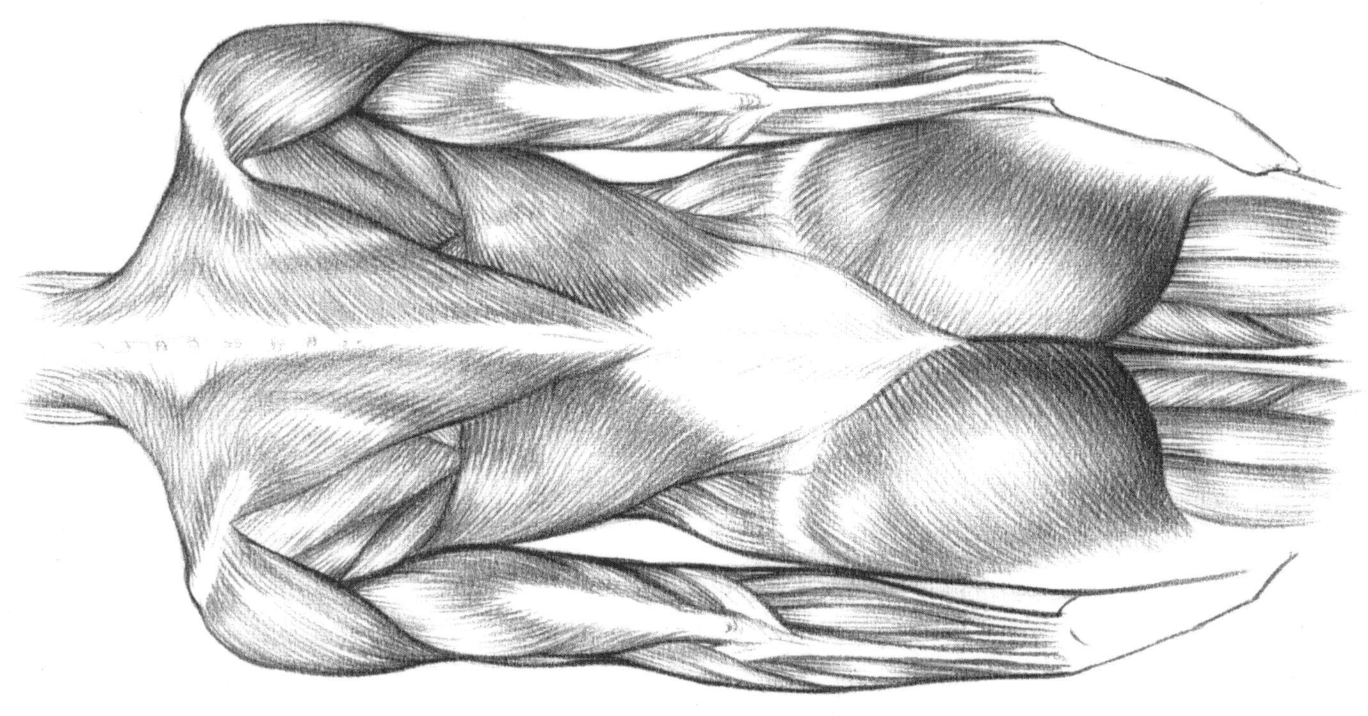

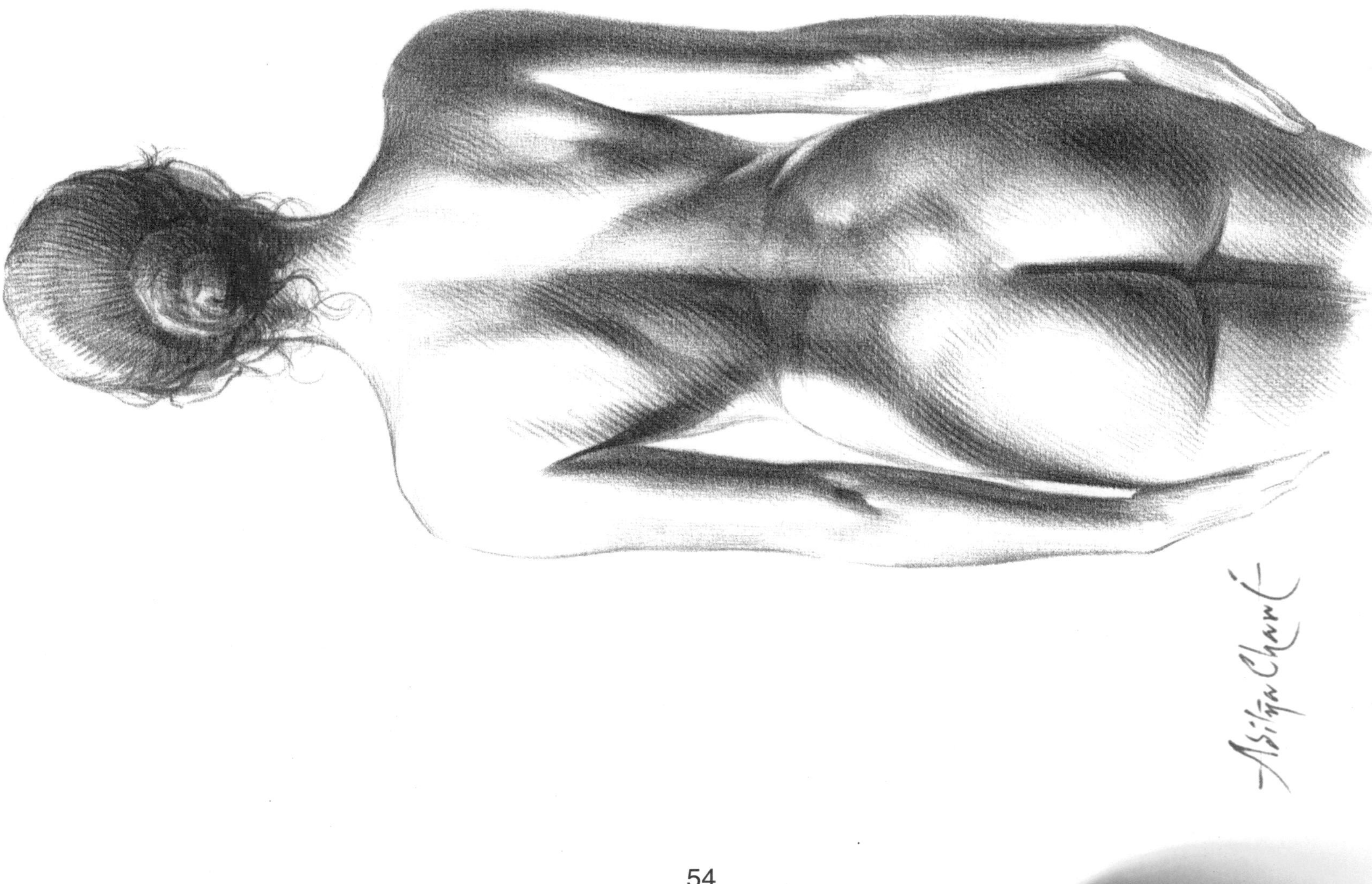

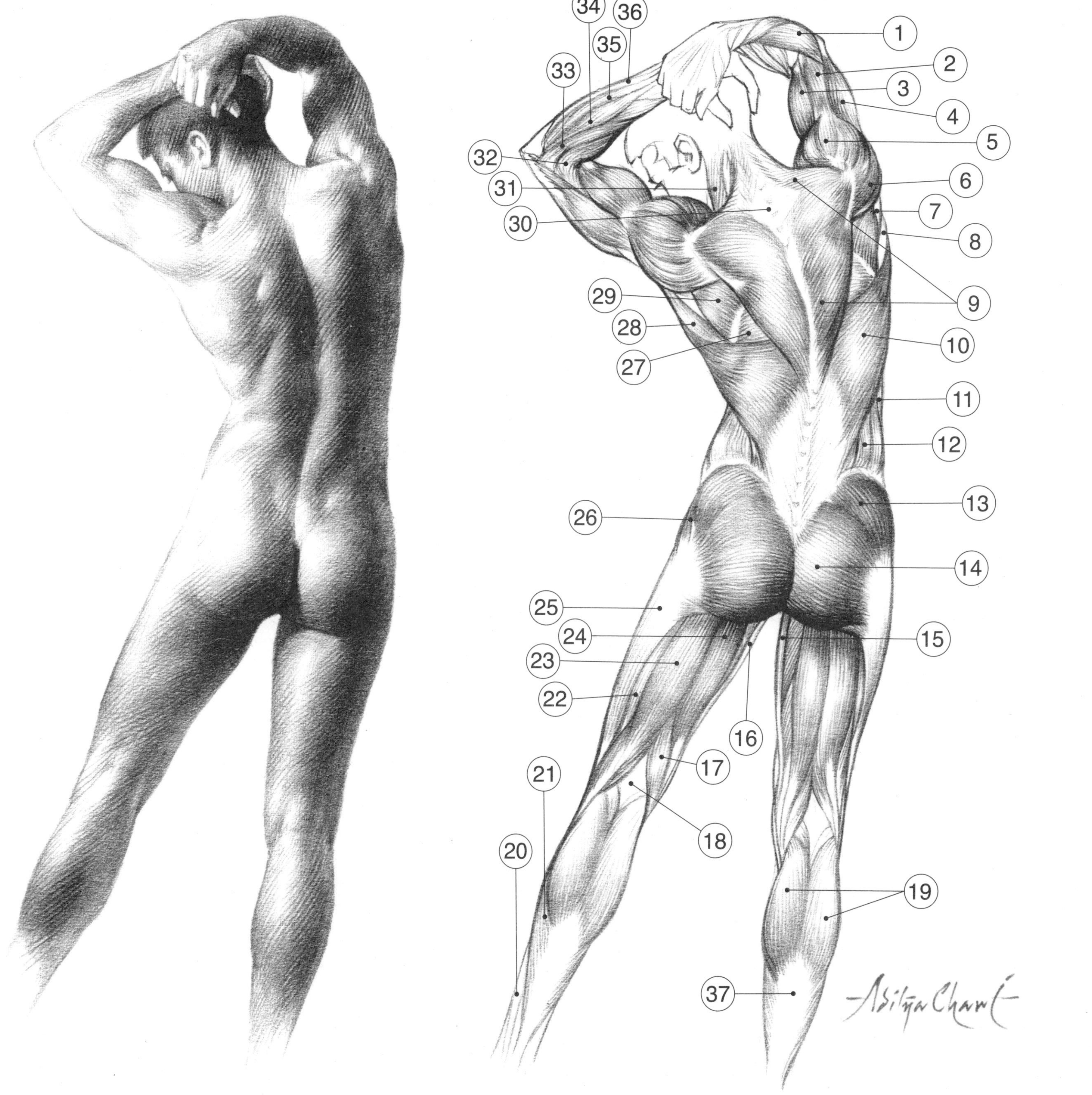

1) BRACHIORADIALIS
2) BRACHIALIS ANTICUS
3) BICEPS
4) TRICEPS
5) DELTOID
6) REAR DELTOID
7) TERES MINOR
8) TERES MAJOR
9) TRAPEZIUS
10) LATISSIMUS DORSI
11) EXTERNAL ABDOMINAL OBLIQUE
12) EXTERNAL ABDOMINAL OBLIQUE
13) GLUTEUS MEDIUS
14) GLUTEUS MAXIMUS
15) ADDUCTOR MAGNUS
16) GRACILIS
17) SEMIMEMBRANOSUS
18) POPLITEAL SPACE
19) GASTROCNEMIUS
20) PERONEUS LONGUS
21) SOLEUS
22) VASTUS LATERAL
23) BICEPS FEMORIS
24) SEMITENDINOSUS
25) ILIO TRACT
26) TENSOR FASCIAE
27) RHOMBOIDEUS MAJOR
28) TERES MAJOR
29) INFRASPINATUS
30) SPINE
31 STERNOCLIEIDOMASTOID
32) BRACHIORADIALIS
33) EXTENSOR CAPRI RADIALUS
34) EXTENSOR COMMUNIS DIGITORUM
35) EXTENSOR DIGITI MINIMI
36) EXTENSOR CAPRI ULNARIS

1) STERNOCLEIDOMASTOID
2) TRAPEZIUS
3) STERNO MASTOID
4) DELTOID
5) TRICEPS
6) BRACHIALIS ANTICUS
7) BICEPS
8) BRACHIORADIALIS
9) EXTENSOR CAPRI RADIALUS LONGUS
10) EXTENSOR COMMUNIS DIGITORUM
11) EXTENSOR DIGITORUM COMMUNIS
12) EXTENSOR CAPRI ULNARIS
13) GLUTEUS MEDIUS & MAXIMUS
14) BICEPS OF LEG
15) SEMITENDENOSUS
16) SEMIMEMBRANOSUS
17) GRACILIS
18) SARTORIUS
19) VASTUS MEDIALIS
20) RICHER'S LIGAMENT
21) GASTRONEMUS
22) TIBIA
23) TENDO- ACHILLIS
24) SOLEUS
25) PERONEUS LONGUS
26) GASTRONEMUS
27) PATELLA LIGAMENTS
28) SEMITENDENOSUS
29) BICEPS OF LEG
30) TIBIALIS ANTICUS
31) EXTENSOR LONGUS DIGITORUM
32) PATELLA LIGAMENTS
33) POPLITEAL SPACE
34) ILIO TIBIAL BAND
35) VASTUS LATERAL
36) RECTUS FEMORIS
37) EXTENSOR POLLICIS BREVIS
38) TENSOR FASCIAS FEMORIS
39) ABDUSTOR POLLICIS LONGUS
40) PALMARIS LONGUS
41) EXTENSOR CAPRI RADIALUS
42) FLEXOR CAPRI RADIALIS
43) BRACHIORADIALIS
44) RECTUS ABDOMINIS
45) EXTERNAL ABDOMINAL OBLIQUE
46) PECTORALIS MINOR
47) PECTORALIS MAJOR
48) STERNO-HYOID
49) OMOHYOID
50) TERES MAJOR
51) LATISSIMUS DORSI
52) SERRATUS ANTERIOR
53) EXTENSOR CAPRI RADIALUS BREVIS
54) ABDUSTOR POLLICIS LONGUS
55) EXTENSOR POLLICIS BREVIS

LIGHT & SHADE

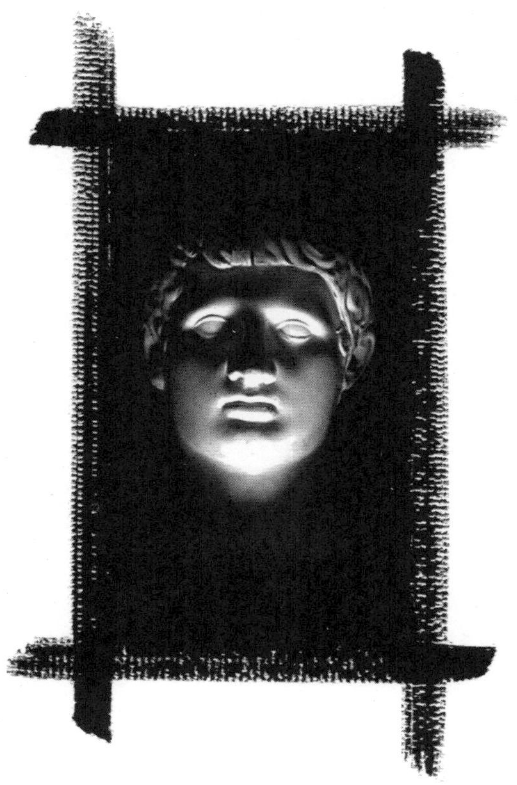

Light is the only reason we are able to see colours and shapes. Without it, we would experience total blackness. Even with the lights out, you can still make out shapes, once your eyes get adjusted to the darkness in existing dim light.

In drawing too, light plays an extremely important role. To give you a classic example, draw a circle on a paper. In order to give that circle a three-dimensional feel you will have to make it look solid. This is achieved only after we highlight certain areas and darken others to illustrate the reflection of light – Right. Light or the reflection of light onto an object is what gives it highlights and shadows. Even shadows have varying shades depending on how far away they are from the light and the degree of reflection. It is this distribution of light that brings out the depth and dimension of forms. As explained in the grey scale, these are different conditions of light.

Light and shade of basic solid objects and how it relates with human figures

Knowledge of grey scale (Fig. A) is very essential for an artist and an art student. In this scale, ideal white is placed at one end and an ideal black at the other end and in between are created seven steps of gradually increasing greys, from lightest to darkest grey. All these steps stand for different conditions of light. The grey scale is also known as value scale. Value means lightness or darkness of the surface the artist in experiencing.

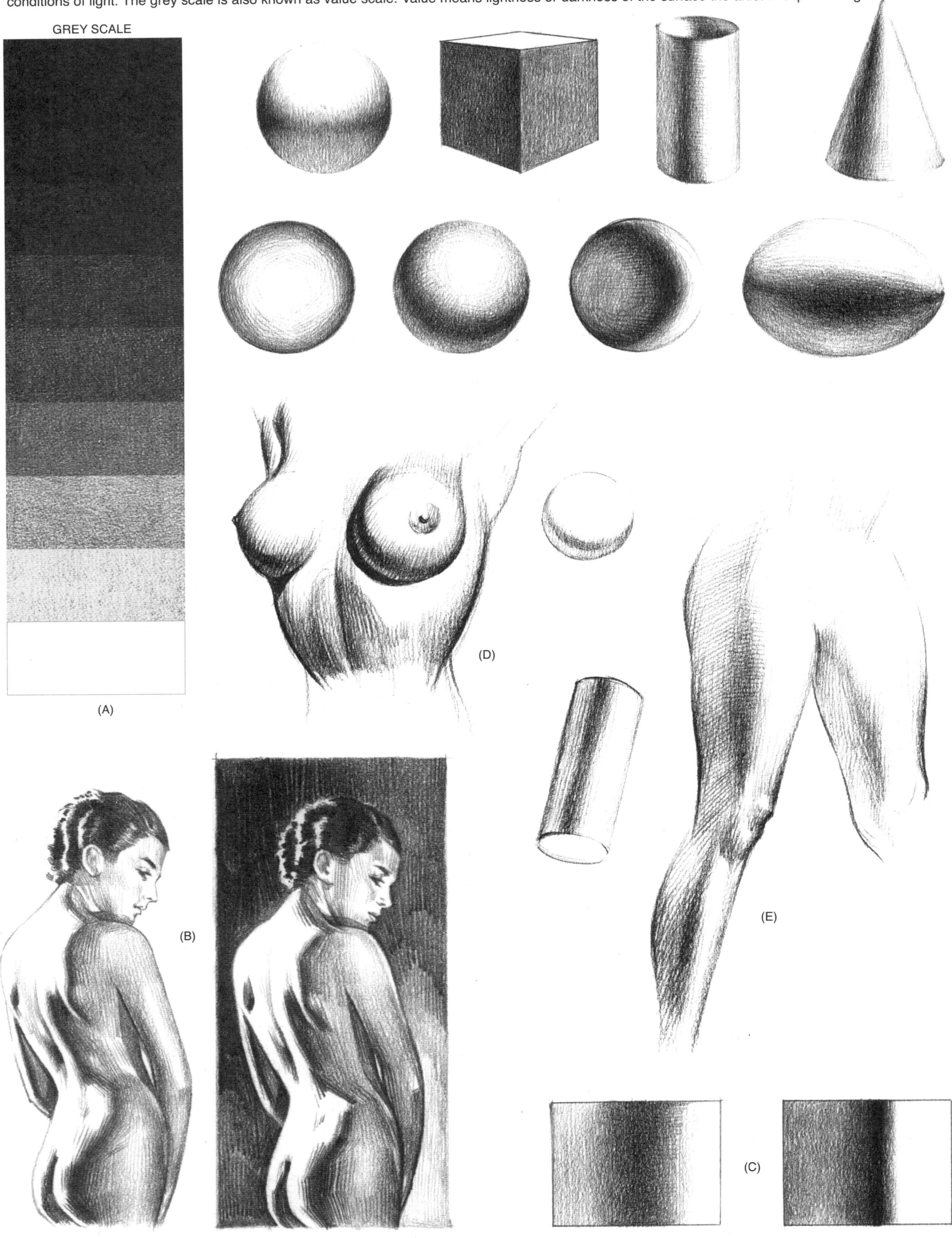

Use of background to enhance the figure

Soft light

Hard light

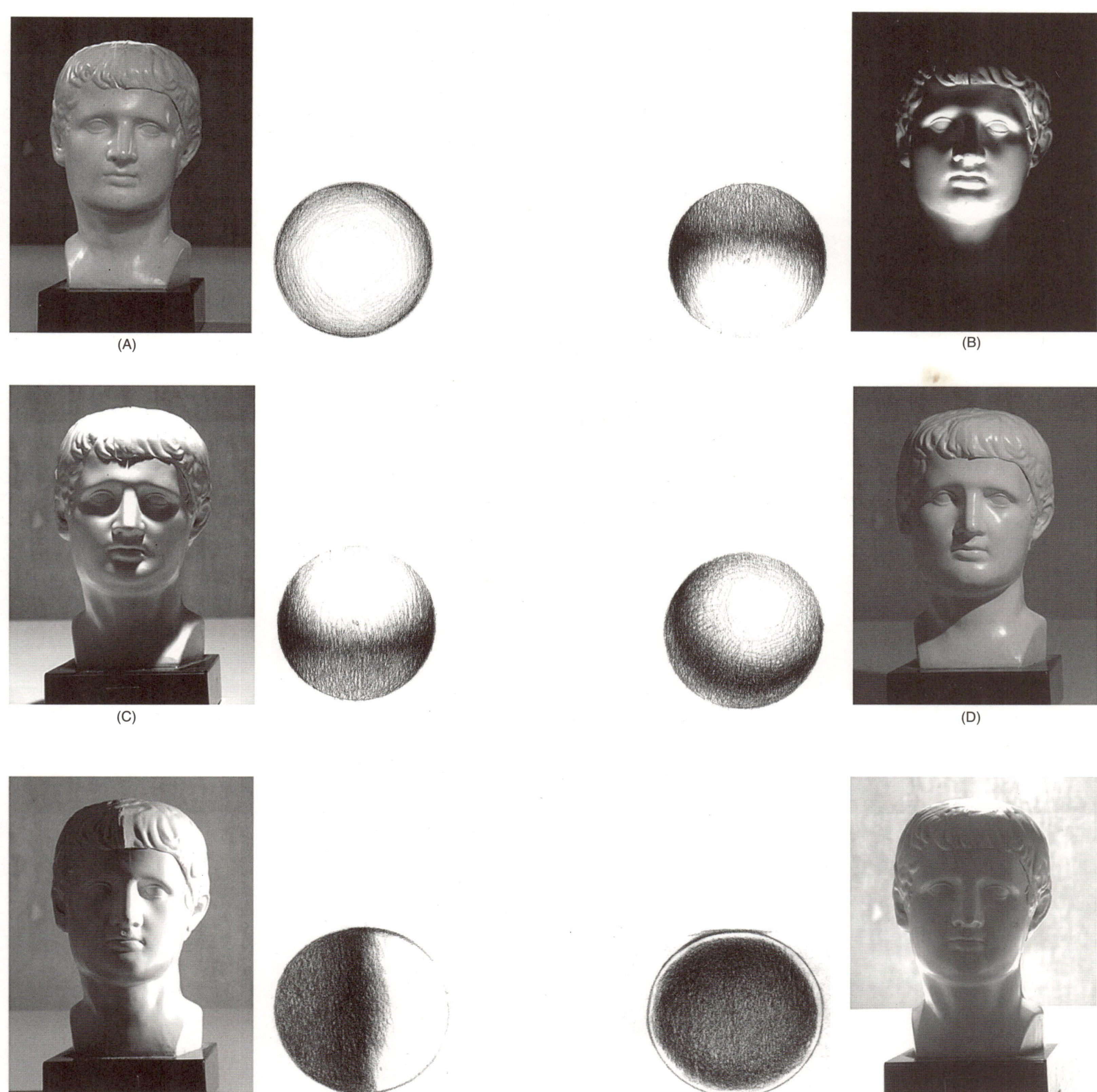

(A) (B) (C) (D) (E) (F)

Here I have taken a bust to demonstrate different lighting and the play of light and shade on it. This exercise could also be done with a simple sphere, with which you would be able to clearly tell every tonal value. When light falls on the sphere, it produces a highlight, a halftone and casts a shadow that is a darker area. (The reflected light compresses the darkness resulting in the cast shadow). These three values: the highlight, half tone and cast shadow, which collectively, make an object, look three dimensional and real.

Depending upon the angle of the light source, the percentages of light and shade differ. For example, if the light is projected from the front of the bust, (Fig. A) there is maximum light and hardly any shadow, resulting in a large amount of light tones and highlights, with a darkening only over the edges. Due to the lack of shadows, the final artwork looks flat, loses its depth and dimensional effect.

When the light is projected from the back of the bust (Fig. F), the entire front of the bust is eclipsed in darkness, with hardly any visible details. Only a narrow band of light is visible which is definitely not suitable for modeling. The phases of light reflected upon the model bust are similar to the phases of light upon the moon, (full, half, crescent etc.)

We see more or less of the enlightened side of the model depending on the angle of light or the angle of view. In the case of a 90-degree angle of light source (Fig. E), the bust has an equal division of light and dark. In this case, half of the bust is in total darkness, losing details, while the lighted part is highlighted. However, if the light is reflecting back over the cast shadow, you will sometimes get a good result, but note that this does not always work.

In a 45-degree angle or the three quarter light source there is a little more light than in the 90-degree light source or half lit view (Fig. D). Most portrait artists prefer this lighting as it leaves most of the face illuminated. Here, the concentration of light decreases from the forehead, cheekbones, mouth and finally to the chin. However, there is enough shadow to convey the feeling of mass and solidity of the bust.

We finally come to the part where we are going to discuss the dramatic source of lighting - either from below or above. If you see (Fig. C), where the light source is from above, you will notice that, in this case, most of the planes of the body/face that face upward gets highlighted, for instance, the head and forehead are greatly lit. The nose and the cheekbones are also some of the enlightened areas. However, the chin gets hardly any light at all. The key areas of expression on the face, namely the eye, lips etc are in shadow. This kind of lighting can be used for sculpted models, but NOT for live models. Similarly, in the case of lighting from below (Fig. B), the reverse occurs. All the planes of the face/body that face downward gets highlighted. In this case of lighting, the model will lose its original character and will be taken as one of the dramatic horror character.

Drawing of a body should always be done with a single light source. This gives you two specific areas - light and shadow. The former lighting is governed by the main light source, or Primary light, while the latter is governed by a much weaker light source (Secondary light), which is actually the reflection of the primary light itself. The area where the light and the shadowed areas meet or adjoin is what gives the drawing a real, three-dimensional feel to it.

There are many kinds of lights. These are mainly divided into Natural light sources and Artificial light sources. Sunlight, moonlight and starlight fall into the former category while tube lights; halogen bulbs, candle lights etc. fall into the latter. You should remember that every light source has its own character, which is referred to as KEY of the light. It is the source of light that will set the mood and feel of your drawing.

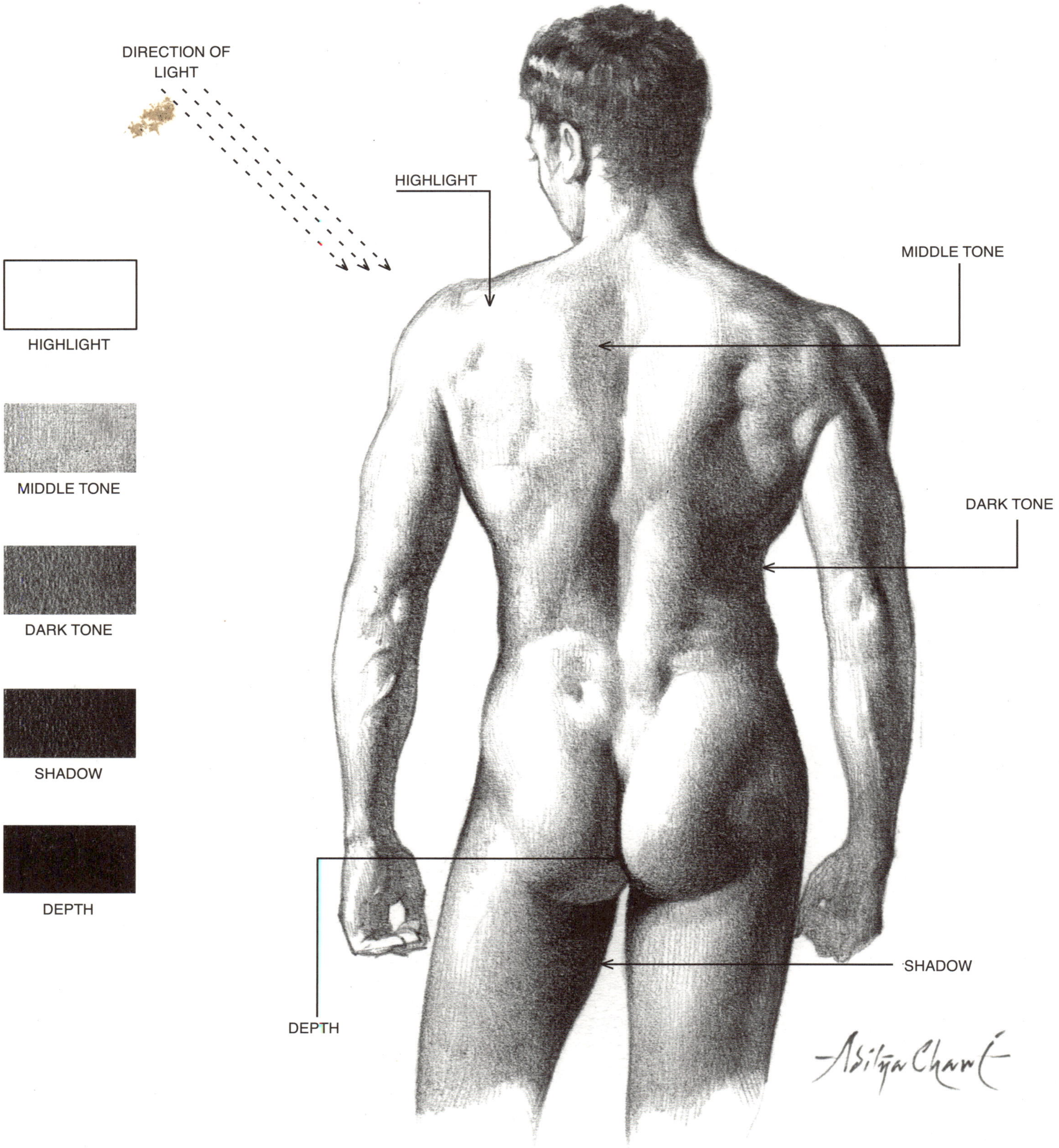

While modeling, the most important factor is the angle of the light source. In short, the degree to which a surface faces the light source determines how much light it catches. The distance and the angle of the light source and how it reflects back are the important aspects that only help to make your work better. A 45-degree angle light is highly recommended for live modeling or for portraits. You should play around with different degrees of light to experiment with the various effects of light and shades on a model.

The best and most preferred light source for modeling is natural daylight. Remember, that even a simple light setup can be very effective if executed well. This lighting gives you the diffused light effect that reflect the original body tones, emphasizing the skin texture ad features and works well for soft skin. This cannot be achieved with harsh lighting

SHAPE

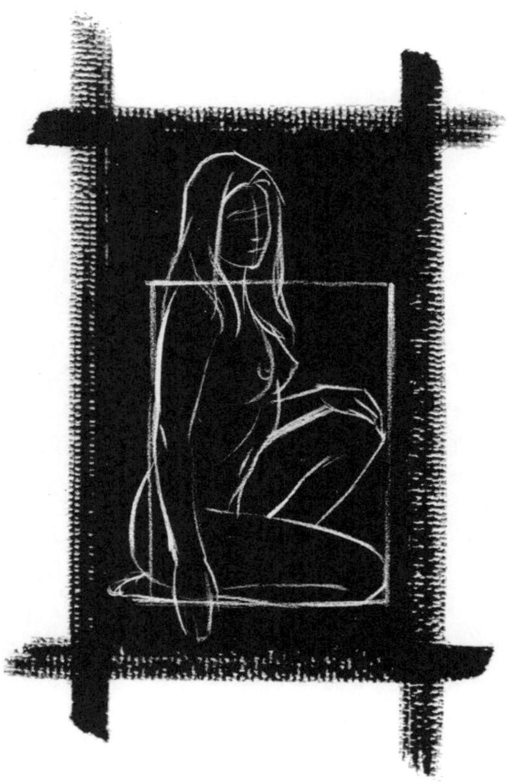

For the first project you should try to do very simple and quick but complete drawings. This exercise will help in developing your ability to see the flow of action and entire shape of the figure in just a glance.

A basic requirement in drawing is the skill to view the real shape of an object without any distortion. One way to achieve this is to train yourself to look for the overall flat shape of an object, rather than evaluating its height and width separately. If an object can loosely fit into a square or a circle, even if it is not a perfect fit, then it is very handy in mentally visualizing it or even drawing a square or circle around it. Triangles, circles, rectangles, ovals and irregular shapes similar to these, are all easier to judge by the eye than linear dimensions.

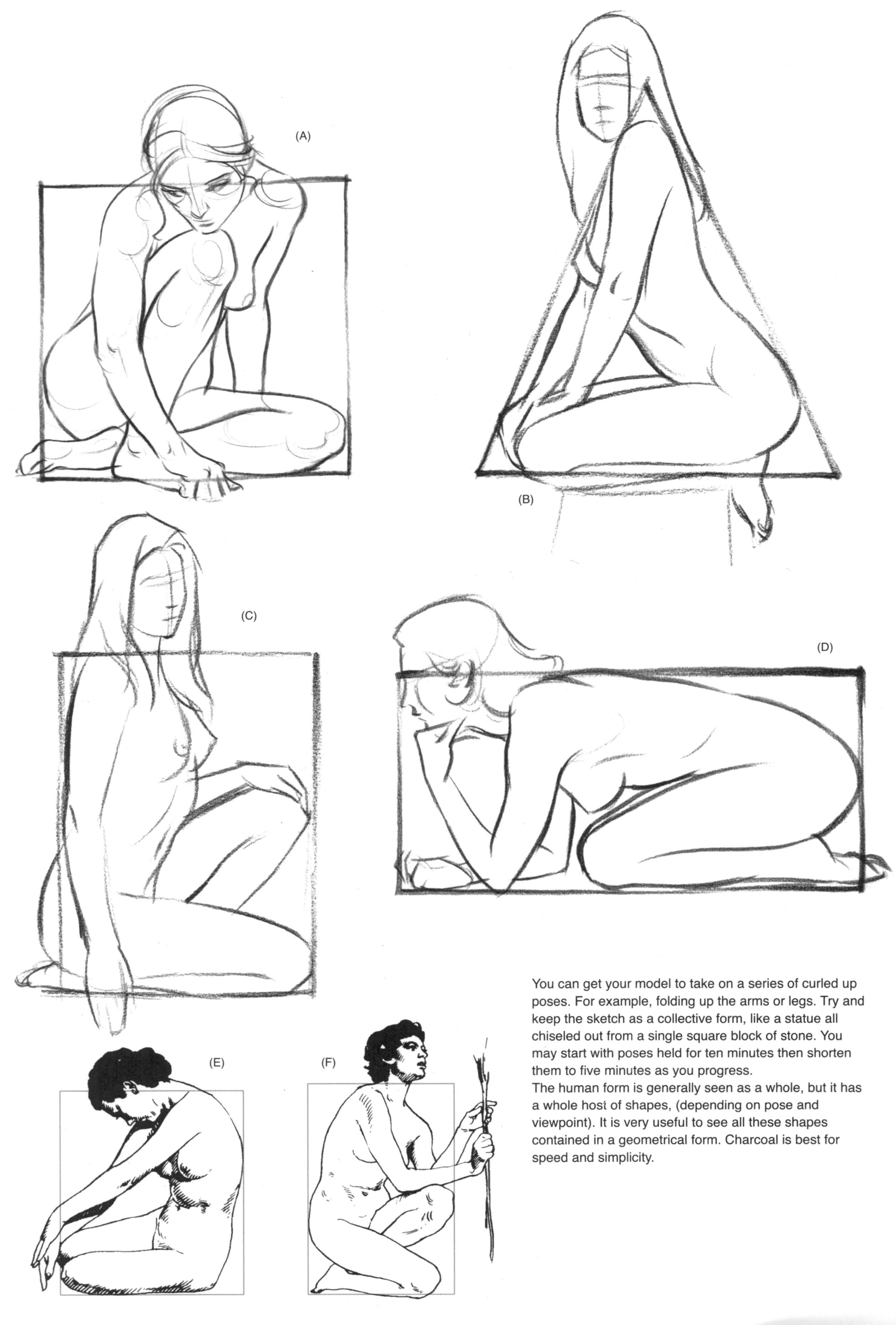

You can get your model to take on a series of curled up poses. For example, folding up the arms or legs. Try and keep the sketch as a collective form, like a statue all chiseled out from a single square block of stone. You may start with poses held for ten minutes then shorten them to five minutes as you progress.

The human form is generally seen as a whole, but it has a whole host of shapes, (depending on pose and viewpoint). It is very useful to see all these shapes contained in a geometrical form. Charcoal is best for speed and simplicity.

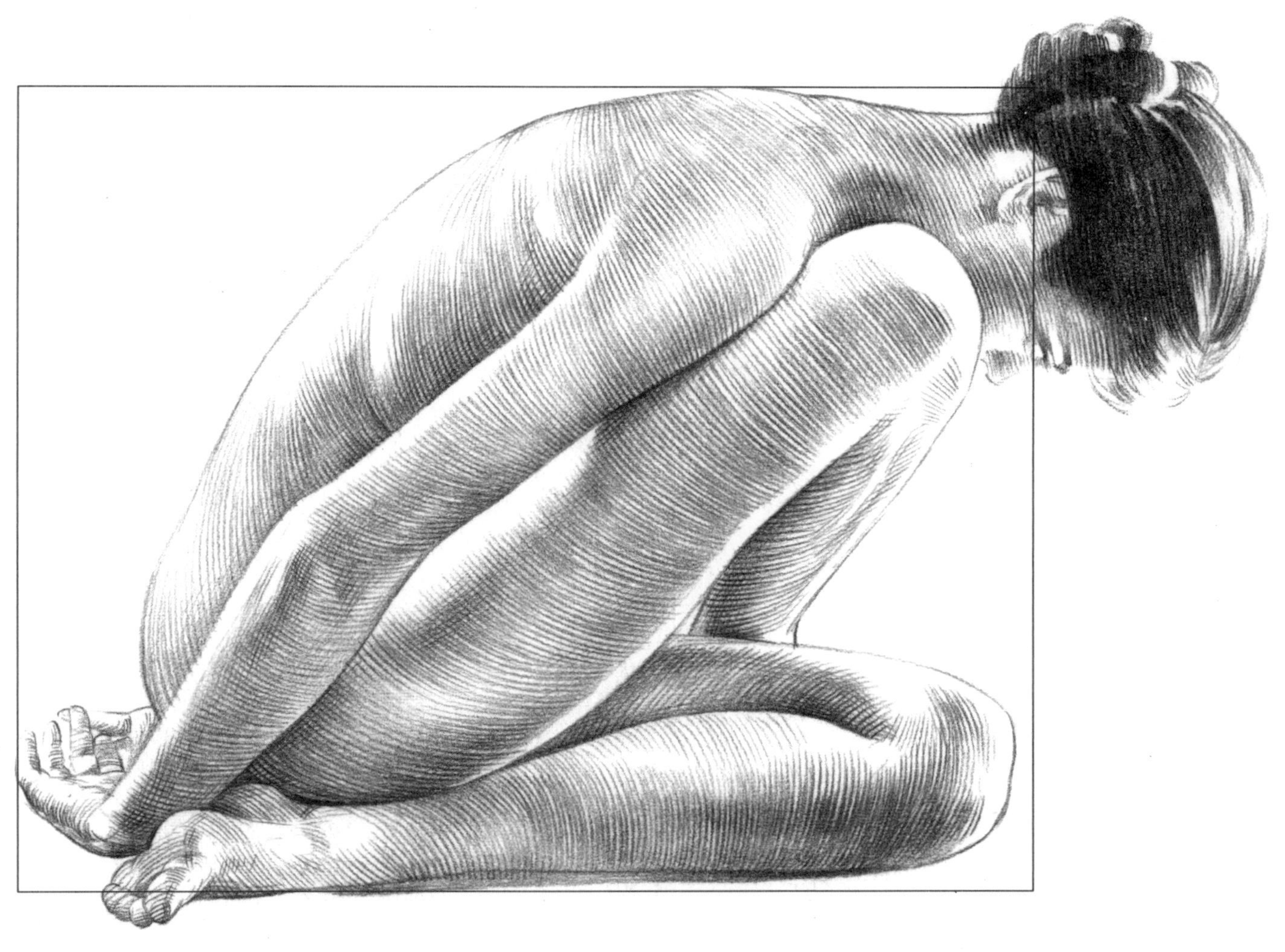

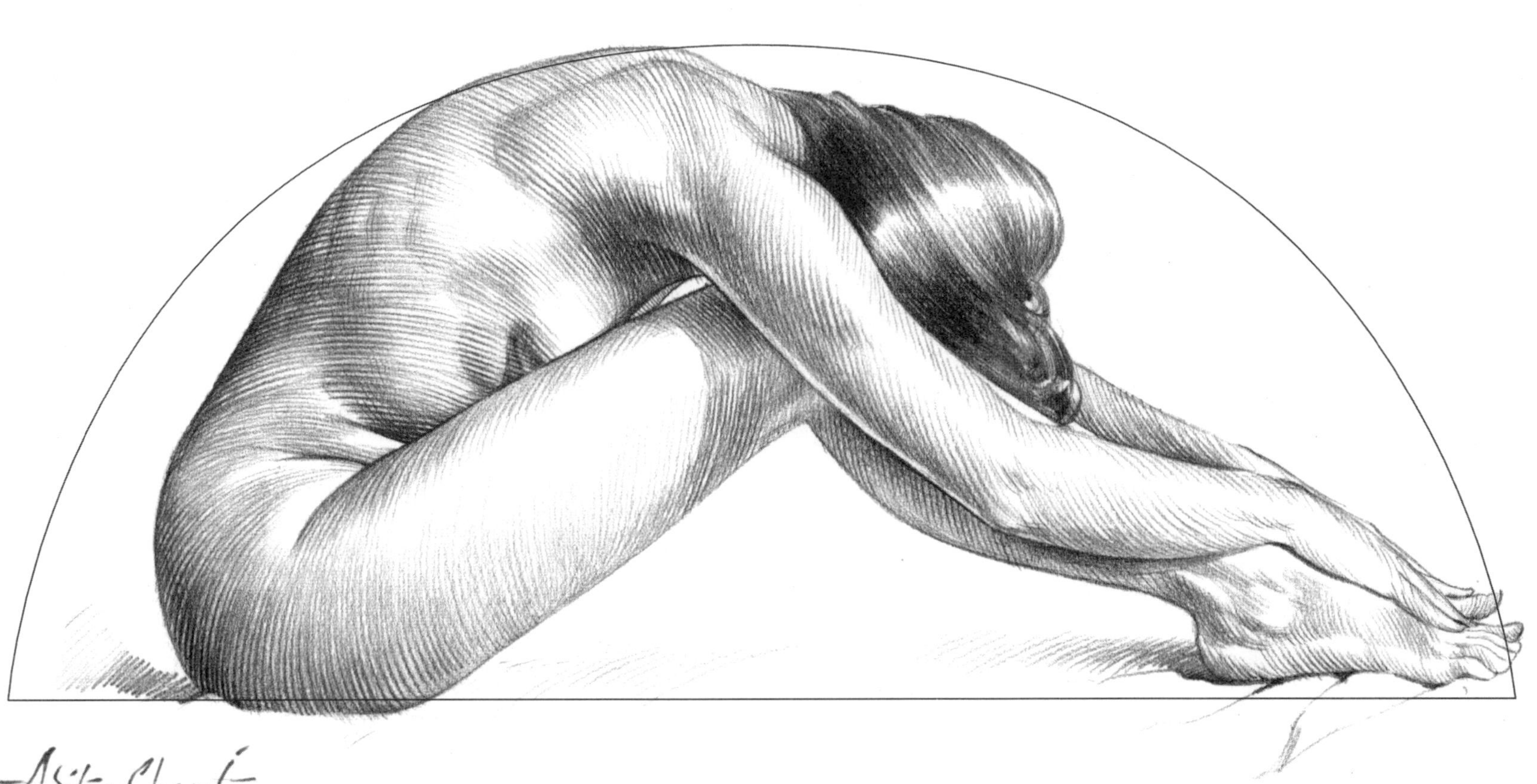
Aditya Chari

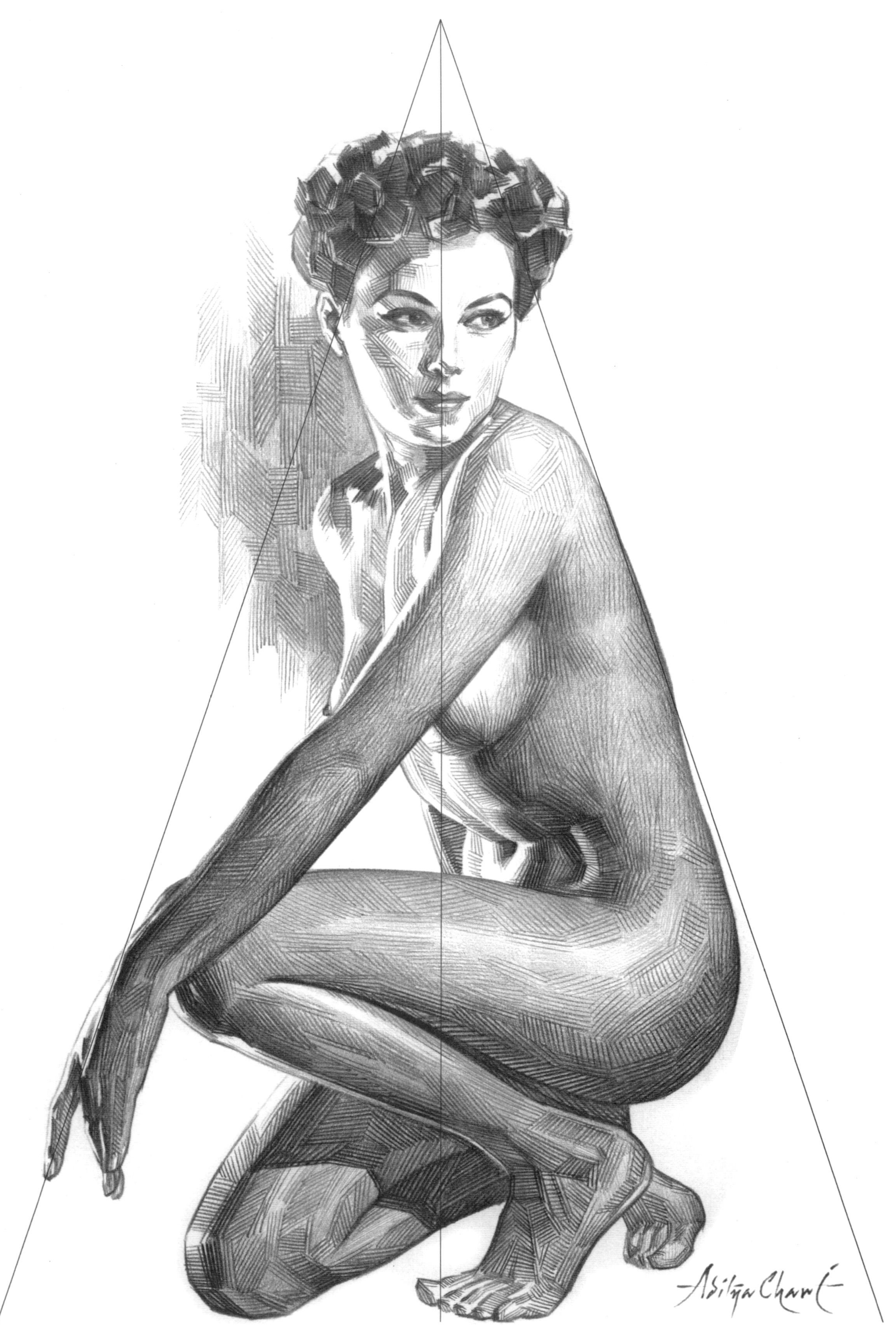

Look at the complete pose and try to figure out which geometrical form it would fit into best i.e. a square, a rectangle, a circle. Then you should draw out the geometric form first and then sketch the figure within it. Do not pay attention to the details - draw what you see, but as one lump or whole form. This may be just a simple outline or silhouette, but must consist of the whole figure. In this exercise it is better to sketch an almost abstract form, which denotes the general outline of the pose, rather than to complete only an arm, hand or head, no matter how skillfully it is drawn out. Do NOT try to complete the drawing, for in doing so you would only miss the point of the entire exercise.

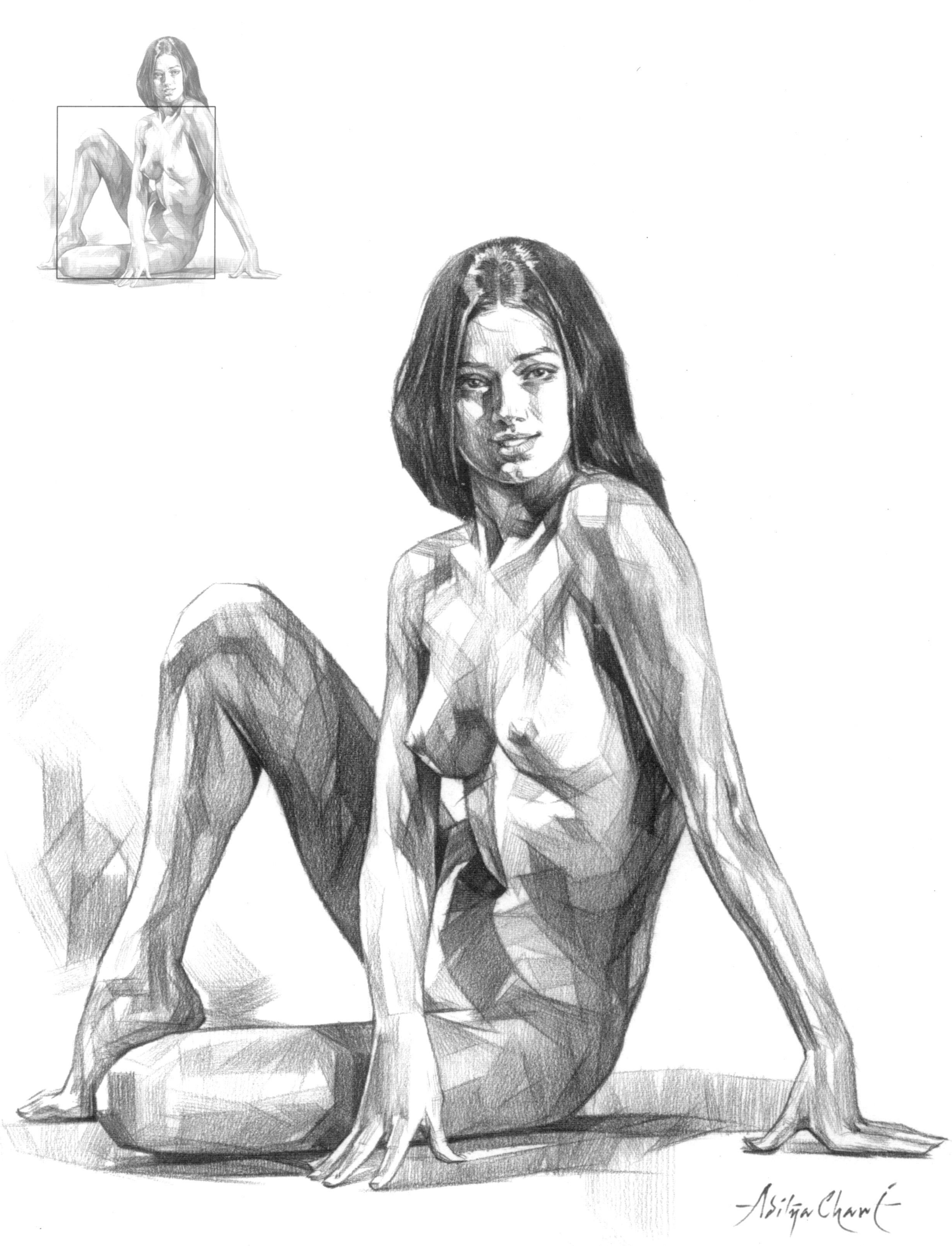

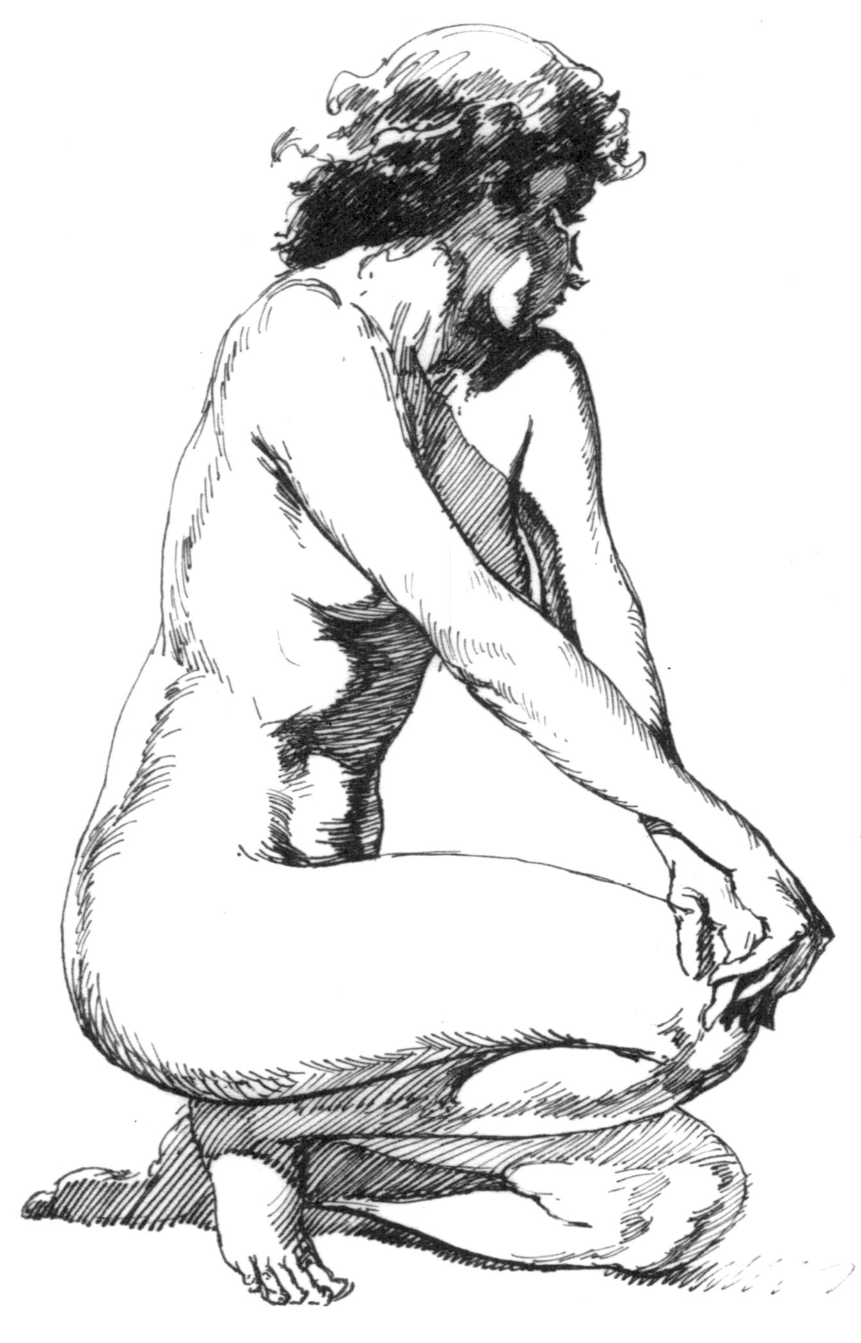

ACTION

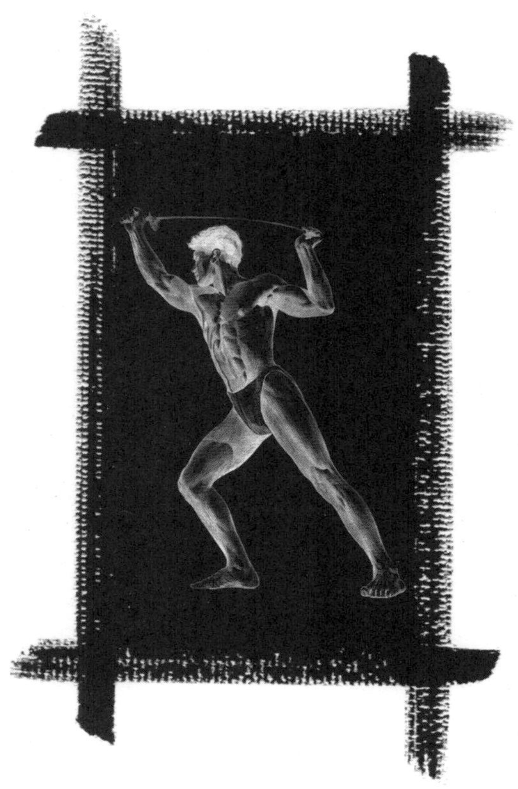

Every drawing of a figure in action has to begin with a Line of Action. This line, often known as the Center line, is in reality, a make-believe or imaginary curved line that travels down the center of the figure. It is this line that determines the flow and sweep of the movement or action. Every figure has a line of action. I strongly recommend drawing the line of action first and then build your figure around it. Sketch the figure loosely, in a gesture style (see Gesture Drawing, page no. 3) always keeping in mind the line of action. Once drawn, the simple Action Line can be used as a reference to draw out the more complex surface and outlines of the figure. It is not easy to note the extreme level of action with normal vision, so in this instance, photographical references or movies can be used. These have proven to be very useful for, you can pause the action, frame by frame, and notice minutely how the various body parts move in an arc formation. For best results, it is advisable to watch an action movie!

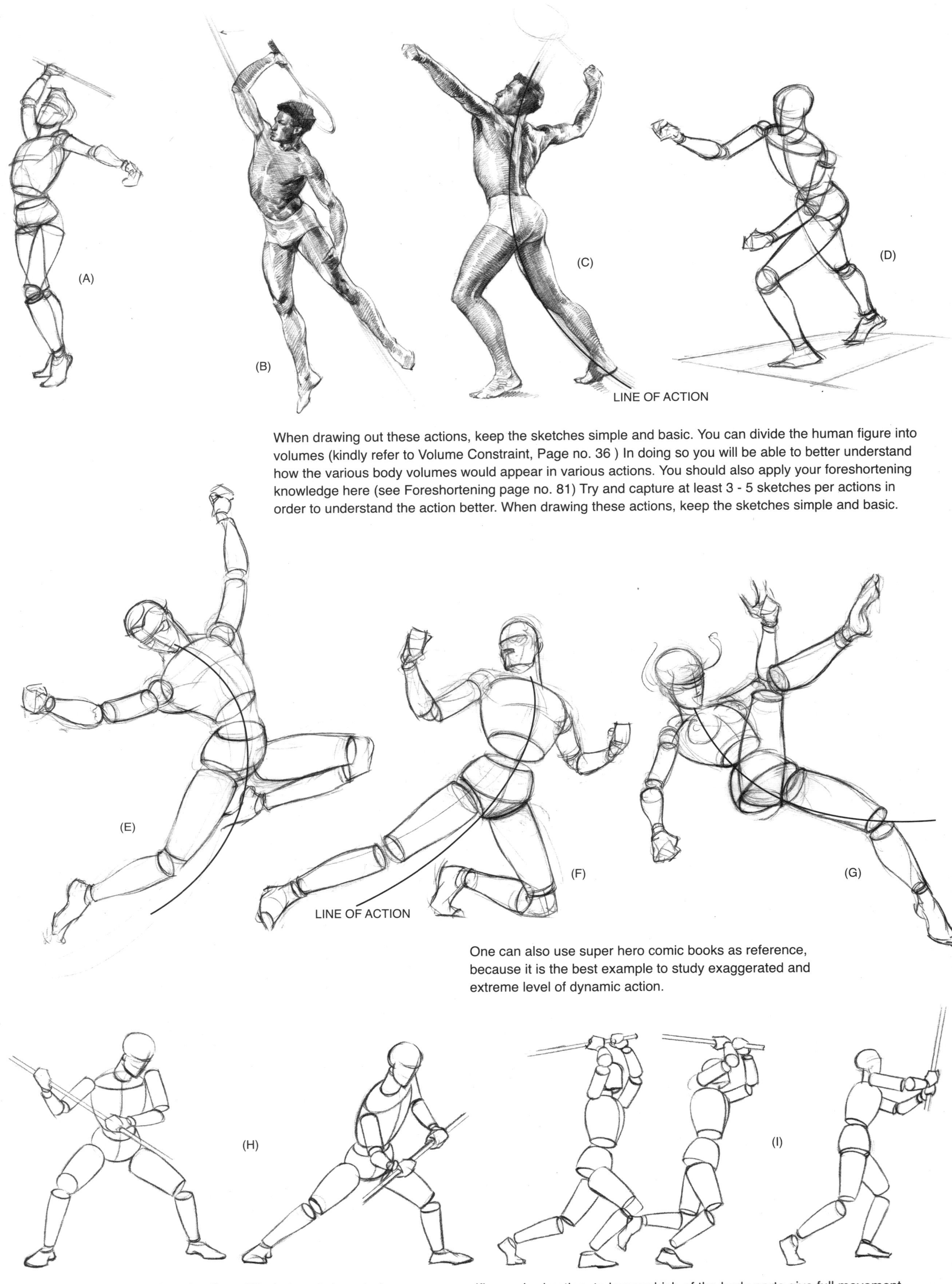

When drawing out these actions, keep the sketches simple and basic. You can divide the human figure into volumes (kindly refer to Volume Constraint, Page no. 36) In doing so you will be able to better understand how the various body volumes would appear in various actions. You should also apply your foreshortening knowledge here (see Foreshortening page no. 81) Try and capture at least 3 - 5 sketches per actions in order to understand the action better. When drawing these actions, keep the sketches simple and basic.

One can also use super hero comic books as reference, because it is the best example to study exaggerated and extreme level of dynamic action.

Taking the reference of movie clips will help to gain knowledge upon a specific required action, to know which of the body parts give full movement and which parts move less.

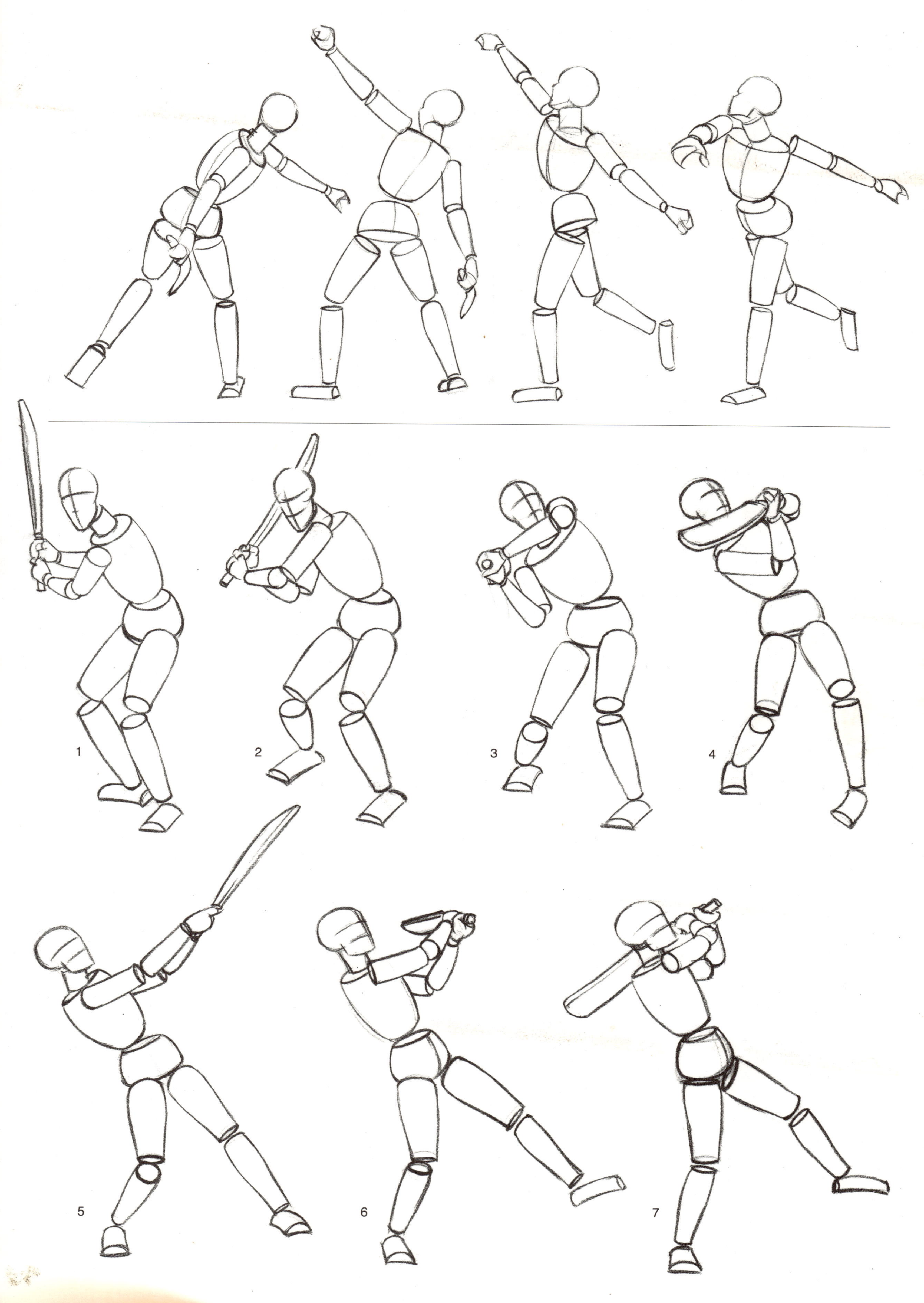
1
2
3
4
5
6
7

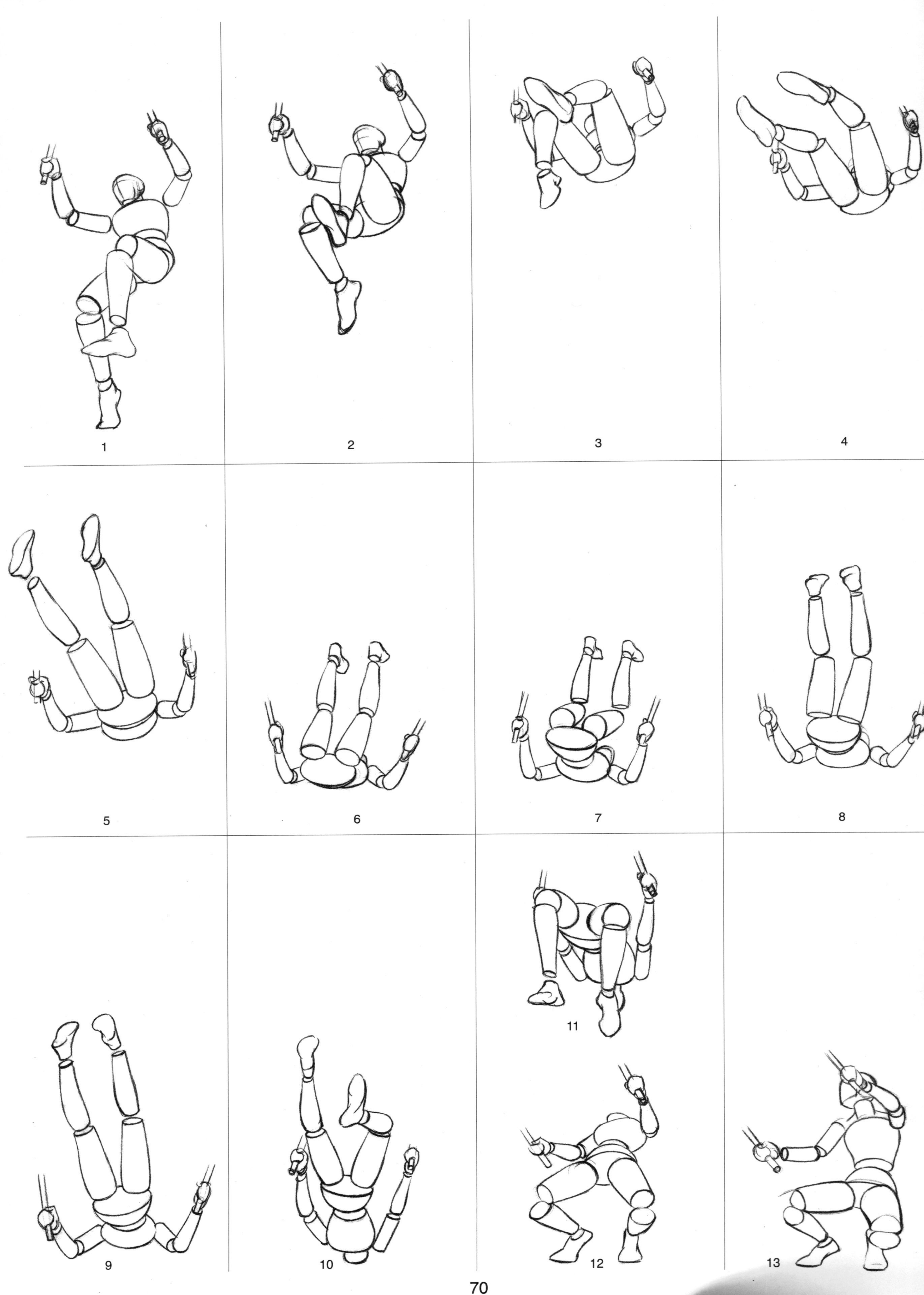
1
2
3
4
5
6
7
8
9
10
11
12
13

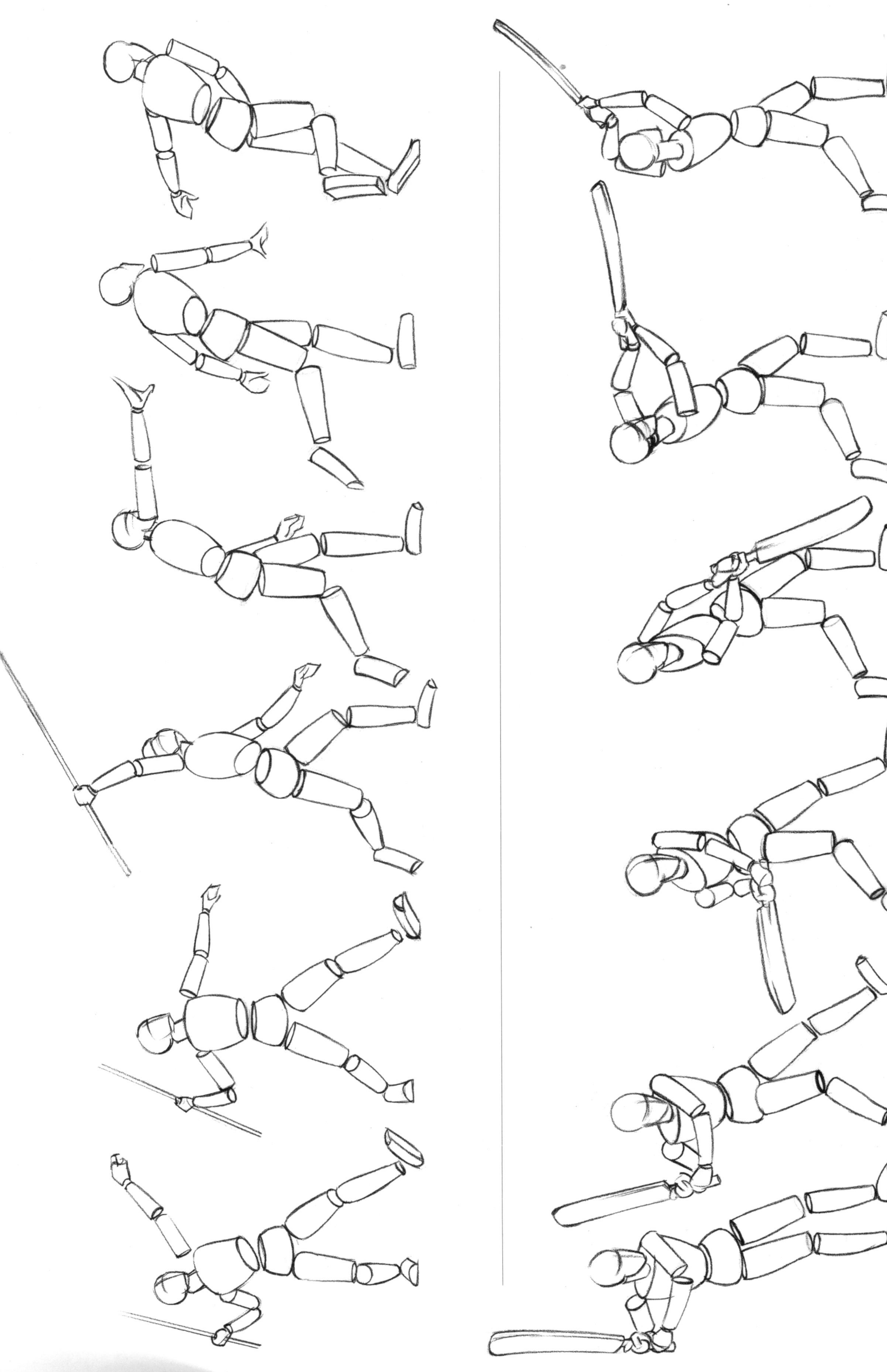

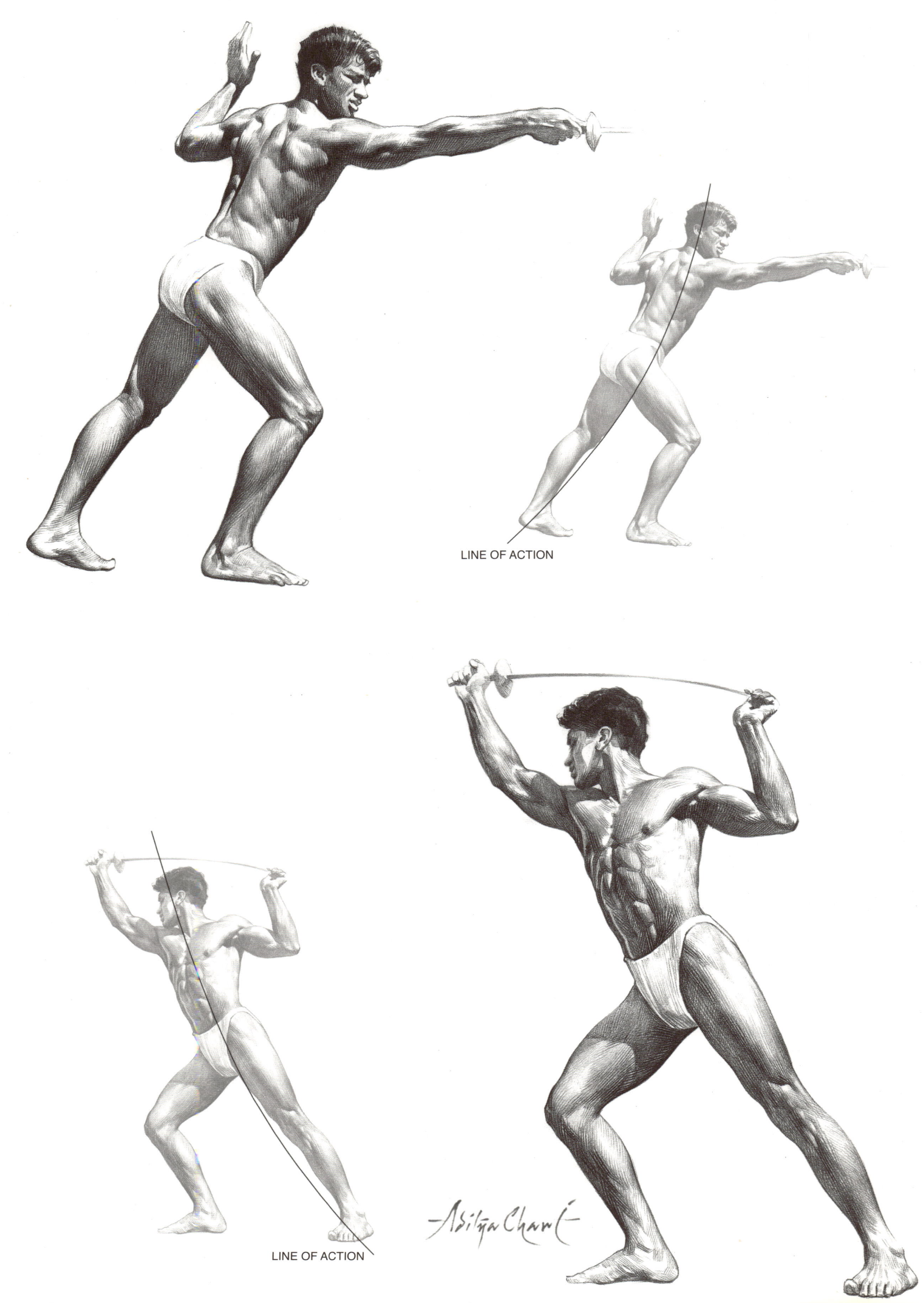
LINE OF ACTION
LINE OF ACTION

HANDS & FEET

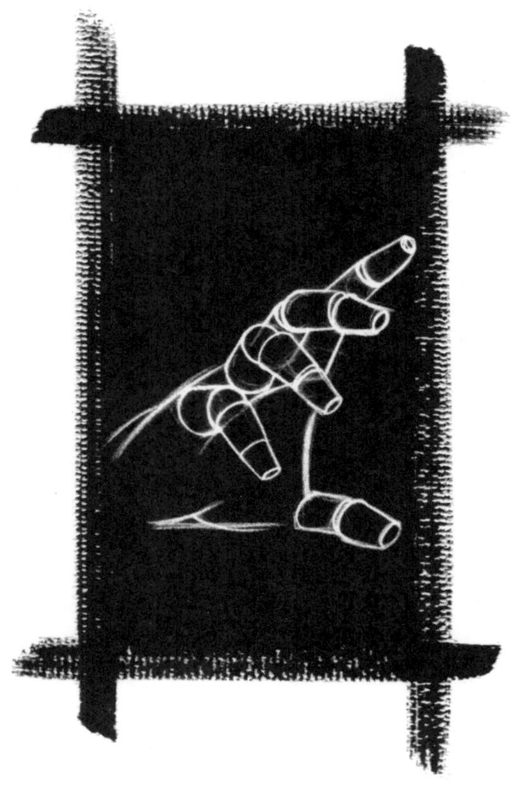

Drawing hands may look complicated, but it is much easier than it seems. The hands may be complex forms, but if their shape is simplified, then the task of drawing them becomes easier. To start this exercise, it is best that you begin to draw hands using simple geometric circles and ovals (Note however, that the shapes of the circles and ovals drawn will change according to the position of the hand). Observation is the key to any and every drawing, be it hands, arms, head etc. The best way to start off is by visualizing each part of the finger as a short cylinder, (depicted with an oval) each overlapping the next, while the overlapping portion is the joint. Once you have done this, you will have to concentrate on filling in the numerous variations of the shape.

For some reason, the hands and feet are the most neglected areas of figure drawing while maximum importance is given to the torso and head. One of the reasons for this is that it is possibly assumed that the hands and feet are difficult and complicated to draw, and therefore people do not attempt to study them.

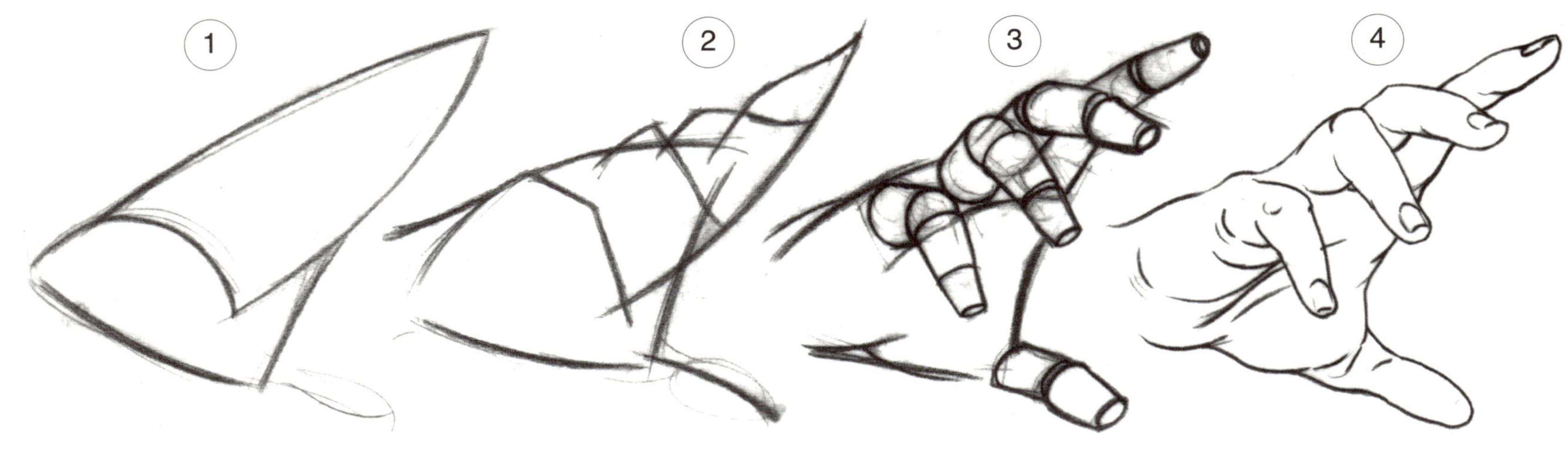

1. Rough in the overall form. Visualize the hand as encased in a tight mitten or glove. Now sketch the basic shape formed by the hand and fingers. Mark the imaginary lines through the joints.

2. Form the fingers. Observing carefully the shape of the space between them, draw and check the comparative size and placement of the fingers and thumb.

3. Before you draw the main out- line of the hand, it is better to sketch out the volumes of each finger, to understand their foreshortened angles.

4. Refine the drawing. Show the main visible creases. Refine the outlines defining the fingers, palm and thumb.

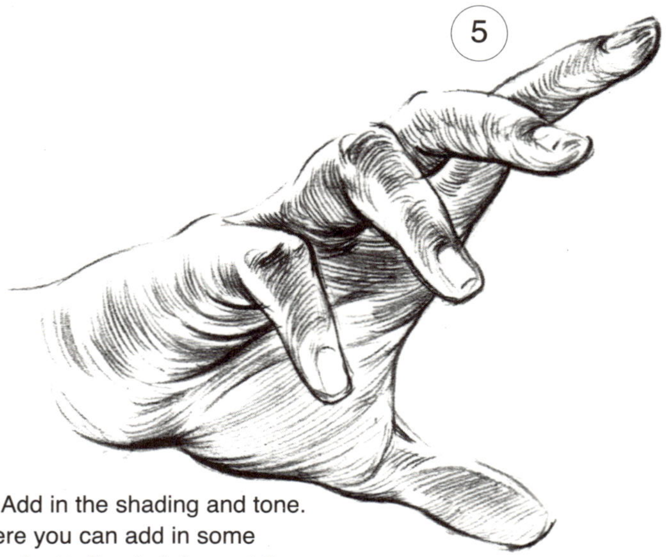

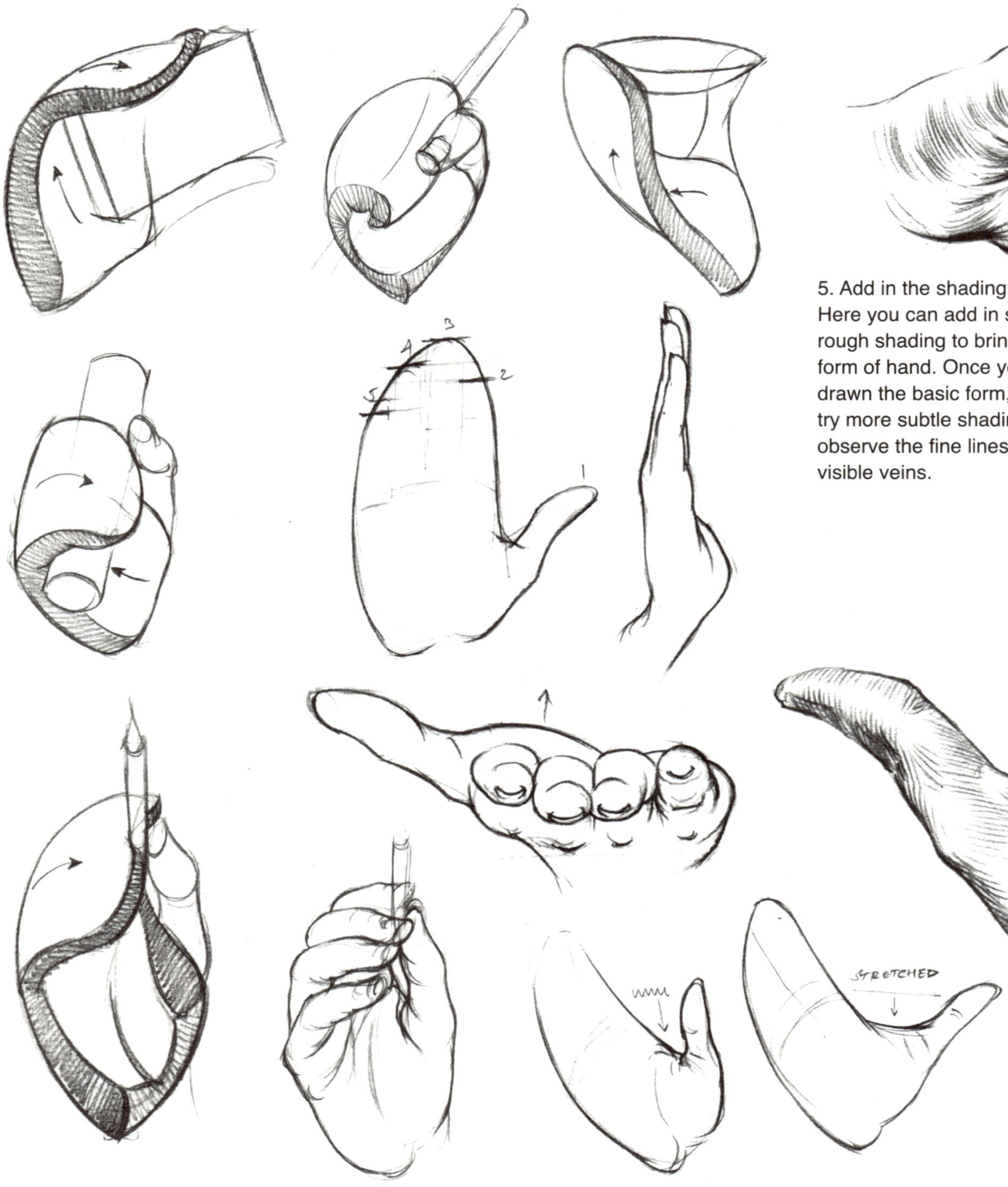

5. Add in the shading and tone. Here you can add in some rough shading to bring out the form of hand. Once you have drawn the basic form, you can try more subtle shading and observe the fine lines and visible veins.

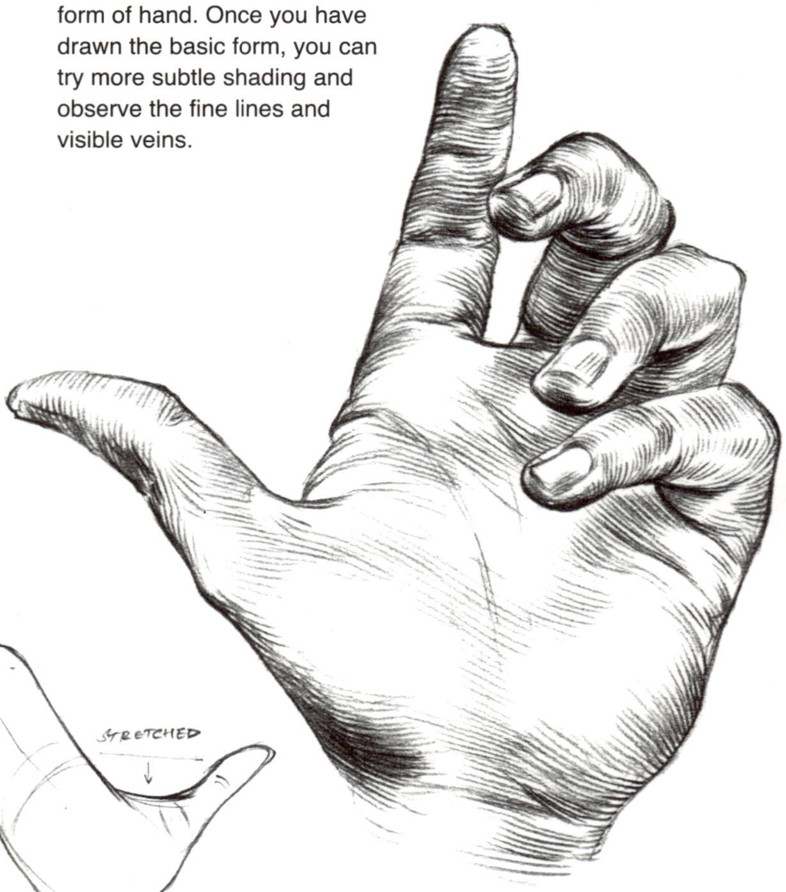

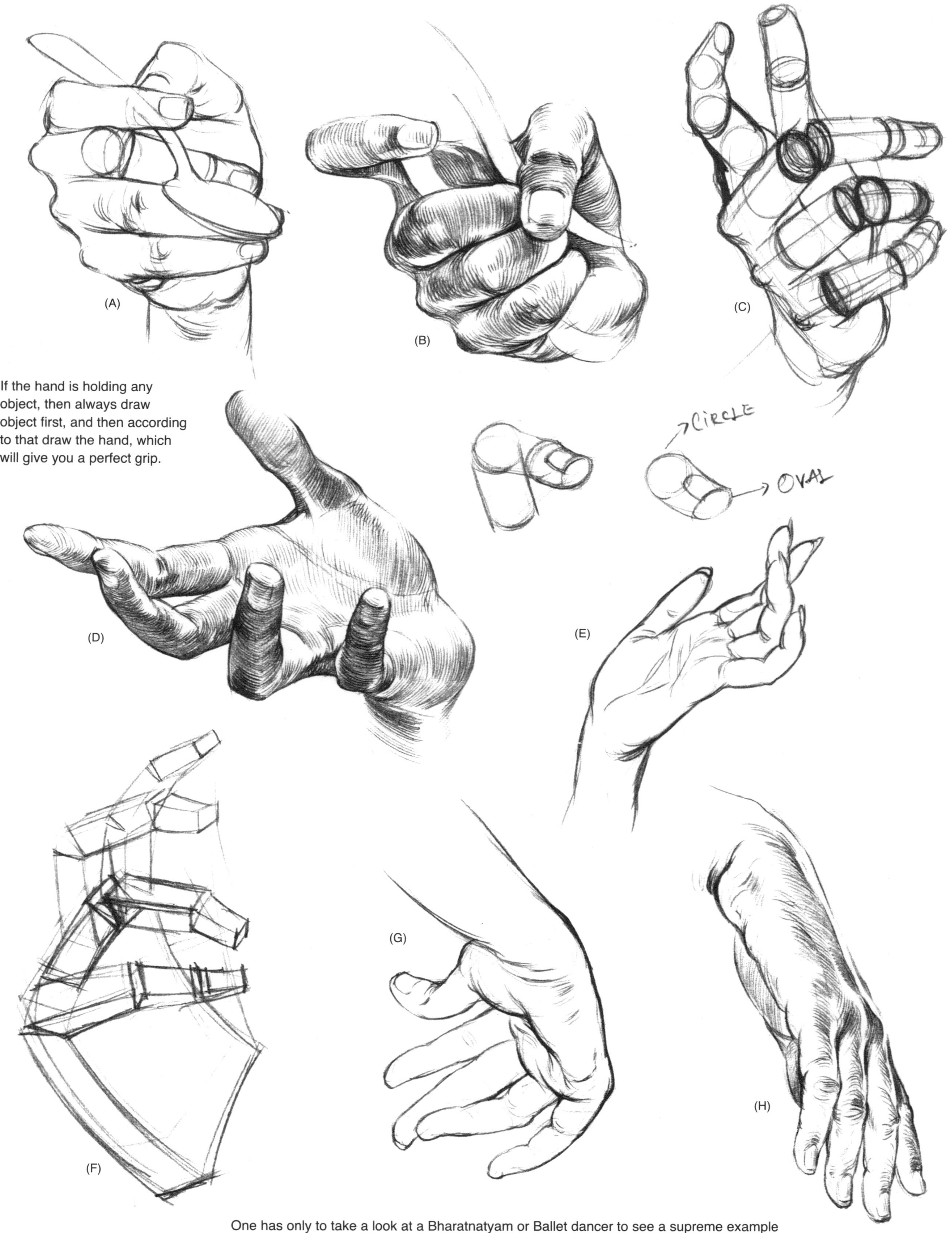

If the hand is holding any object, then always draw object first, and then according to that draw the hand, which will give you a perfect grip.

One has only to take a look at a Bharatnatyam or Ballet dancer to see a supreme example of beauty and expressiveness of the hands and feet.
When you put your hand on your face, palm facing downward, you will find that most of your face is covered! This only goes to show that the hands and feet, like the rest of the body deserve attention when sketching.

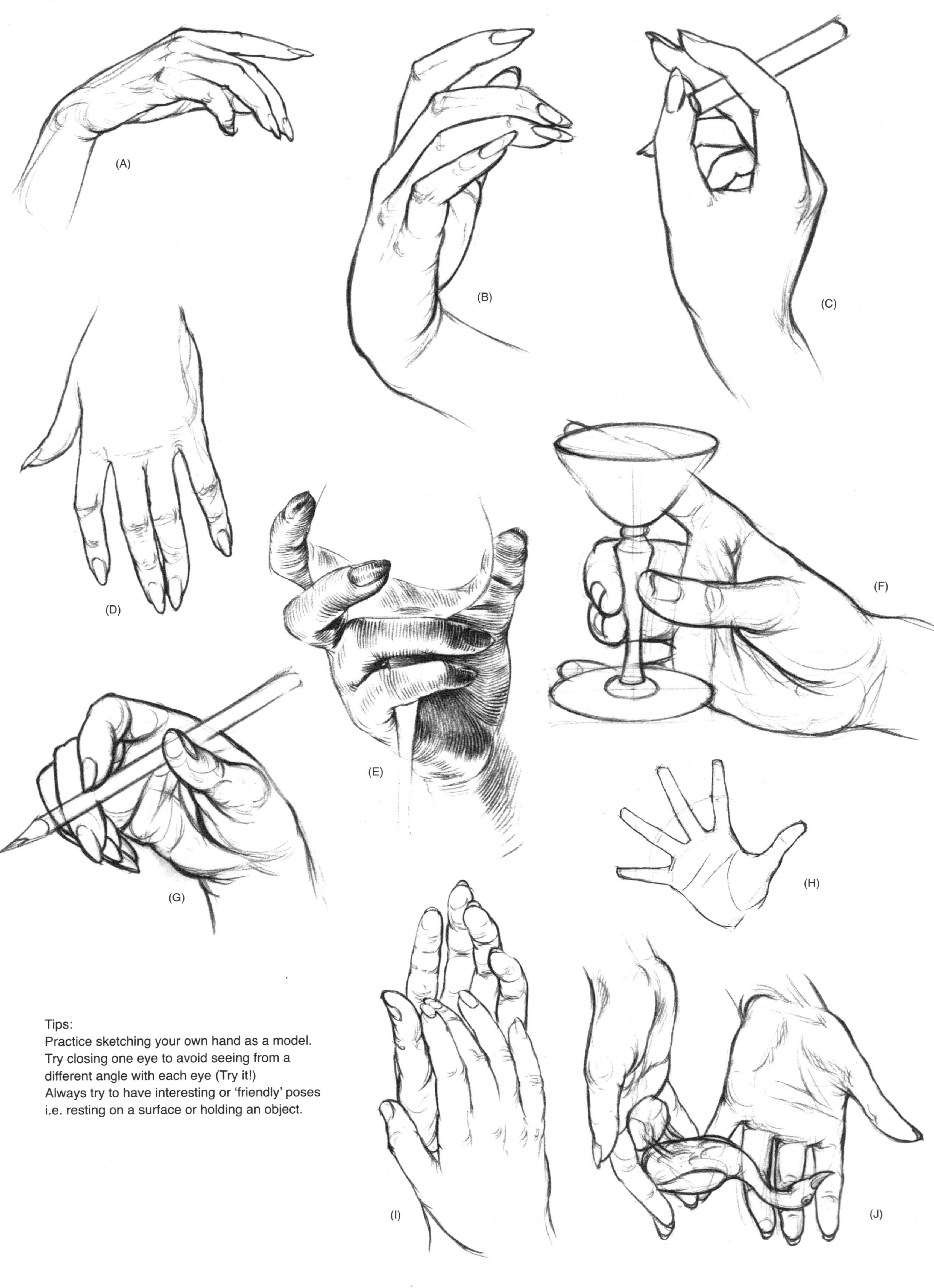

Tips:
Practice sketching your own hand as a model.
Try closing one eye to avoid seeing from a different angle with each eye (Try it!)
Always try to have interesting or 'friendly' poses i.e. resting on a surface or holding an object.

FEET

Feet and hands are very similar in terms of bone structure. However, overlying skin mostly hides the feet. It is only at the toes where the actual similarity of the hands and feet appear. Keep in mind when drawing, that toes are quite active and that they help with the balance of the body. One of the most beautiful aspects of the pointed foot is that it gives a long, graceful sweep from the top of the knee right down to the tip of the big toe. It is the feet and hands that are essential to the rhythm and fluidity of the human figure. Much of the grace and spirit of movement will be lost if they are not studied.

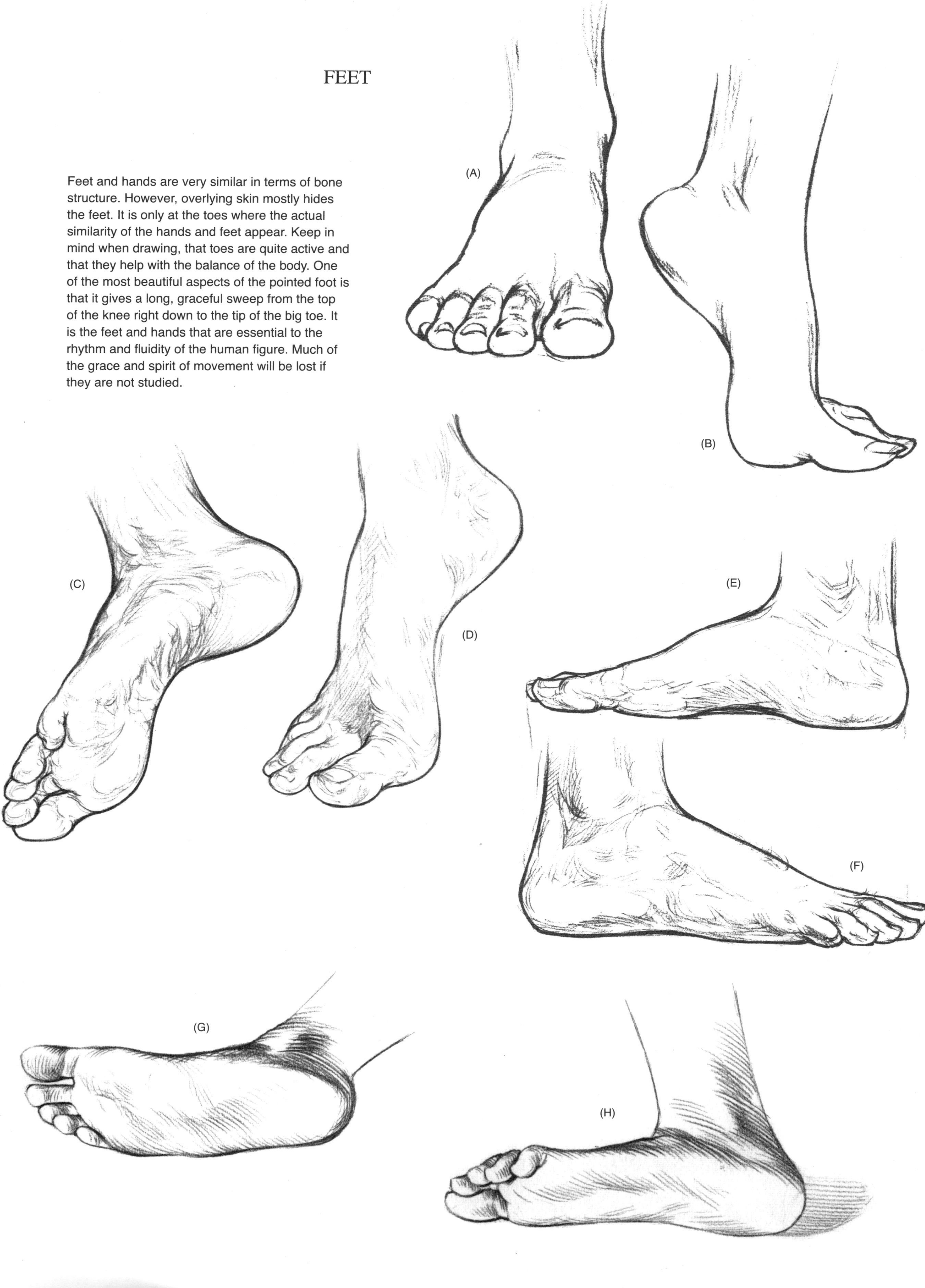

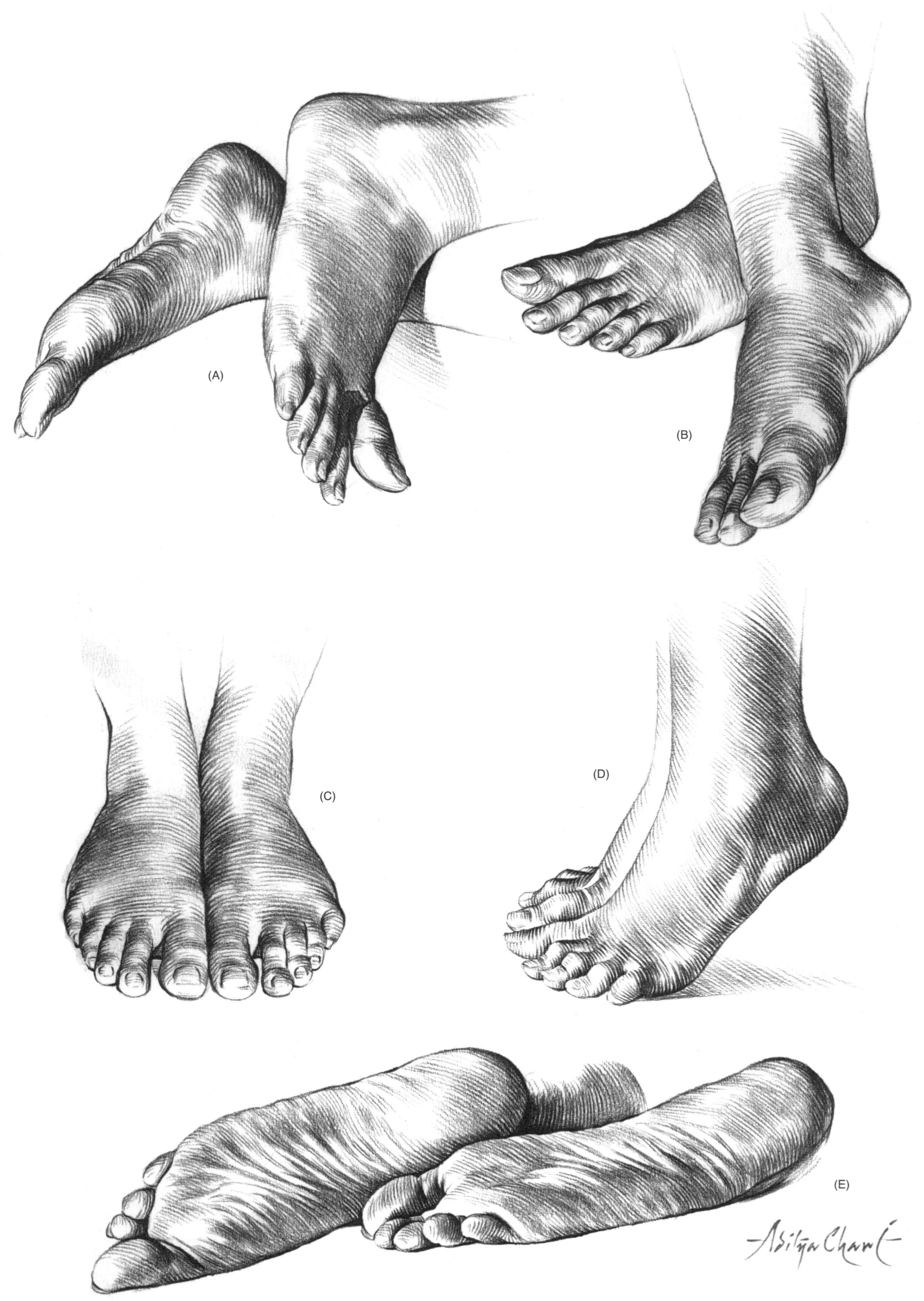
(A)
(B)
(C)
(D)
(E)

FORESHORTENING

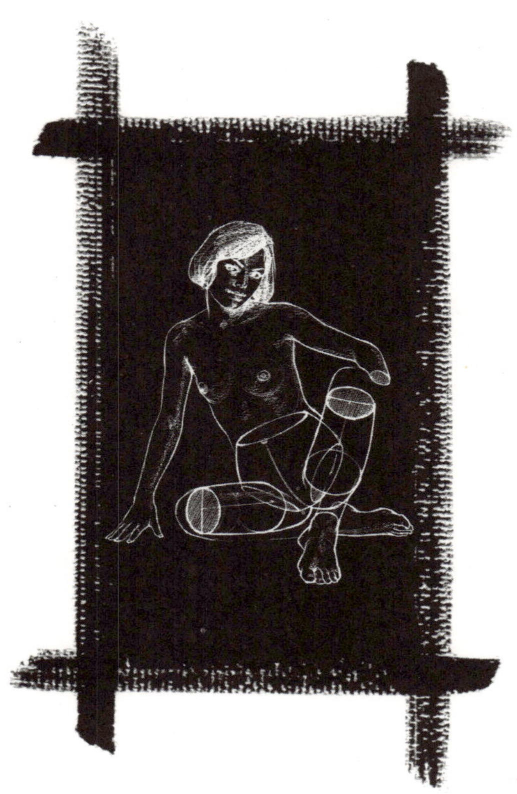

Look at a mug from above: you see a circle. Now slowly tilt the mug and observe that as you turn it sideways, it forms a narrower ellipse. In the same way, if you look straight down at a book, you see a rectangle; but tilt it away from or towards you, you see a trapezoid. Now try sketching some simple objects from various angles to show their change in shape. Drawing the changes in the shape of objects from different angles is called foreshortening, or the creation of an illusion of depth. In order for your drawing to convincingly trick the human eye, it must be executed smartly and with confidence.

Perspective has been closely linked with Foreshortening. However, the latter is used usually when drawing figures (human or animal form), where visual perception supersedes depth or constructed perspective. Foreshortening is not very easy to achieve realistically, especially when drawing a more complex shape – if not done accurately, the end result may look like a distorted object. For best results, practice is the only answer. Do not lose heart because it is not easy. In foreshortening, an object appears compressed especially when observed from a particular position, and the effect of perspective causes distortion.

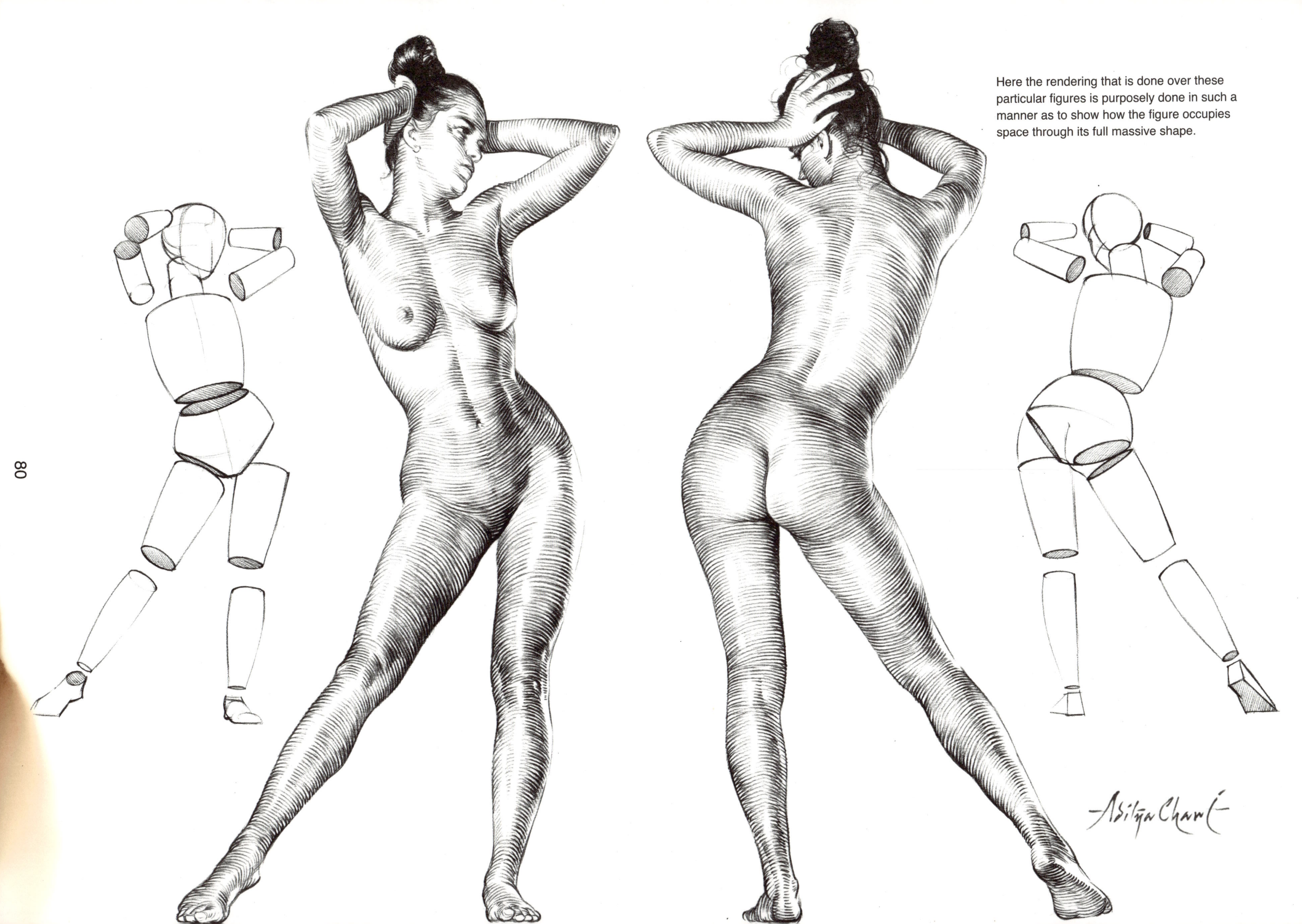

Here the rendering that is done over these particular figures is purposely done in such a manner as to show how the figure occupies space through its full massive shape.

In Foreshortening, whenever an object is viewed in perspective, there is a visible distortion in length and width. For example, an object slanting away from or toward the viewer seems to reduce in size and shape. To realistically portray figures, practice and wholehearted & concentrated observation are fundamental requirements in determining the amount of foreshortening. In Foreshortening, whenever an object is viewed in perspective, there is a visible distortion in length and width.

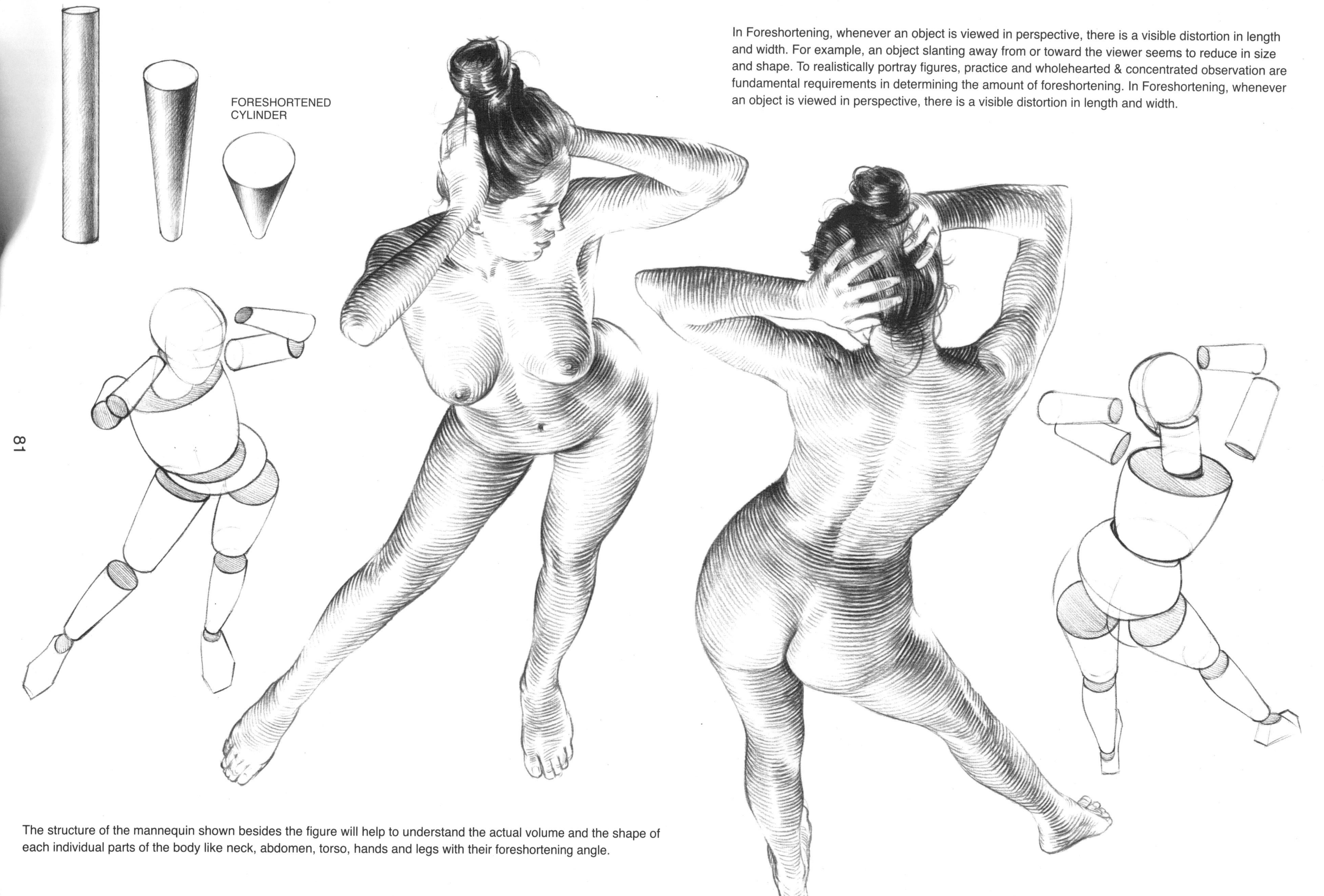

The structure of the mannequin shown besides the figure will help to understand the actual volume and the shape of each individual parts of the body like neck, abdomen, torso, hands and legs with their foreshortening angle.

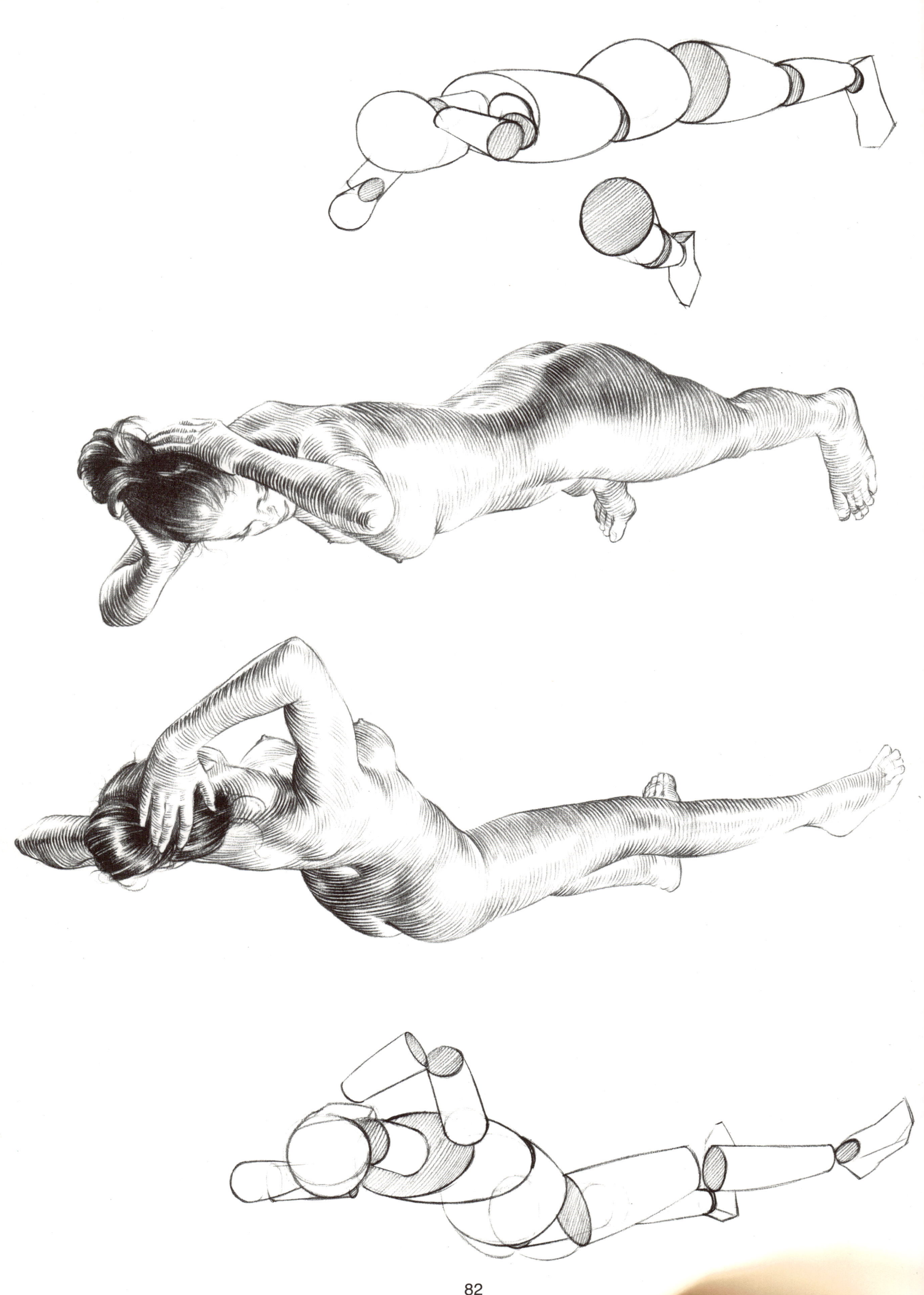

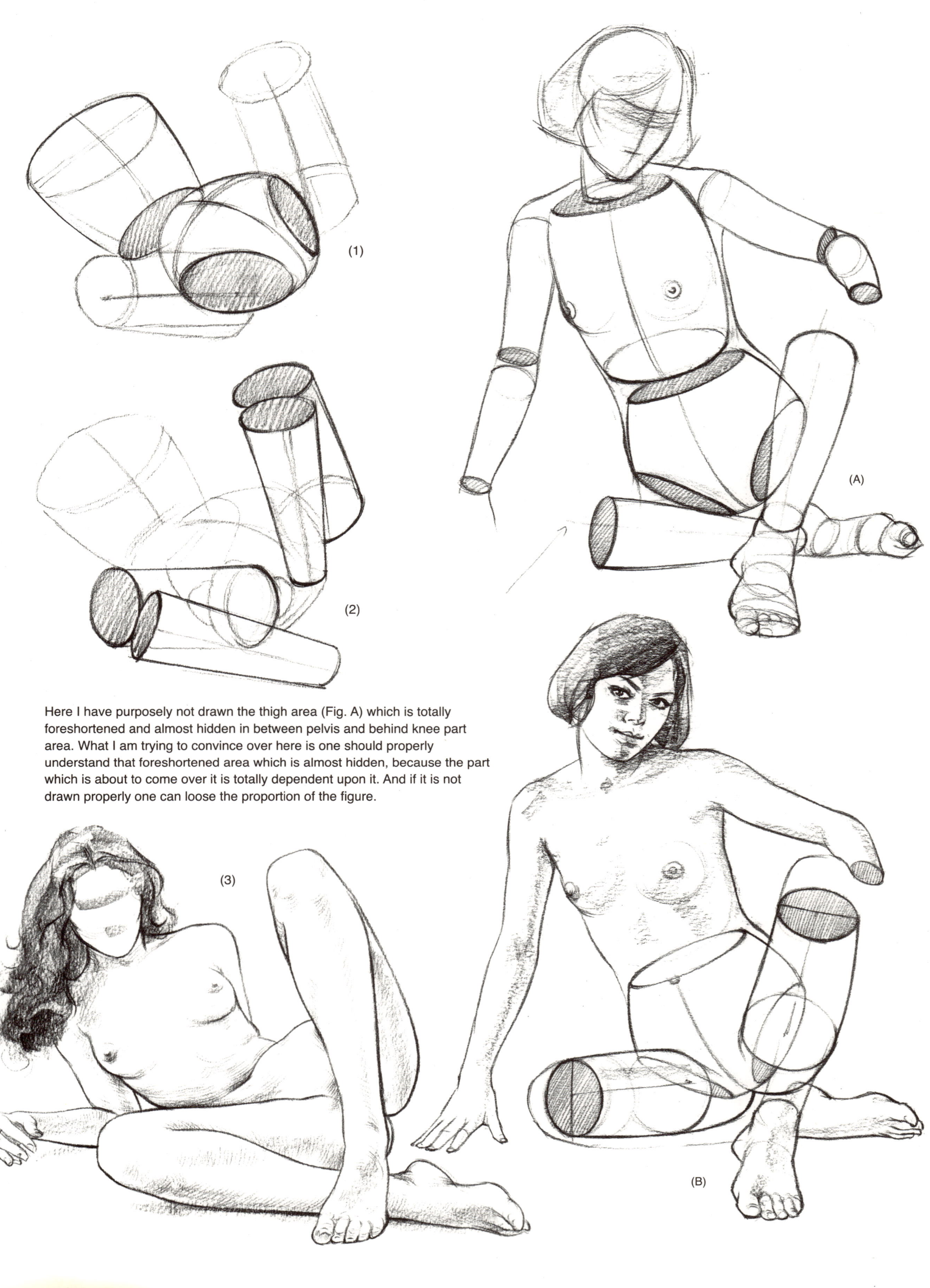

Here I have purposely not drawn the thigh area (Fig. A) which is totally foreshortened and almost hidden in between pelvis and behind knee part area. What I am trying to convince over here is one should properly understand that foreshortened area which is almost hidden, because the part which is about to come over it is totally dependent upon it. And if it is not drawn properly one can loose the proportion of the figure.

The principles of perspective seem to change shape and get smaller in size as they retreat toward the background in Foreshortening. This is used to alter body parts that go toward or away from the viewer in a proportionate manner. This gives a figure a three-dimensional look by creating depth.

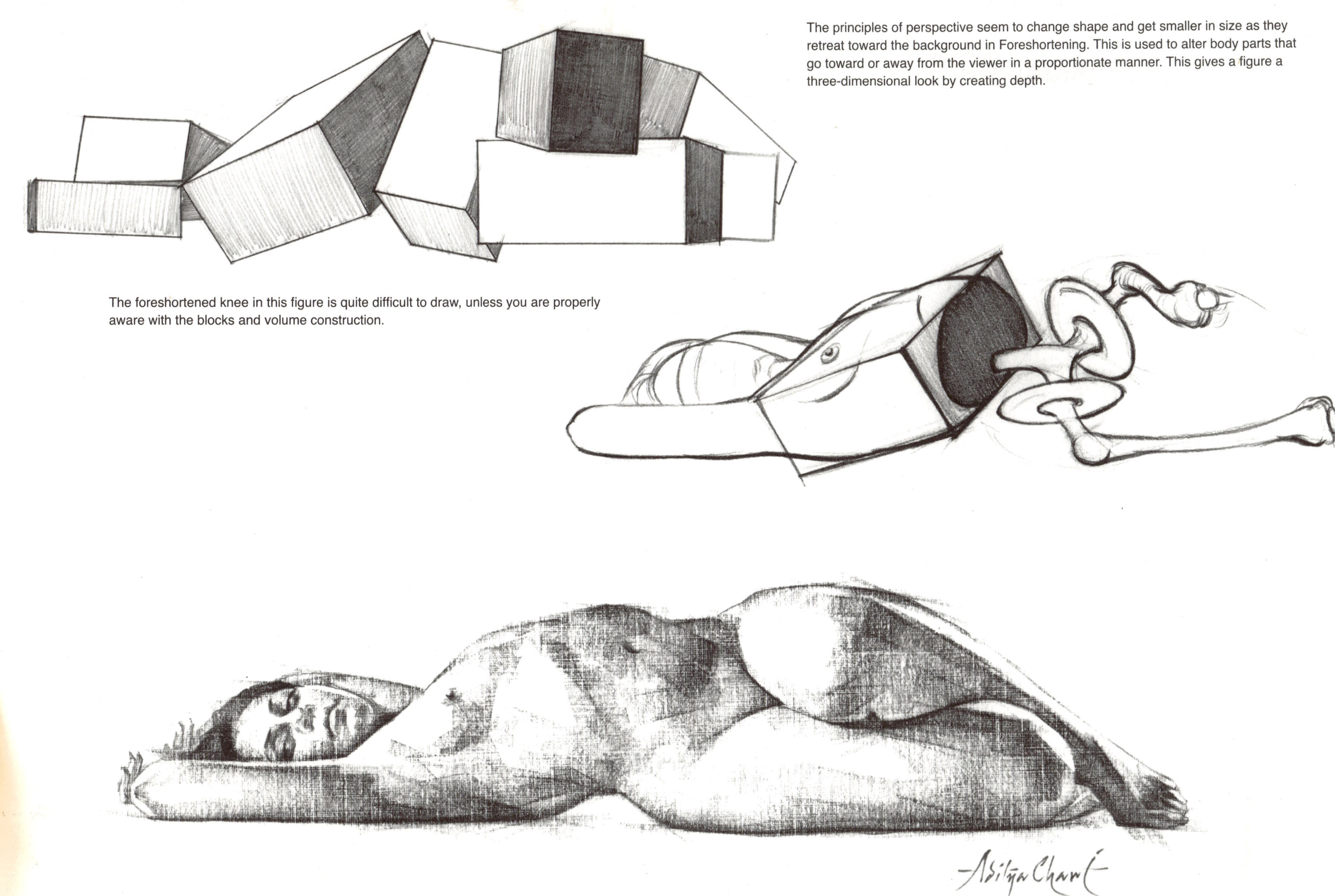

The foreshortened knee in this figure is quite difficult to draw, unless you are properly aware with the blocks and volume construction.

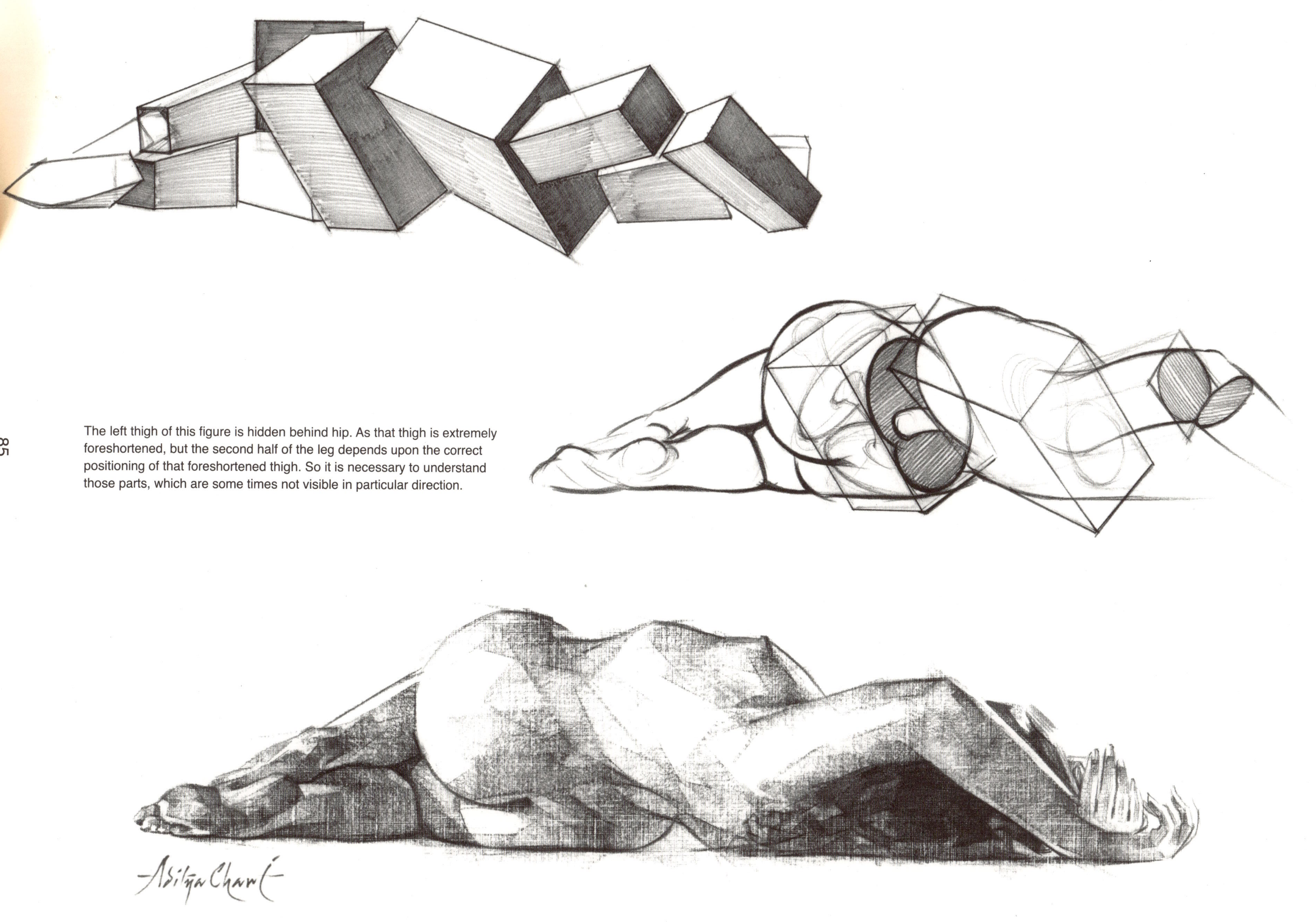

The left thigh of this figure is hidden behind hip. As that thigh is extremely foreshortened, but the second half of the leg depends upon the correct positioning of that foreshortened thigh. So it is necessary to understand those parts, which are some times not visible in particular direction.

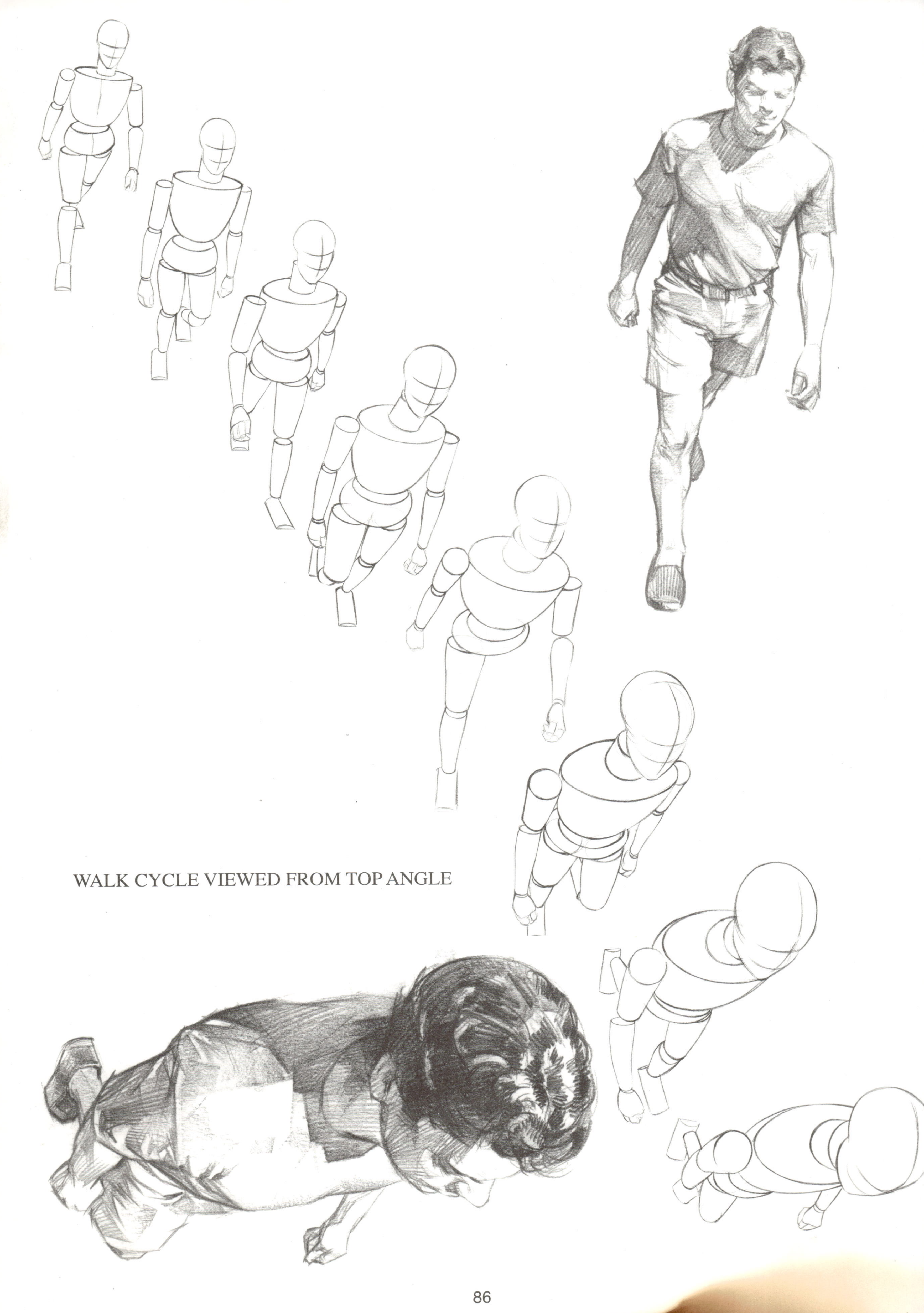
WALK CYCLE VIEWED FROM TOP ANGLE

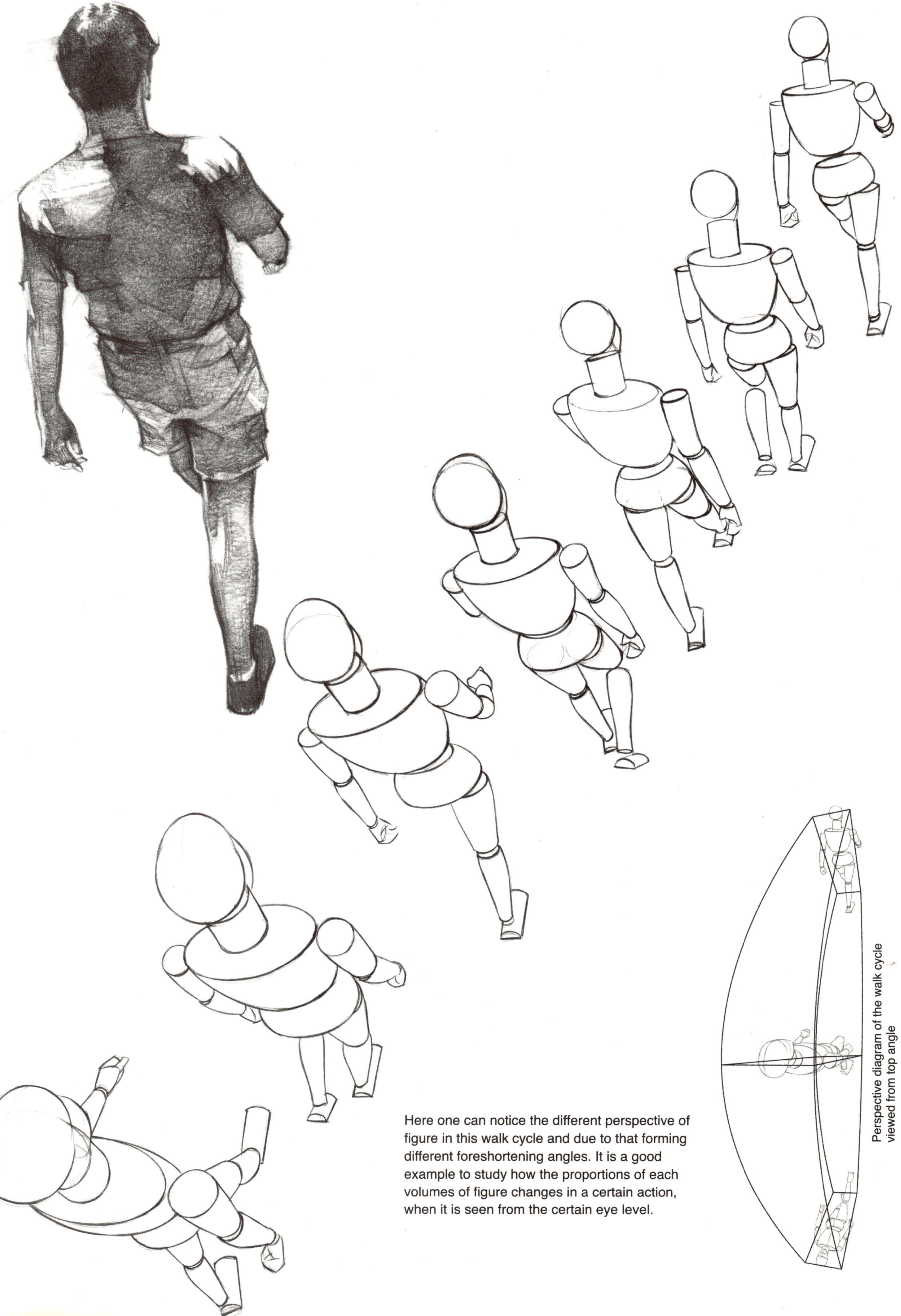

Perspective diagram of the walk cycle viewed from top angle

Here one can notice the different perspective of figure in this walk cycle and due to that forming different foreshortening angles. It is a good example to study how the proportions of each volumes of figure changes in a certain action, when it is seen from the certain eye level.

FORESHORTENED KNEE

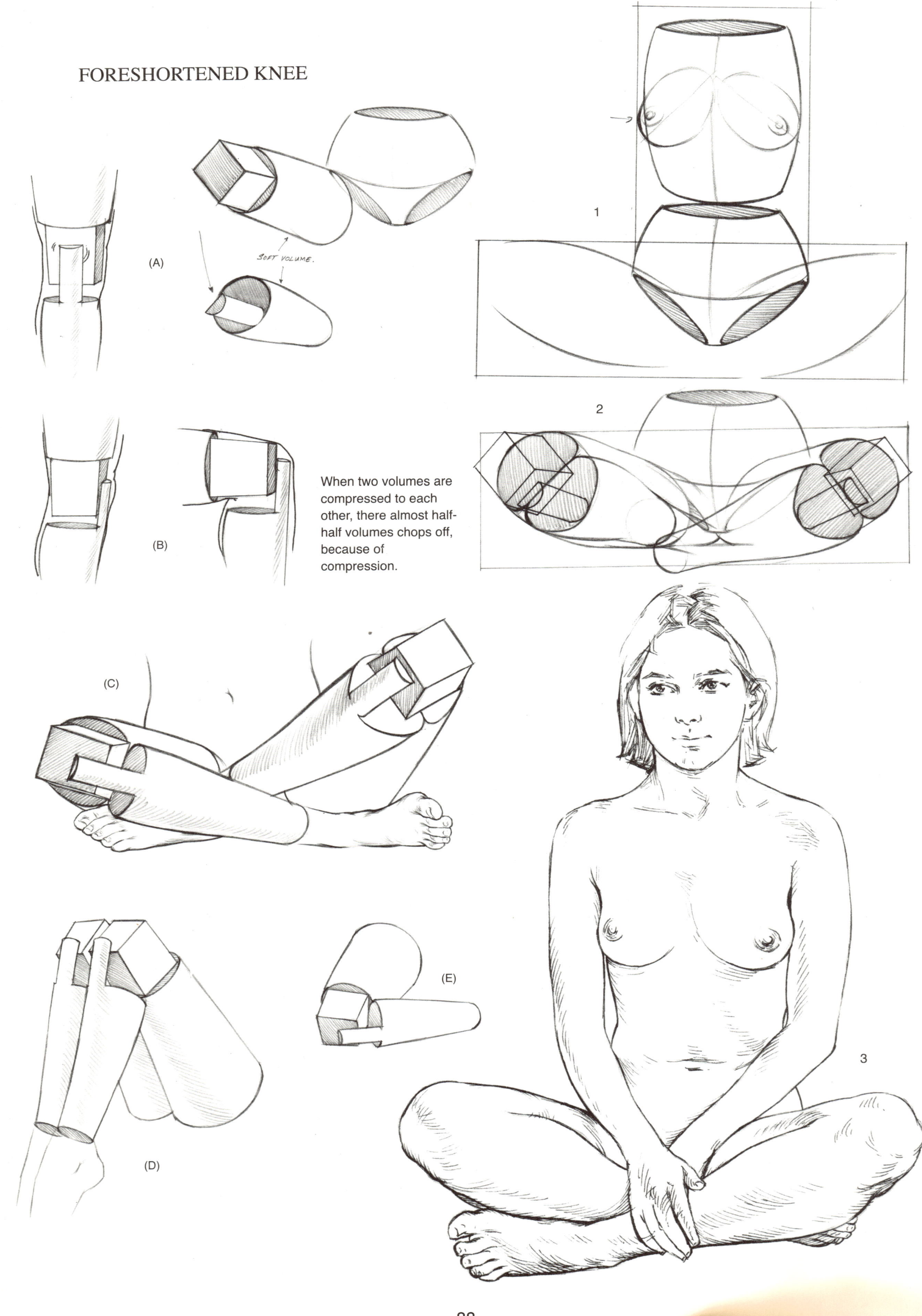

DRAPERY

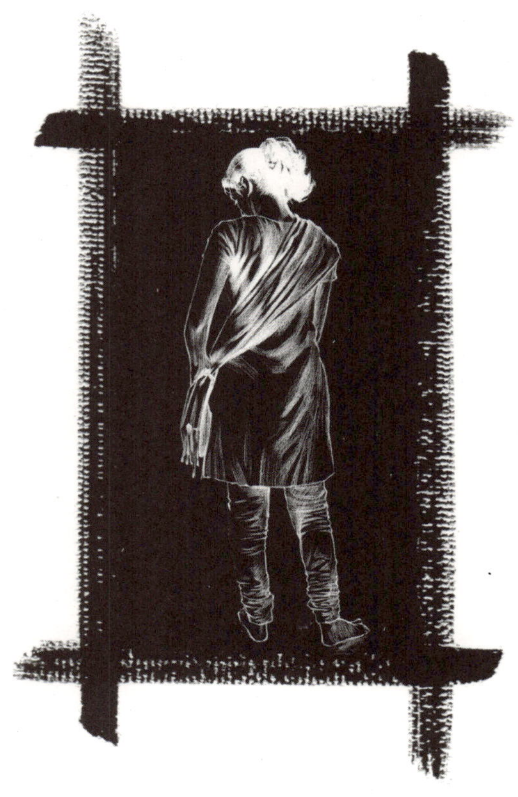

It is always better to understand the human figure more profoundly before attempting to draw clothes on it. Clothes can be thought of as an extra skin or an outer layer. They are never skin-tight, but made to loosely or closely fit the human body. The movement of the clothes or 'outer layer' is directly related to the actions of the body itself. By knowing about the way human skin reacts to movement will only aid in your knowledge of how the clothes will behave to similar movements and stresses.

Twisting of folds always makes various shapes, namely: spirals, acute angles or ovals. Always remember that each fabric or material is different and has its own characteristic, the most important of them being weight and texture. It is the weight and texture of the fabric that is responsible for the movement and speed of the folds of the fabric. You will observe various types of folds. To mention a few; some folds will be straight or V- shaped; folds will fall, cross, or pass each other. Also bear in mind that each drapery has its own set of laws and each must be studied separately and intensely. The drapery greatly depends upon the type of fabric or materials used.

Each fabric will have a different reaction to body movement. For example, cotton will react differently as compared to wool. So too, each fabric will have its own characteristic and this can be denoted in the folds of the fabric. To state an example of this, heavy drapery will have an oval fold while silk fabric will take on an angular or ovular fold. The nature of folds will depend on the fabric used.

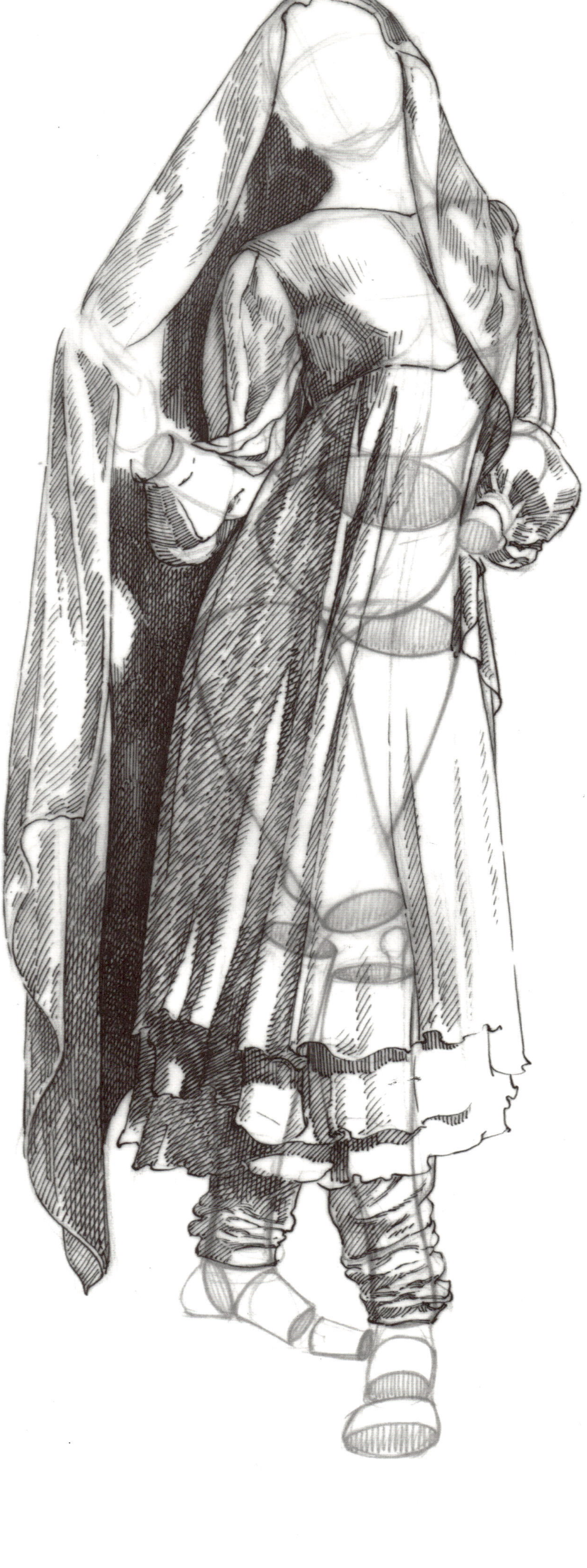

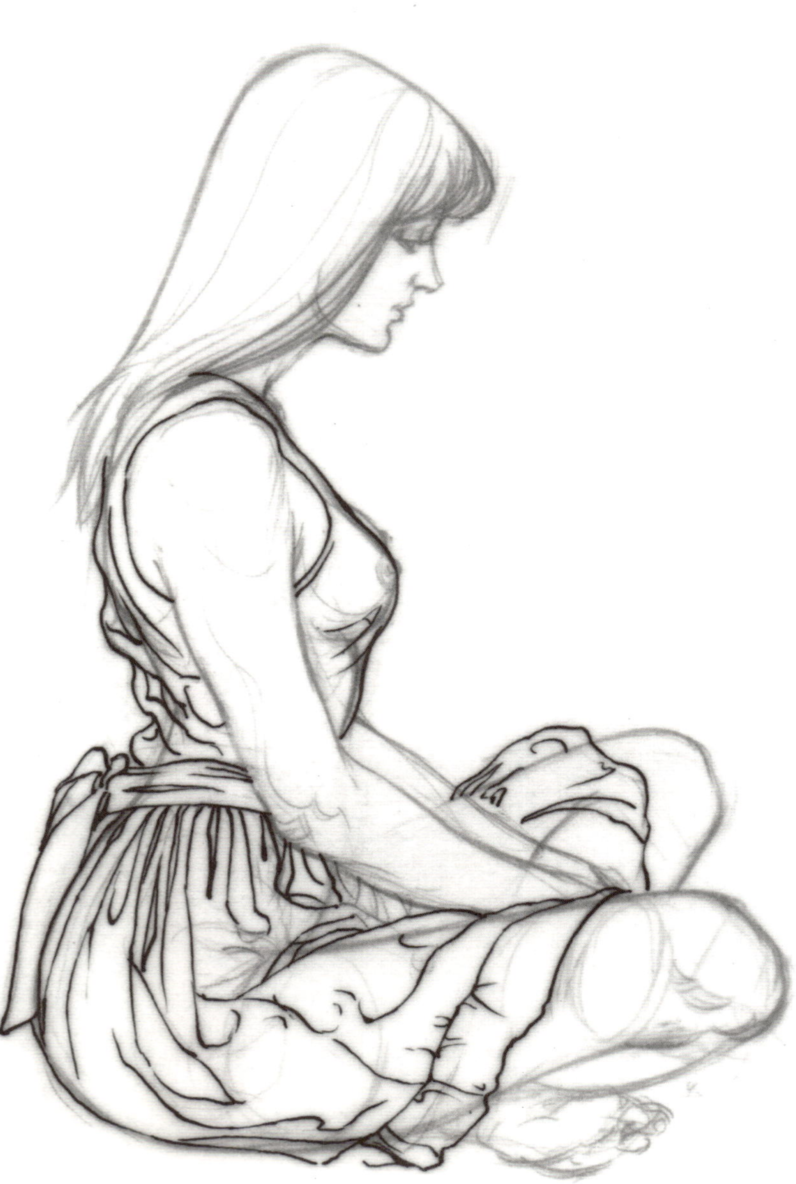

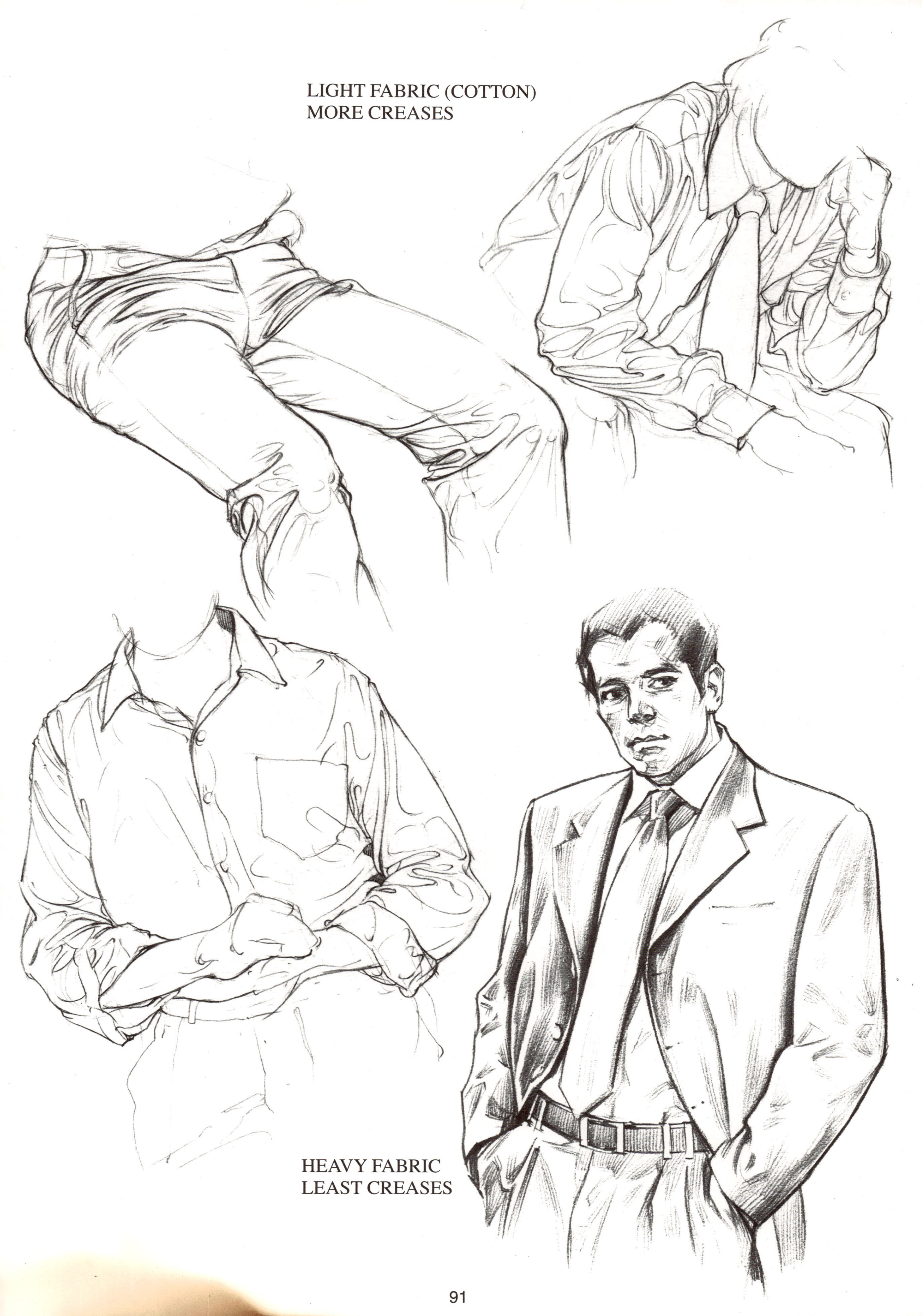
LIGHT FABRIC (COTTON)
MORE CREASES
HEAVY FABRIC
LEAST CREASES

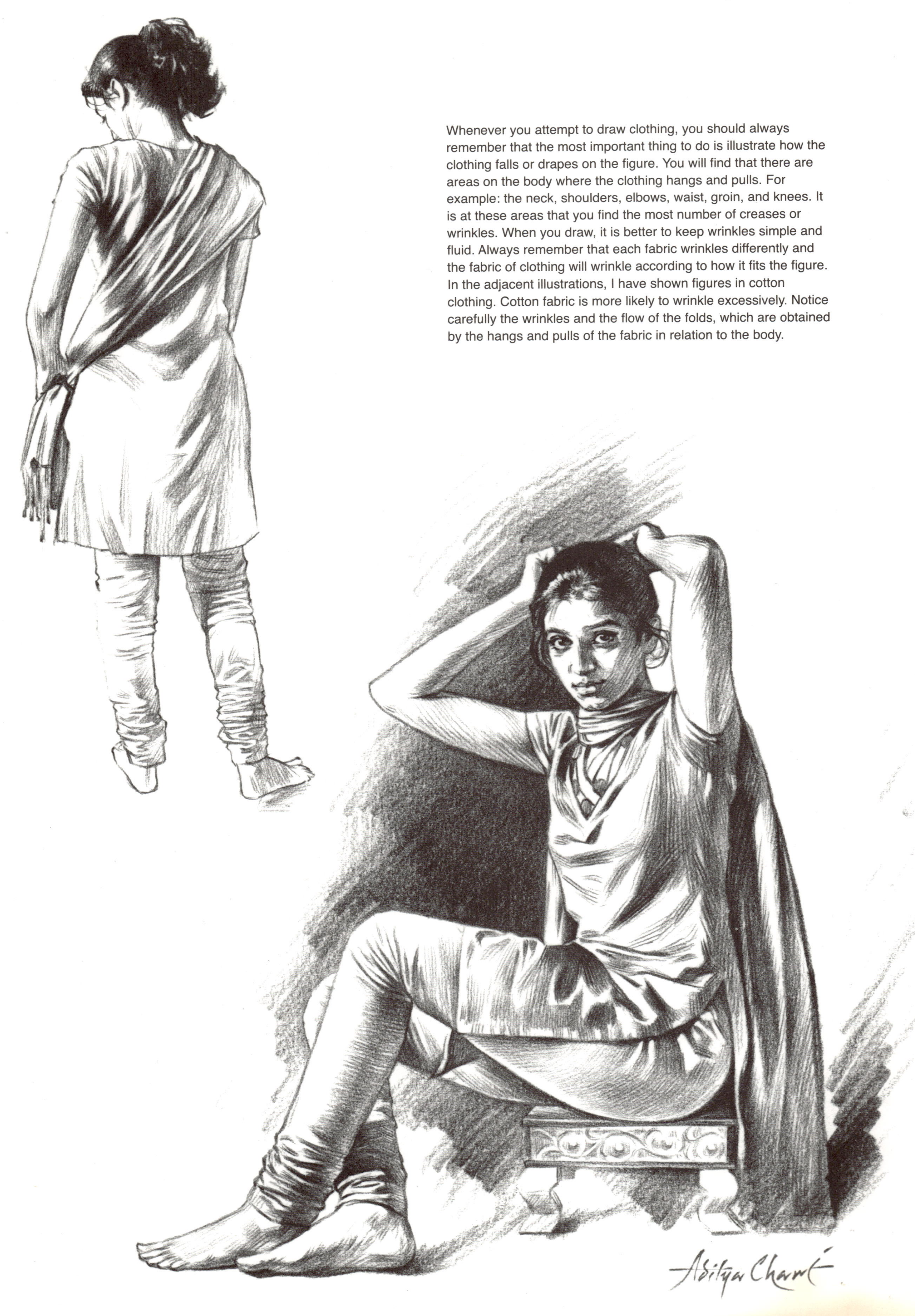

Whenever you attempt to draw clothing, you should always remember that the most important thing to do is illustrate how the clothing falls or drapes on the figure. You will find that there are areas on the body where the clothing hangs and pulls. For example: the neck, shoulders, elbows, waist, groin, and knees. It is at these areas that you find the most number of creases or wrinkles. When you draw, it is better to keep wrinkles simple and fluid. Always remember that each fabric wrinkles differently and the fabric of clothing will wrinkle according to how it fits the figure. In the adjacent illustrations, I have shown figures in cotton clothing. Cotton fabric is more likely to wrinkle excessively. Notice carefully the wrinkles and the flow of the folds, which are obtained by the hangs and pulls of the fabric in relation to the body.

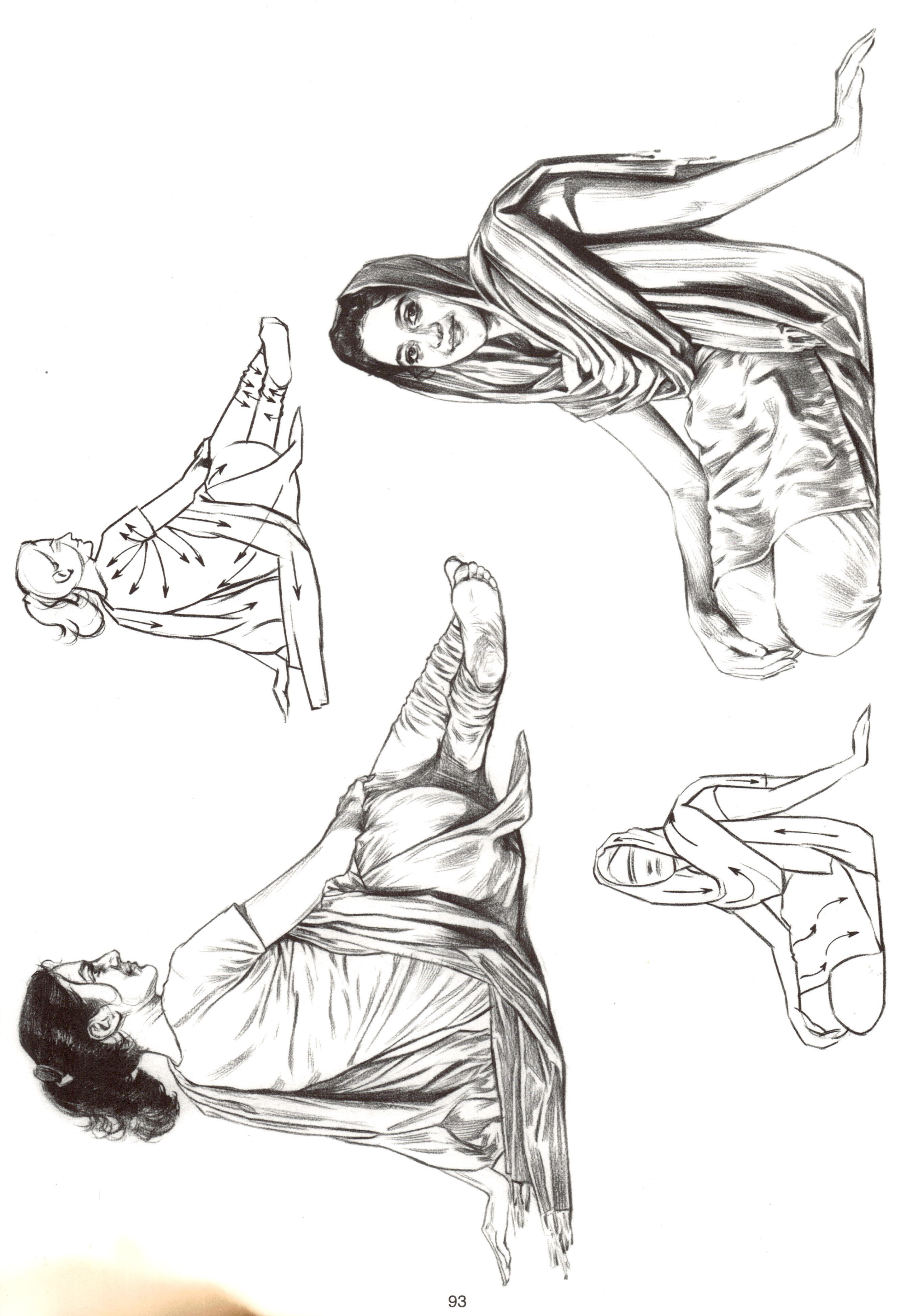

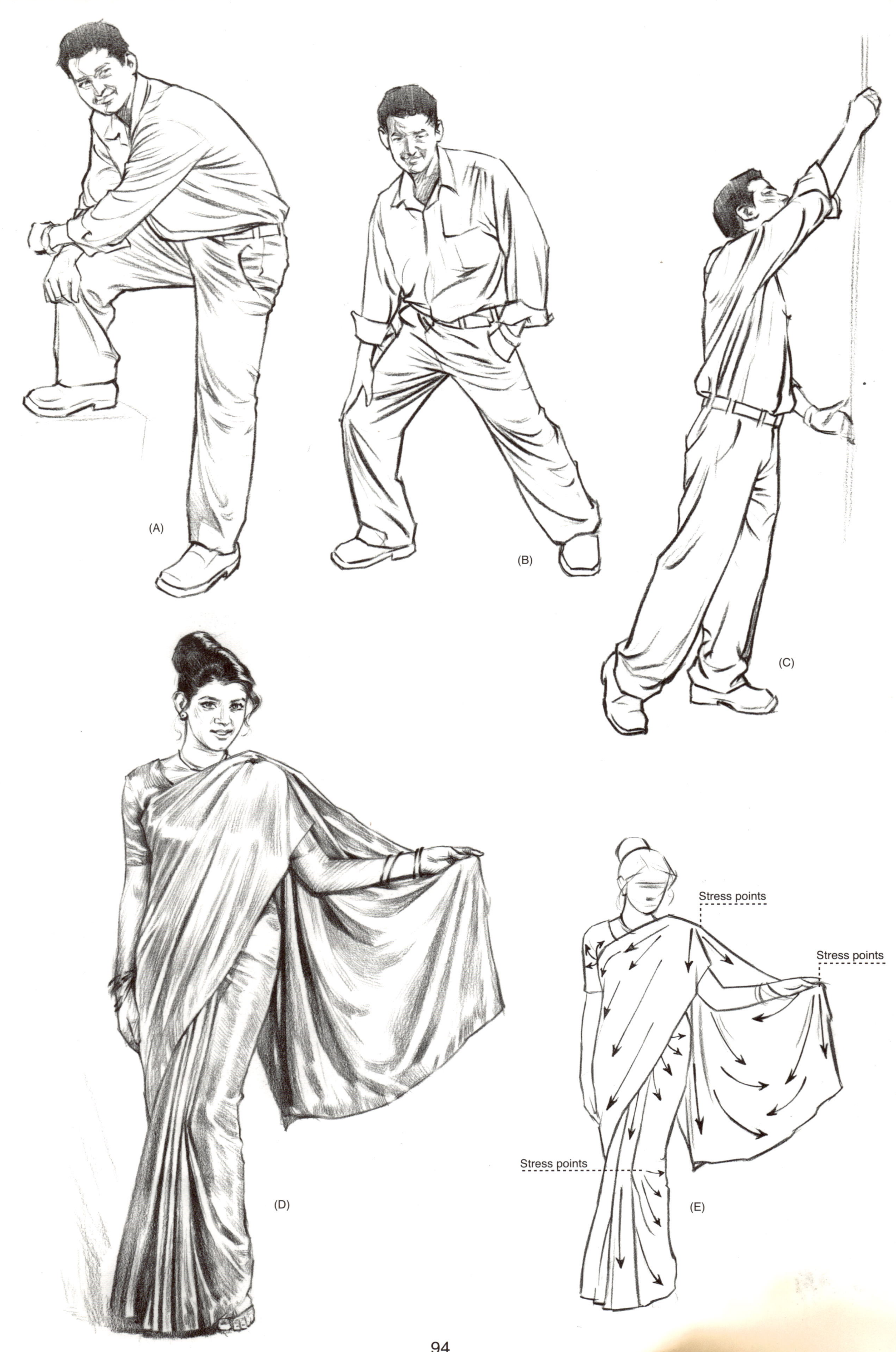
(A)
(B)
(C)
(D)
Stress points
Stress points
Stress points
(E)

RHYTHM
&
GRACE

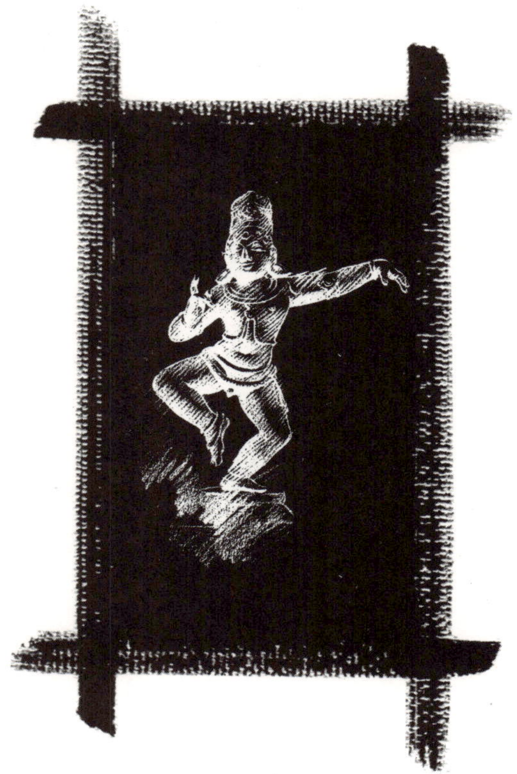

More emphasis is given to "rhythmic form" rather than "symmetry". The human form limits creative expression. An artist's aim is not only to recreate life but also to signify graceful rhythm through his art. I strongly recommend you to practice sketching of Indian sculpture so that you develop the understanding of the eternal rhythm, which is inside of each natural object. It is only through this understanding that you can bring out the inner beauty of each creation of art.

There is rhythm in every movement on this planet, in this universe. It is an integral part of all animal and plant life. There is even movement in speech – the different accented and unaccented syllables grouping and pauses in sentences. Both poetry and music are the embodiment of rhythmical sound. Without rhythm there could be no poetry or music. In drawing and painting too, there is rhythm - in outline, colour, light and shade.

The term "rhythm" used in figure drawing is in reality, an imaginary inner curve or inner path which denotes the line of action. The key to getting motion into the drawing lies in seeing this inner curve and in developing its influence in the shapes of the contour of the figure. These graceful lines that run through the body, like thread, are imaginary. One has to realize that the semi-rigid skeletal structure of the body is never straight; the bones are curvilinear forms, which are highly complex. In addition to this, the band-like soft tissues of the body, namely the muscles, wrap the skeleton and soften all its contours.

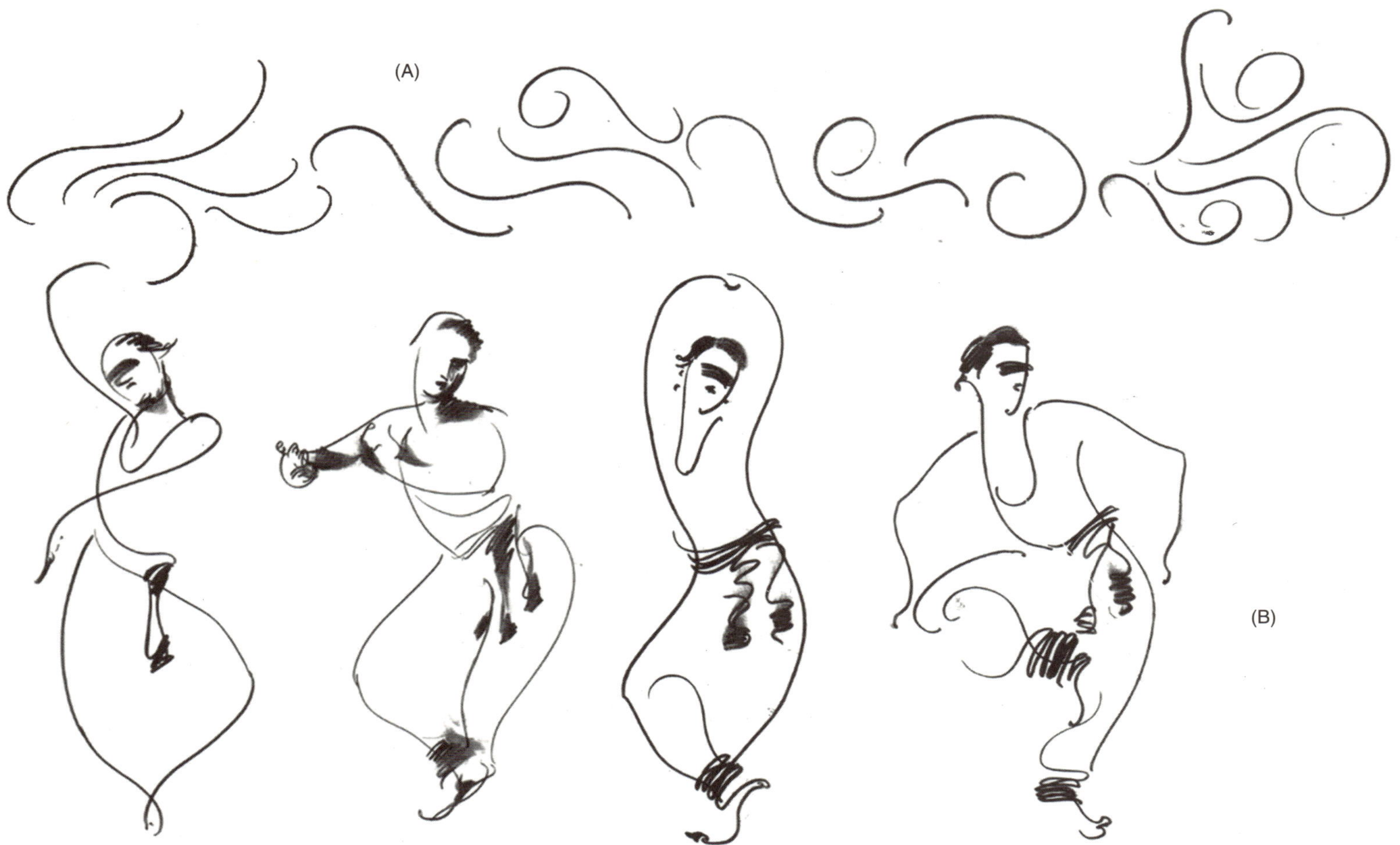

In order to express rhythm in drawing a figure, you have to create a balance in the passive or inactive side and the active or more forceful and angular side in action. Always keep in mind the subtle flow of symmetry right through the drawing. Rhythmic forms are essential to drawing or painting in order to take away the dullness - a figure can only give progressive rhythm because of the different sizes of body components, a hand and leg can form the same line but in varying sizes, there by providing a progressive rhythm. Once you are aware of this, you will be able to position your model to give you this rhythm. As you gain experience, you can slightly alter your figure drawing to give it more rhythm while still maintaining the true structure of your figure.

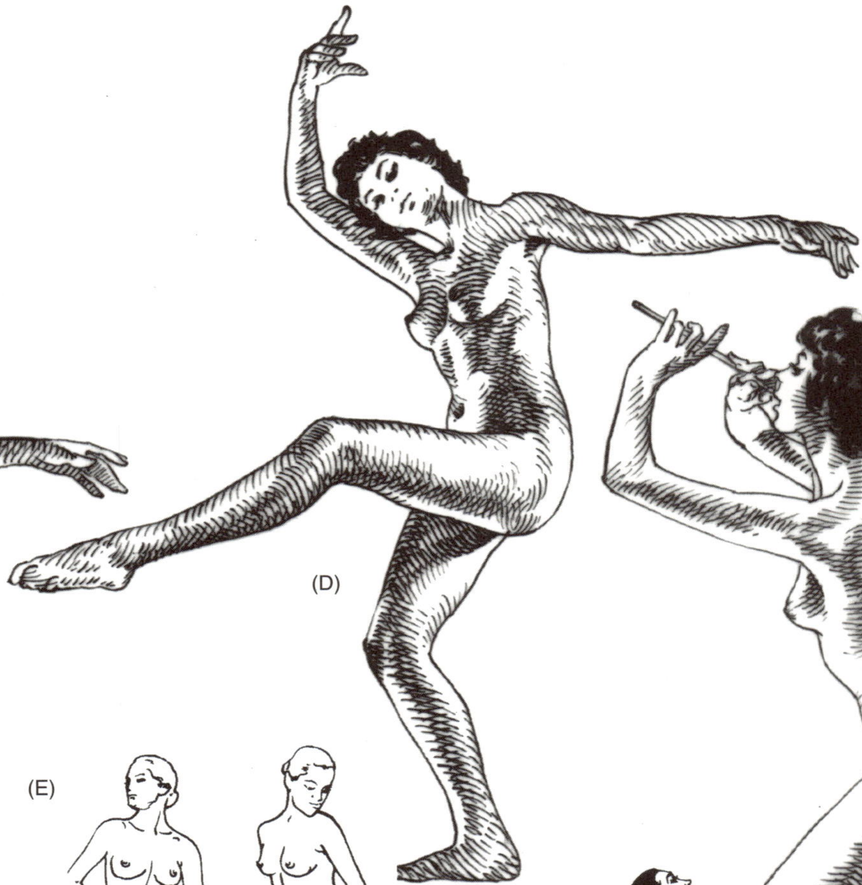

(D)

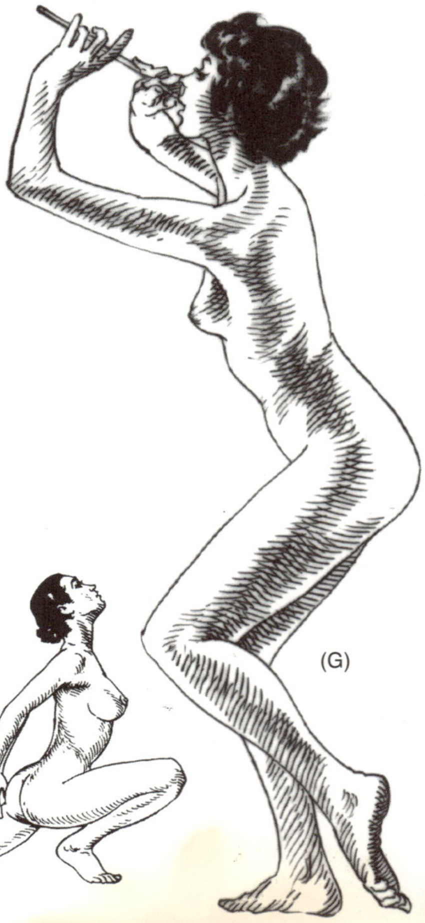

(E)

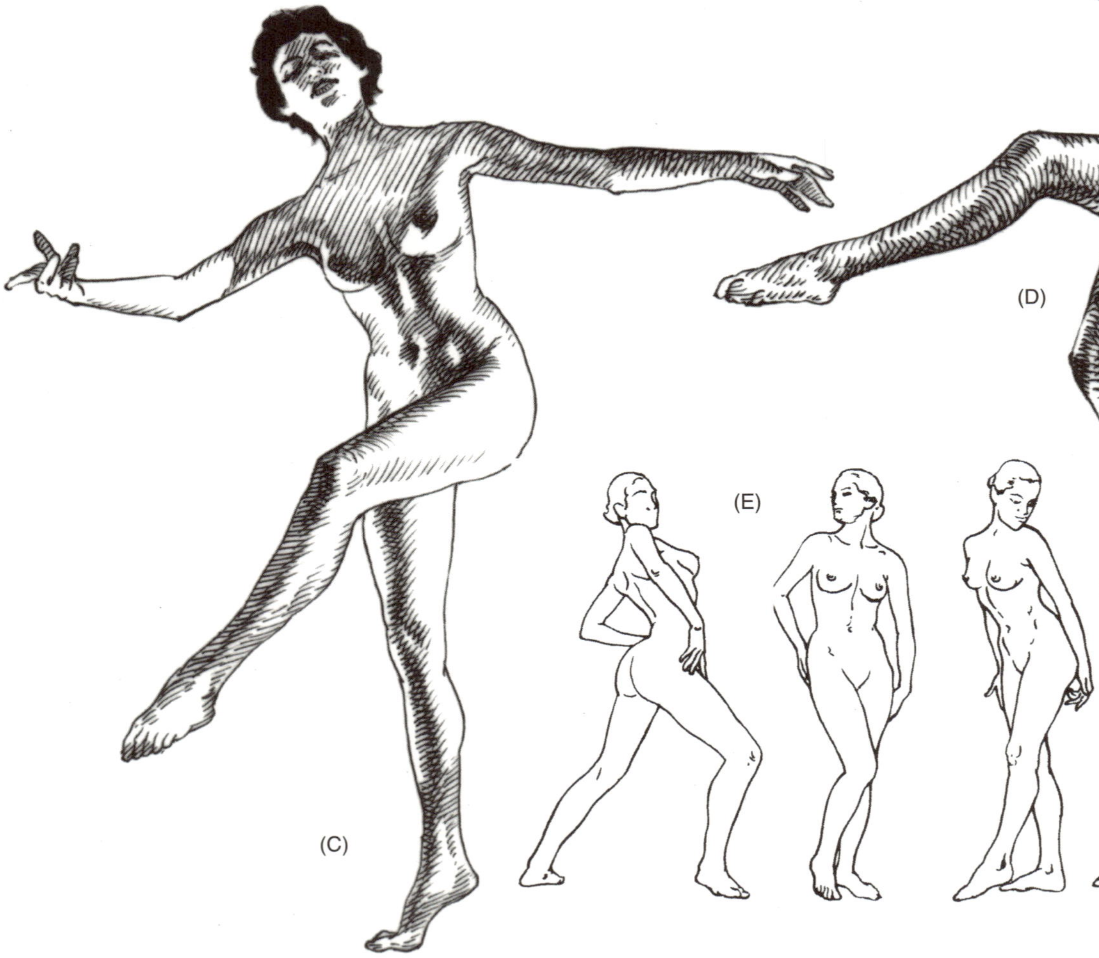

(G)

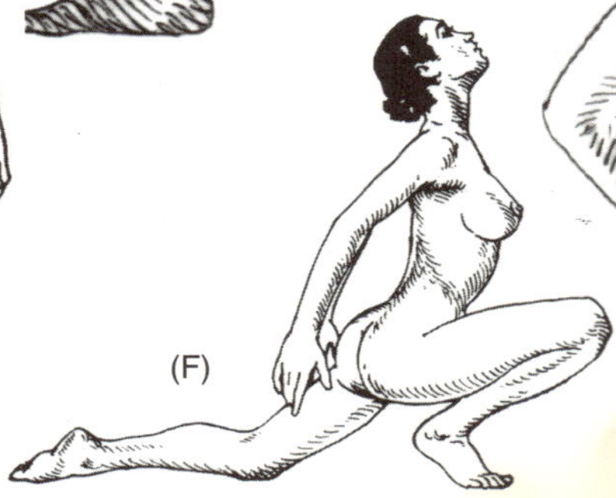

(F)

(C)

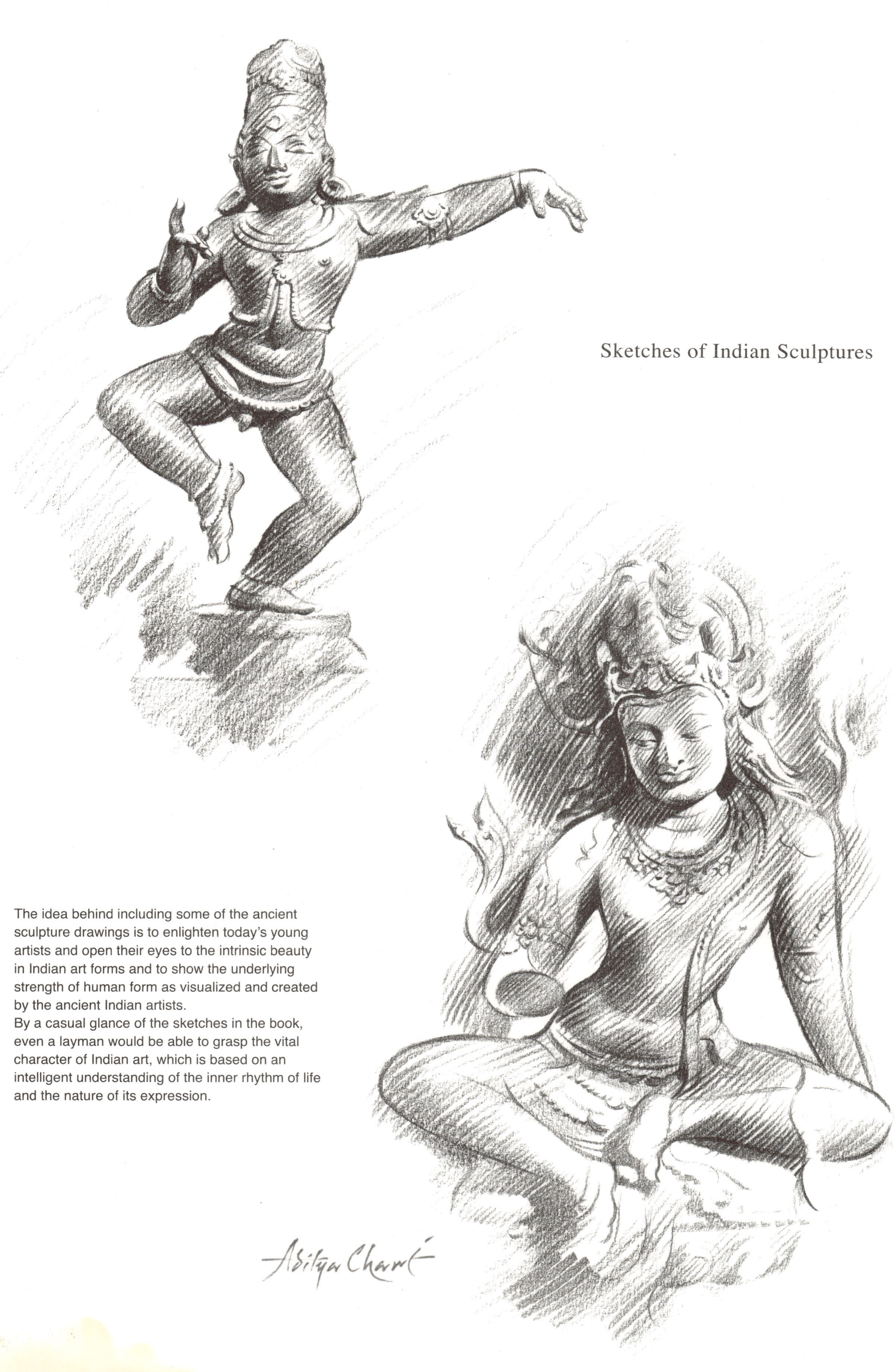

Sketches of Indian Sculptures

The idea behind including some of the ancient sculpture drawings is to enlighten today's young artists and open their eyes to the intrinsic beauty in Indian art forms and to show the underlying strength of human form as visualized and created by the ancient Indian artists.
By a casual glance of the sketches in the book, even a layman would be able to grasp the vital character of Indian art, which is based on an intelligent understanding of the inner rhythm of life and the nature of its expression.

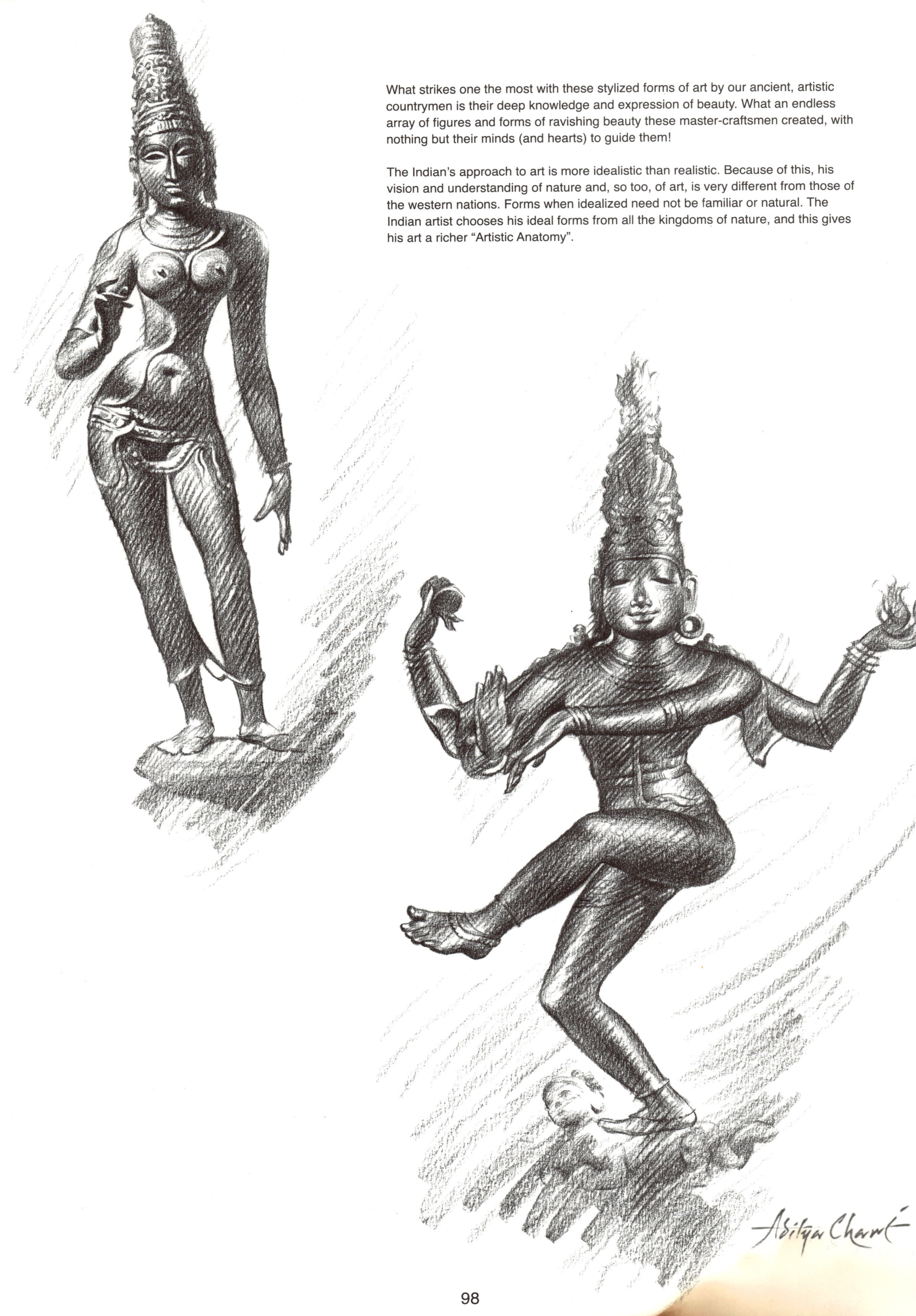

What strikes one the most with these stylized forms of art by our ancient, artistic countrymen is their deep knowledge and expression of beauty. What an endless array of figures and forms of ravishing beauty these master-craftsmen created, with nothing but their minds (and hearts) to guide them!

The Indian's approach to art is more idealistic than realistic. Because of this, his vision and understanding of nature and, so too, of art, is very different from those of the western nations. Forms when idealized need not be familiar or natural. The Indian artist chooses his ideal forms from all the kingdoms of nature, and this gives his art a richer "Artistic Anatomy".

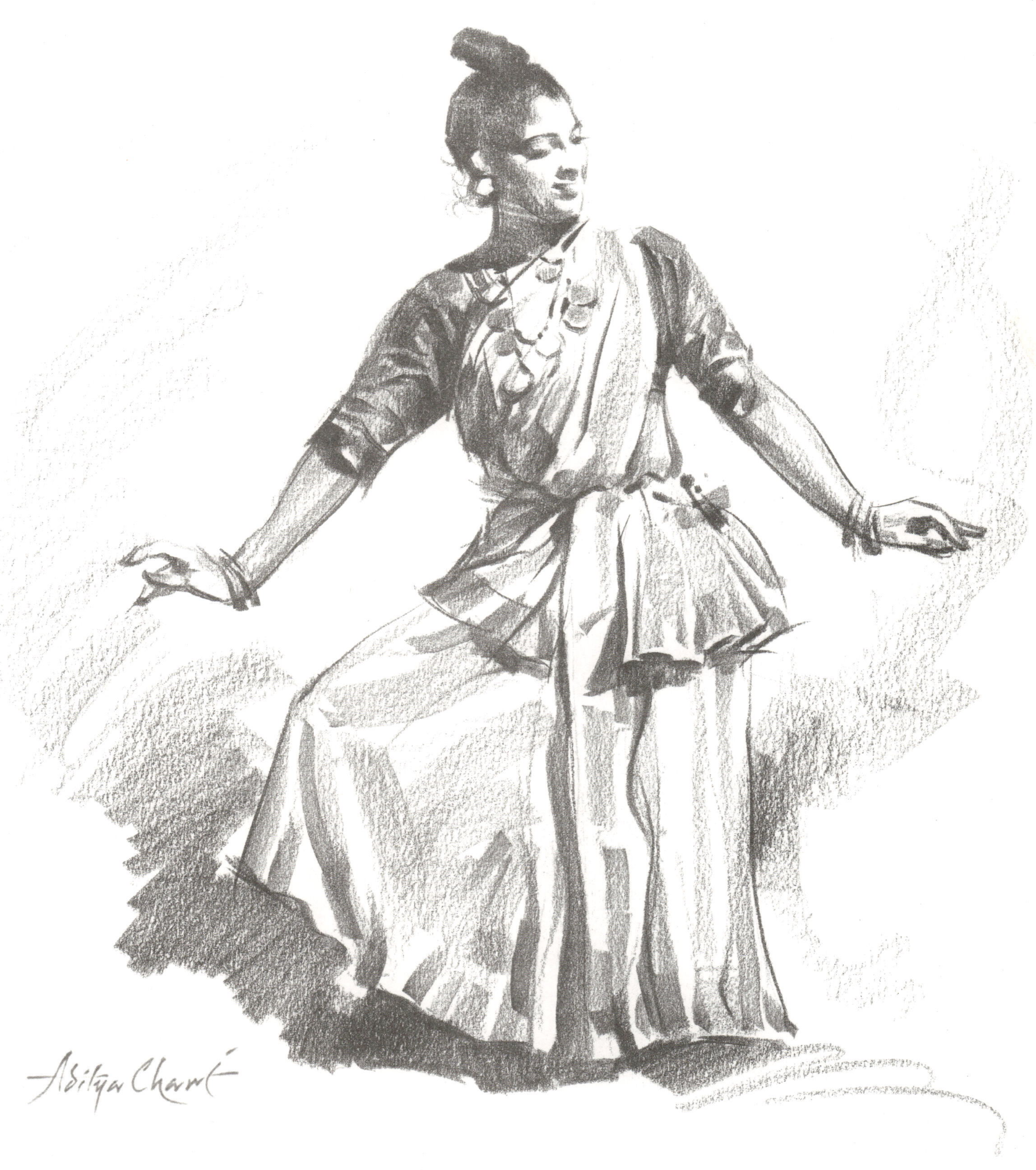

The drawings of Indian dancers have been included, just to show some different ways of rendering styles, how it relates and suits to particular dancer's pose.
The strokes have to be loose and with the flow of action. Force of action has to be maintained through out the figure. No need to give attention into so much of detailing.
The speed and urgency is important to capture the action in a proper rhythm.

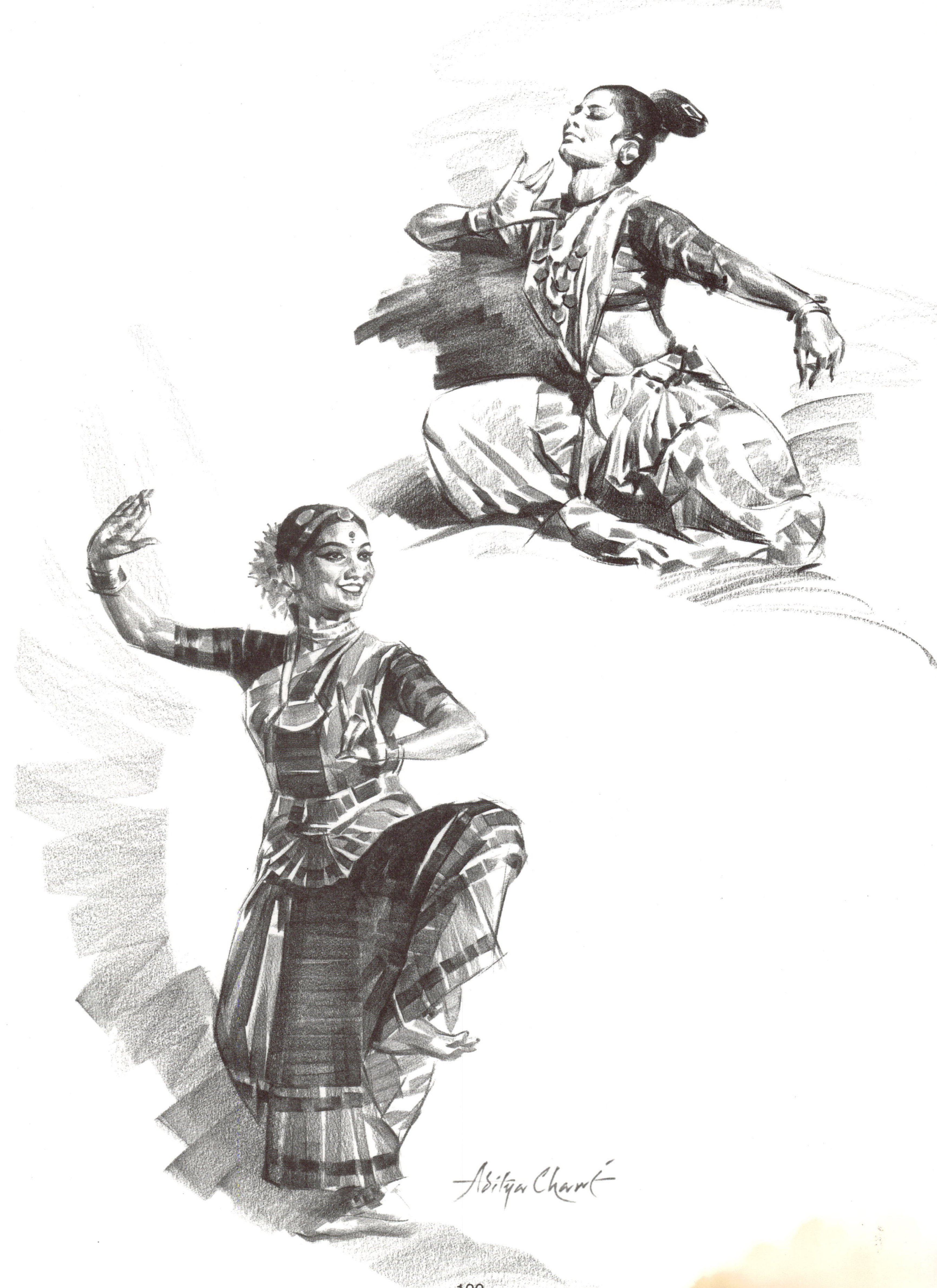
Aditya Chari

BALLET DANCERS

It is also important how you render the particular action figure. The treatment of rendering shown in this particular two figures are treated according to the flow of action, which creates additional movement and grace to the figures.

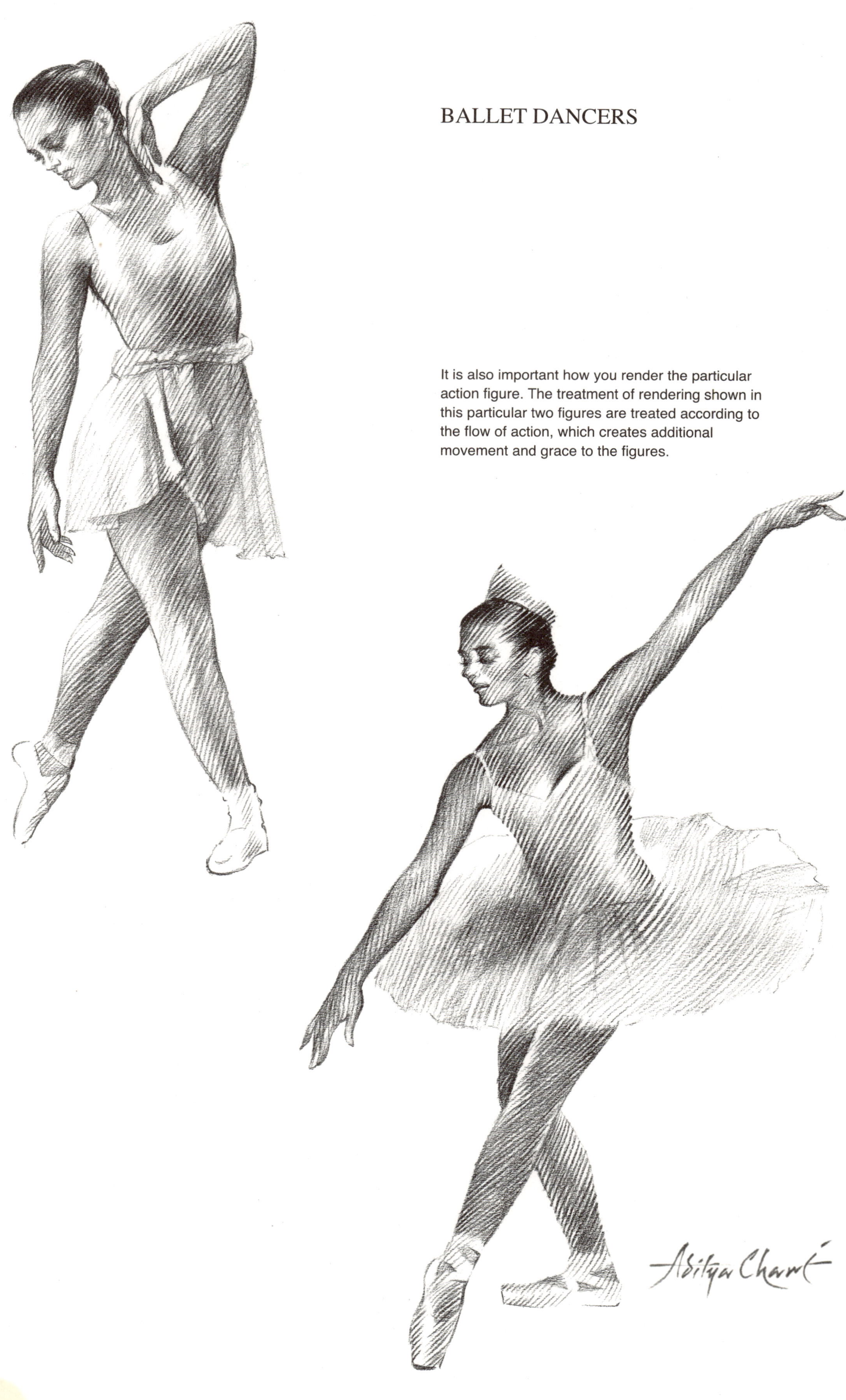

SKETCHES SHOWN IN STAGES

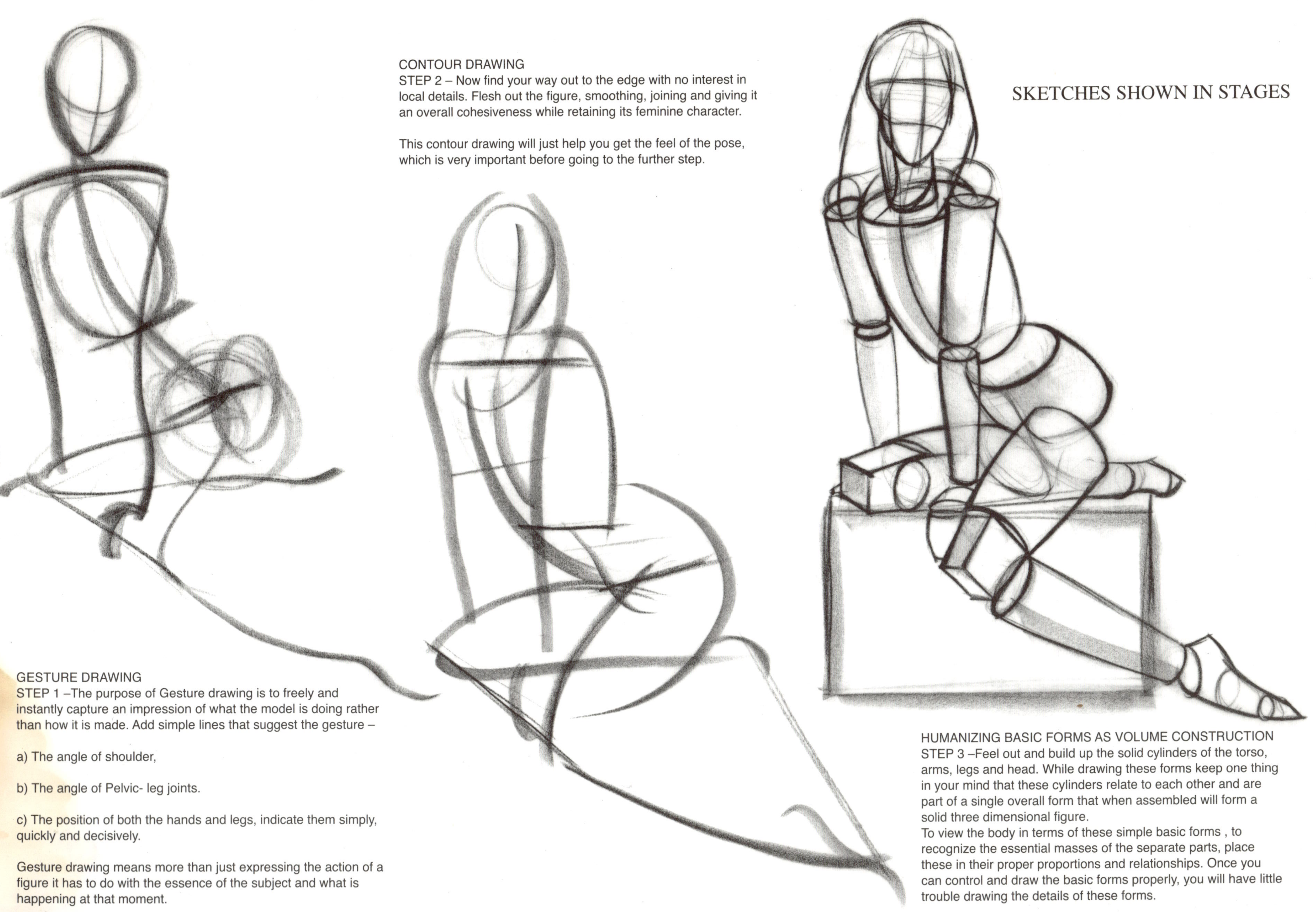

GESTURE DRAWING
STEP 1 –The purpose of Gesture drawing is to freely and instantly capture an impression of what the model is doing rather than how it is made. Add simple lines that suggest the gesture –

a) The angle of shoulder,

b) The angle of Pelvic- leg joints.

c) The position of both the hands and legs, indicate them simply, quickly and decisively.

Gesture drawing means more than just expressing the action of a figure it has to do with the essence of the subject and what is happening at that moment.

CONTOUR DRAWING
STEP 2 – Now find your way out to the edge with no interest in local details. Flesh out the figure, smoothing, joining and giving it an overall cohesiveness while retaining its feminine character.

This contour drawing will just help you get the feel of the pose, which is very important before going to the further step.

HUMANIZING BASIC FORMS AS VOLUME CONSTRUCTION
STEP 3 –Feel out and build up the solid cylinders of the torso, arms, legs and head. While drawing these forms keep one thing in your mind that these cylinders relate to each other and are part of a single overall form that when assembled will form a solid three dimensional figure.
To view the body in terms of these simple basic forms , to recognize the essential masses of the separate parts, place these in their proper proportions and relationships. Once you can control and draw the basic forms properly, you will have little trouble drawing the details of these forms.

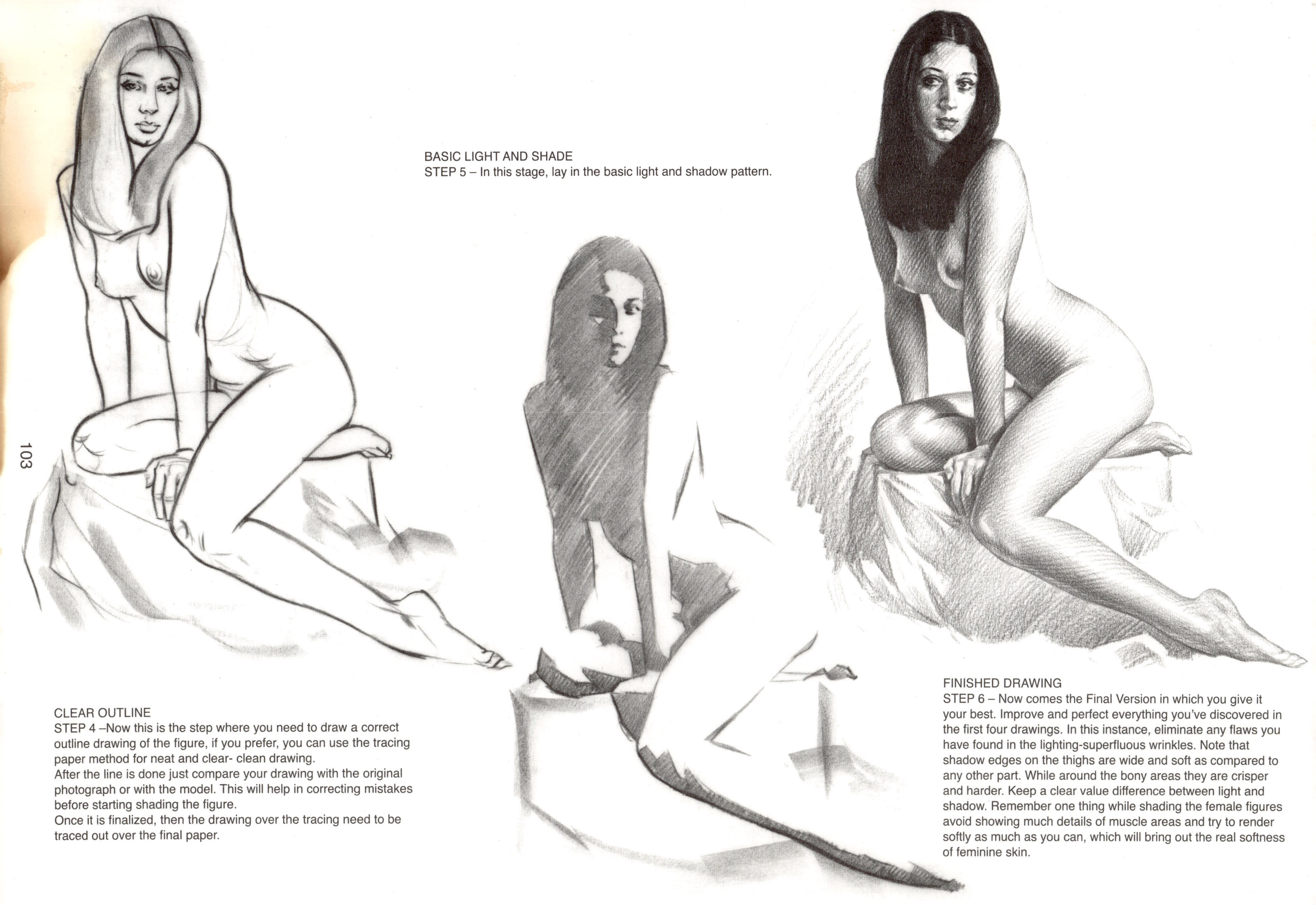

BASIC LIGHT AND SHADE

STEP 5 – In this stage, lay in the basic light and shadow pattern.

CLEAR OUTLINE

STEP 4 –Now this is the step where you need to draw a correct outline drawing of the figure, if you prefer, you can use the tracing paper method for neat and clear- clean drawing.

After the line is done just compare your drawing with the original photograph or with the model. This will help in correcting mistakes before starting shading the figure.

Once it is finalized, then the drawing over the tracing need to be traced out over the final paper.

FINISHED DRAWING

STEP 6 – Now comes the Final Version in which you give it your best. Improve and perfect everything you've discovered in the first four drawings. In this instance, eliminate any flaws you have found in the lighting-superfluous wrinkles. Note that shadow edges on the thighs are wide and soft as compared to any other part. While around the bony areas they are crisper and harder. Keep a clear value difference between light and shadow. Remember one thing while shading the female figures avoid showing much details of muscle areas and try to render softly as much as you can, which will bring out the real softness of feminine skin.

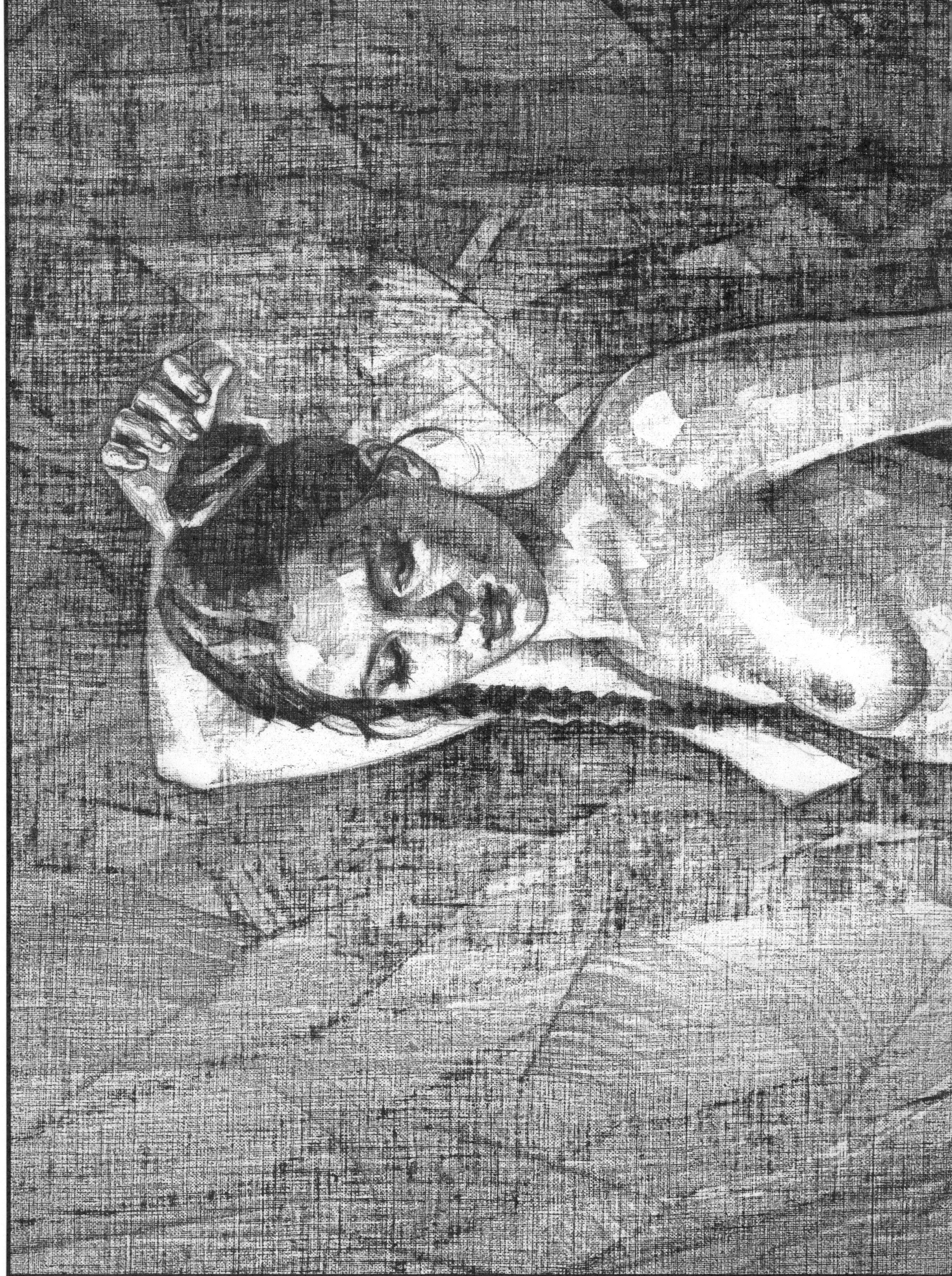

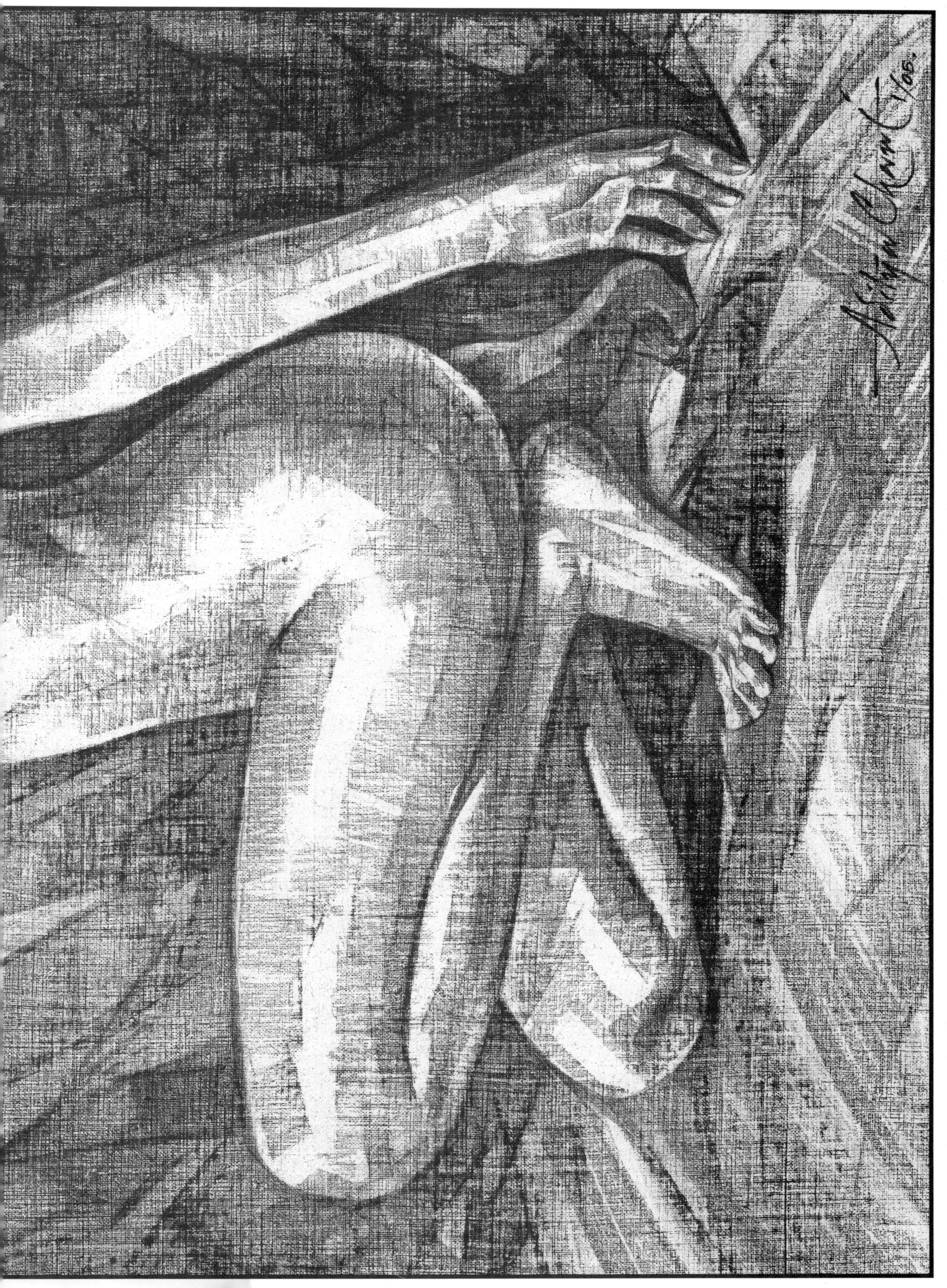